On Becoming a Language Educator

Personal Essays
on Professional Development

On Becoming a Language Educator

*Personal Essays
on Professional Development*

Edited by

Christine Pearson Casanave
Keio University, Fujisawa, Japan

Sandra R. Schecter
York University, Ontario, Canada

LEA LAWRENCE ERLBAUM ASSOCIATES, PUBLISHERS
1997   Mahwah, New Jersey   London

Lawrence Erlbaum Associates, Inc., Publishers
10 Industrial Avenue
Mahwah, New Jersey 07430

Library of Congress Cataloging-in-Publication Data

On becoming a language educator : personal essays on professional
   development / Christine Pearson Casanave and Sandra R. Schecter,
   editors.
       p.   cm.
   Includes bibliographical references and index.
   ISBN 0-8058-2263-1 (alk. paper). — ISBN 0-8058-2264-X (pbk. :
alk. paper)
   1. Language teachers—Training of. I. Casanave, Christine
Pearson, 1944–   . II. Schecter, Sandra R.
P53.85.05 1997
407′.1′1—dc21   96-39504
                                                             CIP

Printed in the United States of America
10 9 8 7 6 5 4 3 2 1

To the memory of Eleanor, a connection lost,
and to Larry, a connection gained.

—*Christine*

For Norman, Jacob, and Zachary,
who have both fostered and unsettled my becomings.

—*Sandra*

Contents

Foreword

D. Jean Clandinin
University of Alberta

As a reader and writer of narrative inquiry, I approached this book with a sense of excitement and enthusiasm: a book of personal stories of language educators, many of whose work provided ways for me to engage in my own work. But even so, I was unprepared for the richness and depth of this carefully edited collection.

Each story, skillfully written, left me wanting to know more about its author. And, as I found myself caught up in each narrative, I was surprised at the power of the stories as they connected with mine and at the courage it had taken to write these personal pieces. When Lily Wong Fillmore described her career choices as "anything but intentional," I knew her plot line. When Sandra Schecter described her unquestioning attitude to university researchers in her classroom, I remembered similar moments. Trudy Smoke's stories of school as no longer a safe place for teachers or for students resonated with the stories teachers tell me of their lives in school. With each new chapter I had to "stop and think," as Hannah Arendt writes, in order to consider my own stories of becoming a teacher educator.

And, as I thought about my stories, I found myself recollecting memories from a time about 12 years ago. A small group of European, Israeli, and North American researchers had planned a conference intending to explore the autobiographical underpinnings of our research programs. Initially, at home writing, I had been excited and wrote about my experiences using a metaphor of finding myself a stranger living in the spaces between my rural background and my home in urban academe, as well as living in the spaces between public schools and universities. Writing the stories, although they were intense and personal, helped me explore questions about personal voices, private voices, public voices, the gendered nature of my experience, the kinds of institutions in which I worked, and the nature of academic discourse about research. I planned to read that paper but, as the conference proceeded and other papers presented did not include personal experience, I realized I did not have the courage. I had another "safer" piece about teacher knowledge and its narrative character. I read that safer paper and nothing changed.

That story has lived with me and I often think about the courage it takes to tell our researcher stories, about how much safer it is to tell stories of the other. I think about how unaccustomed we are to making ourselves vulnerable in the pages of academic texts and at conferences. And yet . . . if we do not do this, if we do not tell our stories, do not make ourselves vulnerable as we explore our storied lives, will the nature of academic discourse ever change?

Christine Casanave connects with my thoughts as she writes of her own struggle to reject the political games that scholars play "on the field of academic discourse as they vie to achieve 'insider' status within a patriarchal education system." Christine feels drawn into the game and fears she does not have "the courage to say no to it," the courage I also lacked as I read my safe paper those 12 years ago.

I now know that if we do want to change the game, we are going to have to take risks, to have "the courage to say no to it." This book of essays is part of coming together as a collective to engage in a courageous new form of academic discourse, one with the potential to change the field. Many of the authors write their stories of having begun their work with voices positioned at the margins. Now, as established professionals, they feel strong enough collectively to risk the telling and, through their telling, to encourage other voices. I too take courage from their willingness to risk, to be vulnerable, to share their narratives of experience. I hope their collection of stories inspires others to continue to change the games played on the field of academic discourse and to encourage others to join the conversation they have begun.

Preface

On Becoming a Language Educator concerns the professional development of language educators. It consists of personal essays by first- and second-language researchers and practitioners in which the writers reflect on issues, events, and people in their lives that helped them carve out their career paths or clarify an important dimension of their missions as educators. It is intended to provide graduate students, teachers, and researchers in language education with insights into the struggles that characterize the professional development of people whose work in educational settings focuses pre-dominantly on language-related issues and activities. Our primary goals are that both readers and authors use the stories told here to view their own professional lives from fresh perspectives—that they are inspired to reflect in new ways on the ideological, ethical, and philosophical underpinnings of their professional personae, and that they forge links between the con-creteness and commonality of the narratives and the potentially profound meanings to be found in human experience. We believe that this kind of reflection leads us, as language educators, not only to find meaning in the narrative episodes of our professional lives, but also to enhance our respect for the nonstatic "ongoingness" of professional development, as reflected in the progressive mood of our title.

By asking authors and readers to look inward, this book fits well within the trends in the professional education literature toward valuing work that is increasingly narrative and reflective (Adler, 1993; Barone, 1992; Carter, 1993; Clandinin & Connelly, 1991; Clandinin, Davies, Hogan, & Kennard,

1993; Connelly & Clandinin, 1990; Elbaz, 1991; Grimmett & Erickson, 1988; McLaughlin & Tierney, 1993; Richards & Lockhart, 1994; Rose, 1989; Ross, 1989; Schön, 1987, 1991; Valli, 1992; van Manen, 1989; Weber, 1993; Witherell & Noddings, 1991). Jerome Bruner's work, in particular, has helped reshape how educators and psychologists view the place of narrative in the study of the human mind (Bruner, 1986, 1990, 1996). We construct ourselves through narrative, according to Bruner, beginning in early childhood, in the process of telling stories that create meanings for us in particular cultural contexts. In tandem with this literature, our book highlights the power of story and reflection in teaching and teacher education, which helps us as storytellers to construct meanings that contribute to professional growth. But in spite of the growing interest in story and reflection, it is still the case that work about narrative takes precedence over narratives themselves (Donmoyer, 1996), and that discussions of how narratives can be used in the practice of research (e.g., Riessman, 1993) appear in print far more frequently than do personal narratives by the authors who are promoting narrative approaches. It is rare to find an entire volume, such as the first-person ethnographies edited by Carolyn Ellis and Arthur Bochner (1996), dedicated to alternative forms of qualitative writing (as they highlight in their book's subtitle), particularly in the field of language education.

   On Becoming a Language Educator, designed to begin filling this gap, is such a collection of first-person narratives by people who teach and engage in scholarship on language. As a whole, the collection depicts the ways in which professional language educators from diverse backgrounds and work settings have grappled with issues in language education that concern all of us: the sources and development of our beliefs about language and education, the constructing of a professional identity in the face of ethical and ideological dilemmas, and the constraints and inspirations of teaching and learning environments. We believe that the stories of language educators need to find their way directly into the language teacher education agenda, and that the issues addressed by such an approach must cross the boundaries that traditionally have separated first-language, second-language, and bilingual education.

   Although *On Becoming a Language Educator* makes wonderful reading for individual educators, it is designed to be used as a primary or supplementary text for courses in graduate teacher education programs that address language learning and professional development (methods, theory, field experience). In particular, it is appropriate in Master's level programs in elementary and secondary language arts, bilingual education, and English as a second/foreign language. It is important for readers to recognize that this book, although theoretically grounded, does not "do" theory, nor is it about theory. It is about people. We do not discuss much of the literature in the field, for example, and we encouraged authors likewise to focus their discussions on themselves and their issues rather than on extensive literature reviews.

We have grouped the essays into five broad parts that reflect their content, although much overlapping inevitably was revealed as we made these decisions. Themes and issues thus carry across the groupings, a feature we hope that readers will take advantage of in their discussions of the essays. Each part contains three to five essays, all of which serve to legitimize the diversity of our experiences and struggles and, simultaneously, to demonstrate a broad range of shared concerns among language educators from different fields. Each group of essays is preceded by a brief introduction in which we highlight the major issues and questions in that part, and then preview each essay. In Part One, "Evolving a Philosophy," the authors dig into their pasts to discover the sources of their beliefs about important pedagogical or theoretical issues and to reflect on experiences that have contributed to changes in their beliefs. In Part Two, "Identity Dilemmas," the authors consider conflicts and contrasts in their lives that have shaped, and are continuing to shape, how they identify themselves and how they are perceived as language educators. In Part Three, "Lessons From Teachings and Learnings," the authors narrate the ways in which past and present relations with students, colleagues, mentors, and even family members have influenced their career choices and helped them shape their professional personae. In Part Four, "Reflections on the Profession," the authors focus on how structural, discoursal, and curricular aspects of their professions have influenced not only their professional development but also their sense of satisfaction in their fields. A final section, Part Five, "Conversations," consists of a selection of communications we have had with some of the authors whose stories appear in the book. These communications show some of the underpinnings of the thinking and writing that went into the essays that contributed to professional insight and growth of both authors and editors.

At the end of each section, in "Explorations," the editors provide suggestions for further discussion that are designed to help readers make concrete connections between their own lives and the issues raised by the authors. The issues are presented as brief commentary, thought-provoking discussion questions, and suggestions for activities such as journal writing, peer discussions, observations, and interviews. We encourage readers to utilize this section well, to take the time to talk together, to write and reflect on the issues brought up and on their own related experiences. However, the suggestions should not be construed as "assignments" in the traditional sense. The format and mode are flexible; it matters little whether readers talk among friends and colleagues, set up class discussions, write personal or assigned journals, or spend solitary time reflecting. The point is that readers can make best use of this book by engaging personally with the material. The questions and suggestions should be seen as dealing with only a fraction of the many possible activities and topics for discussion; we thus urge readers to devise their own questions and activities as befit their particular interests and teaching and learning contexts. In general, we hope that readers will recognize that the fundamentally important human voices in the language education fields include theirs, not just those of published authors.

We believe our book is a valuable addition to the language education literature for a number of reasons. First, our contributors are exclusively language educators in first- and second-language and bilingual settings. They are people whose experiences with native and nonnative languages have helped shape their careers. They are committed to pursuing careers that in one way or another concern language, whether it be written or spoken, the language of children or adults, the languages of home or school, mainstream or minority. Their issues tend to cut across the traditional boundaries in language and education fields. Second, the authors write well, with the result that our book is accessible to a broad audience of readers, including those in the general teacher education field. Third, our contributors talk about themselves, not about others. It is their insights about themselves that will help readers reflect on their own career trajectories. And while our purpose in this book is not curriculum reform, societal change, or theory building per se, we believe that such change and growth can occur only if language educators look inward as well as outward. Finally, in promoting a needed inclusive spirit in our approach to professional development, our book legitimizes the voices of readers as well as authors in the ongoing pursuit of wisdom in the field of language education.

ACKNOWLEDGMENTS

We express our profound gratitude to all who helped shape and produce this book, not the least of whom were: Naomi Silverman, now at Lawrence Erlbaum, who enthusiastically supported this project when the book was still just an idea and saw it through its 5 years of development; to the staff and reviewers at St. Martin's Press who helped us along the way; and to the staff and reviewers at Lawrence Erlbaum Associates for helping to bring the book to its felicitous conclusion. We also thank the many colleagues, friends, and family members (you know who you are) who provided support, guidance, and critical feedback. Above all, we thank the authors for their tenacity, shared vision, and invaluable contributions to this book and to our own professional growth.

—*Christine Pearson Casanave*
—*Sandra R. Schecter*

REFERENCES

Adler, S. A. (1993). Teacher education: Research as reflective practice. *Teacher and Teacher Education, 9*, 159–167.

Barone, T. (1992). A narrative of enhanced professionalism: Educational researchers and popular storybooks about schoolpeople. *Educational Researcher, 21*(8), 15–24.

Bruner, J. (1986). *Actual minds, possible worlds.* Cambridge, MA: Harvard University Press.

Bruner, J. (1990). *Acts of meaning.* Cambridge, MA: Harvard University Press.

Bruner, J. (1996). *The culture of education.* Cambridge, MA: Harvard University Press.

Carter, K. (1993). The place of story in the study of teaching and teacher education. *Educational Researcher, 22*(1), 5–12.

Clandinin, D. J., & Connelly, F. M. (1991). Narrative and story in practice and research. In D. A. Schön (Ed.), *The reflective turn: Case studies in and on educational practice* (pp. 258–281). New York: Teachers College Press.

Clandinin, D. J., Davies, A., Hogan, P., & Kennard, B. (1993). *Learning to teach, teaching to learn: Stories of collaboration in teacher education.* New York: Teachers College Press.

Connelly, F. M., & Clandinin, D. J. (1990). Stories of experience and narrative inquiry. *Educational Researcher, 19*(5), 2–14.

Donmoyer, R. (1996). Educational research in an era of paradigm proliferation: What's a journal editor to do? *Educational Researcher, 25*(2), 19–25.

Elbaz, F. (1991). Research on teacher's (sic) knowledge: The evolution of a discourse. *Journal of Curriculum Studies, 23*, 1–19.

Ellis, C., & Bochner, A. P. (Eds.). (1996). *Composing ethnography: Alternative forms of qualitative writing.* Walnut Creek, CA: Altamira Press.

Grimmett, P. P., & Erickson, G. L. (Eds.). (1988). *Reflection in teacher education.* New York: Teachers College Press.

McLaughlin, D., & Tierney, W. G. (Eds.). (1993). *Naming silenced lives: Personal narratives and the process of educational change.* New York: Routledge.

Richards, J. C., & Lockhart, C. (1994). *Reflective teaching in second language classrooms.* Cambridge: Cambridge University Press.

Riessman, C. K. (1993). *Narrative analysis.* Newbury Park, CA: Sage.

Rose, M. (1989). *Lives on the boundary.* New York: Penguin Books.

Ross, D. D. (1989). First steps in developing a reflective approach. *Journal of Teacher Education, 40*(2), 22–30.

Schön, D. A. (1987). *Educating the reflective practitioner.* San Francisco: Jossey-Bass.

Schön, D. A. (Ed.). (1991). *The reflective turn: Case studies in and on educational practice.* New York: Teachers College Press.

Valli, L. (Ed.). (1992). *Reflective teacher education: Cases and critiques.* New York: SUNY Press.

van Manen, M. (1989). By the light of the anecdote. *Phenomenology + Pedagogy, 7*, 232–253.

Weber, S. (1993). The narrative anecdote in teacher education. *Journal of Education for Teaching, 19*, 71–82.

Witherell, C., & Noddings, N. (Eds.). (1991). *Stories lives tell: Narrative and dialogue in education.* New York: Teachers College Press.

Introduction:
Readers and Authors
in Search of Selves

Christine Pearson Casanave
Keio University, Fujisawa, Japan

Sandra R. Schecter
York University, Ontario, Canada

We believe that language educators who persist in observing, reflecting, and questioning tend to change and grow throughout their careers. They are, in a sense, continually becoming language educators. Many, like us, went to graduate school, but did not find answers there—only more complex questions. Some of us occasionally have awakened in the morning with a sense of understanding that suggests we have arrived—"gotten there," as it were—only to discover later that this was not an arrival, but an insight or breakthrough that further complicated our thinking. We have been struck over the years by the extent to which our lives, and those of colleagues we know personally or whose work we read, are characterized by incredible diversity, richness, struggle, confusion, and complexity. We are thus increasingly convinced that language isn't just words and sentences; it's ideology and identity. Education isn't just a process of acquiring information and answers; it's a process of learning to seek, to explore, and to nurture curiosity in an unavoidably politicized environment.

This book is a collection of first-person narratives by language educators from many fields: English education, language arts, English as a second and foreign language, bilingual education. Many of the authors are well-known, widely published researchers and practitioners in their fields. A few are practicing teachers or relative newcomers to their professions. Although their fields and backgrounds differ, all share an interest in the connections between language and education. They share a belief that the literature in the language teacher education field is missing a fundamental and essential personal voice.

Why did we choose these people and not others? One answer is that we could not accommodate all the people who fit our desired author profile under one cover; there are too many who have insightful stories to tell and who feel passionately about expanding the repertoires of accepted discourse in our fields to include narrative and story. So in one sense it was first come, first served. But as editors, we also selected authors who we felt were dealing honestly with interesting issues in their lives, who did not convey a sense of having discovered all the answers, and who were willing to risk public exposure of private selves in the interest of making the public discourse in our fields more human. By "more human" we mean more peopled, more grounded in issues that connect with the lives of readers who are teaching and thinking about teaching language. As editors, we encouraged contributors to eschew technical jargon and the practiced stances normally associated with the public roles of the professional language educator. Instead, we asked them to explore a personal side of their careers in language education that they may not have articulated before; to take risks; to show us the people behind the prose, in the case of published authors; to convey a directness; and to probe in ways that our professions do not usually encourage in print. As authors, we set the same task for ourselves.

Most of the people we approached accepted the challenge, some curious, some intrigued by the project. But some were not fully aware at first that this apparently simple story-telling task would bring them face-to-face with issues and events in their lives that, profoundly influential as they were, they had not previously dealt with in concrete terms in public. There were few models to turn to for guidance, with the result that, in many cases, the task of writing these essays was not only an adventure; it was downright difficult.

But well worth the effort, as it turned out. We believe that readers at all stages of professional development will connect with these authors as they struggle to understand themselves and make sense out of their professional lives. Of course, the struggles of the authors are unique, in the sense that each story could be told only by the person who wrote it, and only in his or her very individual voice. The collection, in fact, is characterized partly by what may seem like a jarring diversity of voices. As editors, we sought, and found, this diversity, and we now share it with readers in the conviction that it should be celebrated, not censored.

But the struggles of the authors are also very commonplace. The events and issues that they recount appear (to be sure, in many different guises) in the lives of every language educator, whether teacher, theorizer, curriculum developer, or administrator. They are issues that cut across the artificial boundaries that tend to separate practitioners and researchers, the published and unpublished, and the first-language and second-language specialists. They are issues that concern what it means to live, work, and grow intellectually in fields where language and education converge. They are issues that concern how children and adults struggle to make meaning in their lives through written and spoken language, where language cannot be separated from the politically and ideologically charged contexts of schools and workplaces, or from the emotionally and psychologically charged contexts of homes and neighborhoods. We encourage readers to seek meaning in these issues, across contributors, not just to select out those authors who are working in specific fields that may currently match their specific professional arenas of commitment. Appreciate their, and your own, uniqueness, but find the threads that connect you.

We also encourage readers to engage in meaning-making by talking, reflecting, writing, and pondering as they look inside their own classrooms, research settings, and language education seminars. We believe that readers, authors, and editors need to work together to help legitimize the human voice in teaching, research, and study settings, and to push for more serious attention to the human voices and perspectives in the language education literature. Contrary to the fears of some, shifting our focus away from exclusive preoccupation with scientific approaches to the study of language education does not mean embracing sloppiness and noncritical thinking. Rather, the story with the lasting message—the one with the insight that causes readers to nod with recognition or to catch their breath with discovery—is crafted with a precision, a critical perceptiveness, and an eloquence lacking in the more traditional language teacher education literature. Indeed, as all of us have discovered in this project, crafting a meaningful and memorable story is hard work.

One final word before the story-telling commences. We urge those who share these stories with us to seek significance not only in the particulars of each contribution to this volume, but also in the work as a whole. By conceptualizing the work holistically, we will all be able to construct lasting connections between our own lives as language educators and the themes that pervade this book. These themes include the weaving together of personal and public strands of lives; the persistent uncertainty of what one knows and the resultant shifting of beliefs over time; the ideological, intellectual, and personal conflicts and contradictions within ourselves as well as in our work settings; the ongoing struggle to make meaning in the midst of complexity and confusion; and the enormous diversity of legitimate voices inside and outside the language classroom.

Introduction:
Evolving a Philosophy

Our beliefs about language and education evolve from sources that we may or may not fully recognize, and they continue evolving in directions we may not be able to predict or design. The essays in Part One are premised on the belief that our lives as professional language educators become enriched as we delve into the sources of our beliefs, articulating them for ourselves and others to reflect on. We see much value in this kind of exploration, that is, in work that seeks to elucidate the belief systems of educators. Such efforts not only allow us to consciously rethink and refine our beliefs, but they also serve to foster needed discussion about what we assume to be the goals of language teaching and learning, and about the realities of power relationships within a professional community.

Another reality that we confront as educators concerns our beliefs about what knowledge is and does. In our view, knowledge is not something that we acquire and then suddenly possess, even though our educational experiences may trick us into believing otherwise. Looking back on our own intellectual development, we can all probably cite countless occasions where we held fast to beliefs that we later disowned, outgrew, or modified. What seemed certain at one time comes to be viewed later as tentative, only partially true, or blatantly misguided. This sense of destabilization is often followed by a new sense of "arrival."

However, the metaphor of "arrival" misleads when we consider that it implies that growth and change have ceased and that the dynamic process of knowledge construction is now complete. Such a view of knowledge contradicts all that we can observe in the lives of insightful and inspiring language educators whose lives are characterized by periodic shifts in beliefs and understandings that result from ongoing inquiry. The essays in Part One depict some of the ways in which the knowledge and beliefs of the authors have shifted over time—about themselves, their fields, their missions. The impression is not one of arrival, but of incompleteness, anticipation, and curiosity as to where the next step will lead.

As is evident from the essays, the ways are diverse in which the authors are constructing their belief systems—their conceptions of what is real, what has value, and what is possible—as diverse, in fact, as are the many distant and recent sources that feed into them. Common to these very different accounts is the notion that the sources of our belief systems surround us, infusing many aspects of our lives, including our words and other forms of practice. Once articulated, our beliefs can be put to effective use. They can assist us in formulating consonant pedagogic practices, of course. But they can also produce the kind of professional catharses that lead us to reconsider our theories of teaching and learning, theories that, as practiced ideas, have wide-ranging implications for the classroom experience.

Carole Edelsky takes us back to her early years and her sense of estrangement from the mainstream, as well as her passionate commitment to rectify injustice and unfairness. Her passion and sense of injustice appeared early in her life, but were not focused until much later. She eventually reshaped this passion into her own version of a whole-language approach to language education. Michèle Foster reflects on how her French Catholic school background influenced her views and teaching practices at all levels, from elementary through community college and graduate school, and how she worked these experiences into her identity as an African-American educator. Lily Wong Fillmore, through her childhood language-learning experiences as a disenfranchised Cantonese-speaking immigrant child in the migrant worker farm country of California and her trial-and-error tutoring of migrant children, reveals how she developed an early belief about how second-language acquisition works—a belief she later learned to articulate and explore in her university education and in her research. Peter Paul describes the ongoing evolution of his views on the literacy education of hearing-impaired students, based on the struggles and conflicts he has experienced in his own life, and on inquiries he has conducted into theories and practices of literacy. Jim Cummins reflects on memories from his childhood in Ireland and on how linguistic, political, and religious issues intertwined to shape his views on literacy.

Working on the Margins

Carole Edelsky
Arizona State University

MISSION, IMPOSSIBLE OR NOT

People have accused me of taking on whole language as a mission.[1] I say "accuse" because having a mission isn't quite respectable these days. Actu-

---

[1]Whole language is a take on education based on particular theoretical and political premises. A major theoretical premise is that characteristics of language and language learning (as seen through a sociopsycholinguistic lens) should guide decisions about curriculum, evaluation, educational materials, instructional interactions, and so forth. Some major guiding characteristics of language and language learning in a whole language educator's theoretical perspective include: (1) language-in-use is always whole; that is, language subsystems like phonology or syntax function in interaction with other language subsystems and within particular social contexts. Therefore, whole language educators refrain from separating language into multiple subskills and teaching or testing bits of language; (2) language is social; therefore, communities and histories are always implicated in language use and language learning; (3) language is learned by using it for communicative purposes; therefore, whole language educators make students' purposes for using language a central concern; (4) written language is language and, thus, is learned like language is learned; therefore, whole language educators work hard to engage students in reading and writing for real, for some reason other than instruction for instruction's sake or evaluation for evaluation's sake; and (5), language is generally learned for something else; therefore, whole language educators make the something else's the focus, helping students become more skilled language users as they focus on their own concerns.

Whole language's political stance is to promote justice and equity and oppose injustice created by systems of domination. That political stance appears in whole language's: (1) opposition to standardized tests of reading and achievement, which use a separate-skills view of language as a means of ranking and sorting people; (2) emphasis on using language for

3

ally, I think my accusers are both misreading the case and understating it. I think what they're responding to is passion, not mission. It's true; I do write strongly. My emotional responses are intense in person, too. No smooth brow for me! My brother-in-law always warned me not to play poker for money; my face betrays what I have in my hand.

I suppose I shouldn't quibble; passion is as out of fashion as mission. It's the flip side of reason, conjuring up "the mob" (Peller, 1987). It is impolite in academic writing (Stotsky, 1992). In fact, in general, it is downright unacceptable. In a satire on the public's indignation over Phoenix Suns player Charles Barkley's passionate displays about the officiating at a basketball game, E. J. Montini, a columnist for a daily newspaper in Arizona, noted that people who are passionate about something frighten us. What an irony! Me, scared-of-my-own-shadow me, scaring anyone else!

If my rhetorical, interactional passion is going to earn me the reputation of having a mission, however, at least the mission should be correctly identified. My mission (if I play the game and accept that terminology) is not as limited as merely to promote whole language. It's to change the world. It's to help make the world a more just, more equitable, less oppressive place for all who live in it. It's to follow one of the oldest roots in Jewish culture; that is, to take seriously the notion that because the world can and should be different than it is, it is necessary to work for *tikkun*—to work, that is, to mend, repair, or transform the world. In a more modern but reduced American version, it's to abide by the Girl Scout principle to always leave a place better than you found it.

My mission—though I prefer to call that driving force my agenda or my project—is both grandiose and humble. Yes, change the world. But not singlehandedly, not with some definitive static answer, not even necessarily within my lifetime. Change the world by being part of the eons-old struggle to continually transform it in the direction of justice. Change it by contributing to the effort, joined by many people around the globe, to lessen disparities and end the suffering that ensues from them. Change it, in some small measure, through my chosen work.

I chose language education as my work. Or perhaps it would be more accurate to say it chose me (more about that later). But at least I am aware there was a time when professional choices were made. That is not true of

---

communicative purposes rather than doing exercises with it, which undermines an entrenched basal technology based on language exercises and that prevents teachers and students from having control over their own teaching and learning; (3) support of the sociological view that all knowledge is social, which reveals the subjectivity behind the supposed objectivity of tests and other facts; (4) preference for looking at students' language strengths, which results in honoring home discourses, expanding what can count as cultural capital, and lessening just a bit the privilege of dominant groups; (5) view of reading as a transaction in which what readers bring is as important as what texts offer, which gives power to readers, not just to texts and authorities.

the mission/agenda/project itself. I didn't *decide* to be sensitive to injustice; I didn't *choose* to want to lessen it. As far as I can tell from my early memories, I've had that stance from childhood, though not in so many words. Rather than being able to articulate an agenda, what I remember was more of a wail: "It's not fair!"

Some of what wasn't fair was the usual litany, from "they won't let me play" to "why'd you have to bring that new baby home?" Some of it wasn't. Like why should delusional Uncle Isaak have to keep running from the Nazis he thought were coming to finish off the job begun by the real ones who shot all his relatives in front of him in Poland. Some of it was what I saw out of a young but critical eye (who knows where that came from): My daddy's word was law, even when he was wrong; my mommy's ideas were overridden even when she was right.

Now surely there are people who have endured, first-hand and much more directly, far greater inequities in their early lives who did not develop a progressive consciousness. Likewise, at least some of those who devote their lives to progressive activism have had little direct experience with oppression (e.g., the upper-class man who, traveling abroad, truly sees poverty for the first time when it is exotic, goes through a profound awakening, seeks out all the teachings he can find about class struggles, and switches sides). I don't know what combination of factors sensitizes one person but not another to see and want to eliminate injustice. I've never been very good at pinning down original causes. But as for being able to describe what goes into the pot—now that's another story.

HISTORICAL GROUNDS IN THE POT

My particular pot, the one that continues to refine and shape my political agenda as it shows up in my work on language education, contains one sea-changing event and an intertwining of several themes and characters. The event: a divorce; the themes: (in)justice, aesthetics, antipretense, and marginality; the characters: family members and friends/colleagues. Before sorting out this mix, I want to highlight another one: the interconnectedness of biography and history.

Tying my political agenda so closely to my personal experience may make it sound like I'm reducing politics to biography. It would be more adequate, I think, to place my politics—anyone's politics—within personal experience located, in turn, within history. For example, it matters if *social action* means saving pennies to buy bonds to support a war (my World War II era history–biography mix) or marching with parents to oppose one (the history–biography mix many children lived during the Vietnam years). History and biography, that is, bleed into each other.

The same goes for political agendas and biographical correlates. Neither history nor political agendas are simply matters of impersonal forces. A feminist slogan from the 1970s was: The personal is political. But the political is also personal—it has faces, names, memories.

I was born at a time when people "took others in." It wasn't just "cultural." It certainly wasn't a "lifestyle choice" (as it was decades later when communes sprang up). It was materially necessary. Where was the low-cost single-person housing and, besides, who could afford to do otherwise? Thus, at one time, my father's father slept in the living room of our flat, my mother's mother shared a room with my sister, and an aunt slept with me. My coming-of-age years were spent in a predecessor to suburbia during the McCarthy era. There, first- and second-generation immigrant Jews, trying to make it, dissociated themselves from any previous radicalism and tried to imitate the idealized apolitical—indeed oblivious—way of life portrayed in *Good House-keeping*. (Nearly half a century later during the Reagan years, the essential message of that ideal would be put to music: "Don't worry, be happy.")

When I taught fourth grade in integrated schools bordering Black and White segregated neighborhoods in the late 1950s and early 1960s, I had never heard of the Language Experience Approach. Open Education had not yet made headlines in the United States. The theoretical underpinnings of whole language had not been developed. I didn't begin to think seriously about language education until the Civil Rights movement was well underway. The timing, the historical setting, is part of the pot. Indeed, much of the work I've done in language education, with its explicit attention to political projects, may well be considered extreme only because it occurred during the Reagan/Bush swing to the right that made centrism seem liberal and liberalism seem left wing. In other words, a life history, or more pertinent here, the story behind my intellectual work, may seem (is) intensely personal and idiosyncratic, but it is infused with history writ large, shaped by material and ideological conditions.

THEMES AND CHARACTERS

(In)Justice—and My Father and His Mother

If my father were still alive, I doubt I would say what I'm saying now. Not because I would be afraid he'd read it. I don't think he ever read anything I wrote, though he always carried around a reprint of one of my published articles or a flyer about a keynote address I gave and showed it off in the win-status-through-your-children contests he must have been entering since I went to kindergarten, if not before. As far as I can tell, no one ever won those contests, least of all him. (Among his friends, academic work took a decided back seat to income.) If the evidence he displayed listed me as Associate Professor, one of his friends would needle, "So when is she going to be a full Professor?" After I sent him a copy of my first published book, he wanted to know when I'd become a Dean, a question I'm sure one of his friends planted in one of those see-what-my-daughter-did/big-deal-she-didn't-do-*X* exchanges. No, I wouldn't be writing this particular story because it took my father's death for me to begin to understand the extent to which he was an unwitting party in what I think and do in language education.

Life with Father. My favorite book when I was in high school. If my own life were a story, that could well be its title. My father was certainly the main character of the household (my mother's mother competed for the role). And our dramas, too, were played out in a community. But I don't remember the characters in the book being driven by the same engine that was driving ours: comparing each other's statuses. The primary yardstick for status in our community was money. Profession (except for doctor, which occasionally could even outrank money) was secondary. My father, who worked 6 days a week unloading crates of eggs and selling them wholesale and who never had a vacation until his store in the Eastern Market was torn down to make way for a freeway, ranked near the bottom: He never earned much and he had no profession.

I knew early on that this was shameful and also that it was undeserved, that my daddy was just too honest to make a lot of money (my mother's story). And I also learned in my heart, my gut, my bones, my pores—wherever young children learn important truths without words—that hierarchies that demean a little girl's daddy are unjust.

It sounds like we were close, my father and I. In fact, I do remember when I was very young that when my father came home, it was as if the lights had been turned on. But from school days on, our relationship was problematic at best. We acted out the same screaming fight scenes until I was in my teens. No matter how they started, they ended with me being punished for being a big mouth and not showing respect by accepting his views. In later years, our conversations were often like dialogue in bad TV sitcoms. For example, in a long distance phone call 4 years ago:

Me: Daddy, I'm shouting. Why can't you hear me?
Daddy: There ain't nothing wrong with my hearing!
Me: When did you last get your hearing checked?
Daddy: Wha(t) . . . ?

I can remember cringing at his racism and talking back when he described the Black teenagers who walked by his store as sounding like monkeys jabbering to each other in giant unintelligible words. (Twenty years later, Bereiter and Engelman [1966] came out with a similar description of the language of Black children, though they refrained from making the cross-species comparison. I cringed doubly when I heard their description—first for its blatant racism; second for its familiar ring.)

And yet, when I was 12 and I complained about having to walk through part of the Bowery where drunks were passed out on the curb, in order to get to a Saturday morning art class, it was my father who told me I shouldn't be afraid of poor people. It wasn't a crime to be poor, he said, but it was a crime that in this country, people were *allowed* to be poor. It was my father who spoke favorably about politicians and laws that helped regular people rather than the rich. At a time when none of us in that neighborhood knew any woman who had ever gone to college, my father took it for granted that I would go; he even urged me to consider medical school or law school (he'd find the money somehow, he assured me). Now, this goal for me most likely was also for him; that is, being able to refer to his oldest child as "my daughter, the college graduate," or better yet, "my daughter, the doctor," might earn him a bit of that status he hungered for. Nevertheless, he had genuine confidence—more than I had—that I could do it. Years later, when I went through a divorce and had no confidence of my own that I could succeed at anything, it was my father's confidence in me that I managed to borrow, though just barely. And of course, I also borrowed his solution to problems he didn't understand: Go to school.

My father inherited his faith in schooling from his mother. Faith and more. She also gave him (and me, by way of the stories I heard about her) an aching view of opportunities denied by injustice. Bubbe Luba lived the character Barbra Streisand played in the movie *Yentl.* When she was 7, she too dressed up as a boy and slipped out of the ghetto in Odessa because she was so desperate to go to school and learn to read. She managed to sit in a classroom for over a year until she was found out. However, the school she smuggled herself into taught in Russian, not Yiddish. And my Bubbe Luba only spoke a little Russian, a little of a nonstandard, nonschooled variety of Russian at that. Once her disguise was discovered, she never went to school again and never learned to read English after she came to the United States. The family story is that the Detroit Public Library in the 1920s had one book written in Russian, an operatic libretto. My Bubbe Luba, surrounded by other unschooled women and many children in an urban slum but desperate for a literate life, checked that one book out over and over again.

Aesthetics—and Aunt Ethel

My Aunt Ethel considered herself an *artiste.* Waving long scarves (*shmattehs,* my other grandma said. "Rags"), she danced around her apartment with me when I was 3. I remember the filminess and the colors. Aunt Ethel wrote poetry ("a wind upon the heart," she said). Later, when she spent all those years in the Eloise Insane Asylum—the name has now been changed—her brother showed the psychiatrist her published poems and tried to persuade him that her paranoid flights were partly creative outpourings. The psychiatrist dismissed them both, my uncle and the poetry ("ravings and delusions," he said).

Aunt Ethel bought me pastels and drawing paper and urged me to send the pages of the cut-out dolls and cut-out doll clothes I drew to *Jack and Jill* magazine. She sat with me and savored details of my drawings, along with phrases of her poems. When I was 5, it was Aunt Ethel who gave me my first book, Robert Louis Stevenson's *A Child's Garden of Verses*, illustrated with full-page sepia photos. I kept it under my bed and memorized the photos as well as the words.

Color, design, texture—on paper or fabric, in movement or sound—have always touched me deeply. Maybe I learned to tune in to language, to savor the well-turned phrase, to attend to it closely because of the aesthetic press from Aunt Ethel or the comic nudges from some of the other relatives who were amateur stand-up comics. Or maybe I hung on to words because in a household where my sister and I were frequently used as pawns, pulled one way and then the other in verbal battles between my father and grandmother, words could stand still (or so I thought in my pre-Bakhtinian innocence). "But you *said!*" I could hurl back at the shifting figures. "But they *said!*" I could console myself when I had guessed wrong about what was going on.

Antipretense—and My Mother

My mother wore housedresses—Depression-era, button-down-the-front housedresses. And black Enna Jettick shoes. With white socks. No-nonsense clothes for working in the house. The other mothers on the block wore the new clothing called sportswear. Still, she was a modern woman. She gave us vegetables. The other mothers didn't serve such "rabbit food."

In many ways, my mother was a shadowy figure, hovering in the background, often caught in the middle between two bosses: my father and my grandmother. Nevertheless, she had certain powers. She knew about "good taste." She may have worn housedresses at home, but she knew smart attire for going out didn't include gaudy prints. The few mothers who were recent immigrants didn't always know this. And she instructed me on why the frilly white Communion dresses I coveted were not only in poor taste but were *goyishe*—an unfortunate equation she taught me well.

My mother was particularly good at "seeing through." She was contemptuous of anybody who put on airs and even of anyone who today we would say had high self-esteem; that is, someone plain-looking, for instance, who had the nerve to act as though she were pretty. "*P'shaindel,*" my mother scorned. To claim beauty, you'd better really be beautiful! To this day, I don't dare claim or even believe I know something unless I know it thoroughly. To claim to know, I have to really know. No pretense of knowing, no activity that's merely disguised as knowing, no "knowing" for me.

Marginality—and the World at Large

In my family, I was decidedly odd. I read, I drew. My grandma scolded me for thinking too much; others noted disapprovingly that I didn't think enough—about making money, about my appearance. Ironically, I've devoted considerable professional effort to studying and thinking about appearances and, to some degree, money; that is, studying people's presentations of self through language and studying their talk and reading/writing in relation to social class. But that's not what my family meant.

As a Jew in a Gentile society, I'm an "Other." Those idyllic images of small-town America marked by church steeples, of Christmas trees and silent nights sold as universal messages that include everyone are not my images, and in the end, they do not include me. As a female, I rarely saw myself in what I learned in school about "Man and His World," and I rarely see myself even today in most movies scripted and shot from a male perspective, in editorials and ubiquitous ads, even in studies testing the drugs my doctor prescribes for me.

With roots in the lower middle class, I could never quite carry off "doctor's wife" when I was one. And those same roots make me an immigrant, not native born, prone to be too loud, too direct, too candid, too something—prone, in other words, to make mistakes about which academic fork to use—in that elitist, class-sorting, WASP institution that is the university.

THE SEA-CHANGING EVENT

Presleep fantasies at the age of 5 about the wrongness of people being killed in a faraway war. Years of working on student councils to help create a better school community (never mind that it was the school adults who determined what counted as better). I was an involved citizen with an eye out for what was fair from an early age. I read Betty Friedan's *The Feminine Mystique* (1963) between my second and third babies, nodding my head in agreement, sometimes saying "yes" out loud as I resonated with what I was reading. Why hadn't I seen all that before? After all, it was as plain as the nose on my face—which had been surgically altered to please my husband. And why couldn't all the women I urged it on see what Friedan was talking about? Not that I changed anything in my own life in response. But the new insights went into the pot, a pot that boiled over with the end of my marriage.

I was divorced in 1971, when divorce was only beginning to be common, and started graduate school in New Mexico, where the 1960s didn't hit until the 1970s. So I was on my own (though not exactly, because I had three small children by then) and on a university campus when the women's movement was on the rise and consciousness-raising groups were easy to find, when students questioned and demonstrated, when many (myself included) tagged along with if they didn't join the Black Panthers, the Brown Berets, and Students for a Democratic Society, when the New Left—with all its wit and eloquence and particularized vision—came onto the scene.

I was divorced not really believing in divorce, believing instead that my husband was my family and family members were supposed to stay family members forever. As great as the emotional anguish was this intellectual disbelief. (Years later, I experienced a similar disbelief, but without the anguish, when I moved to Phoenix and found the temperature remaining at over 100 degrees at midnight. When it's dark, it's supposed to cool off.)

A HEADY AFTERMATH

The divorce had two immediate benefits: graduate school and radicalization. Once again, I gave up my plan to go to art school. I had given up that childhood plan before, when I enrolled in college for the first time. Pinned (a state of having received your boyfriend's fraternity pin, being engaged to be engaged. That was the 1950s, remember?) to someone who was beginning many years of medical school, internship, and residency at almost no pay in those days, I knew I would have to support us. My practical self saw that being an artist was out of the question. This time, I gave up the art school plan for the same reason, except now it was to help support myself and three children instead of a husband.

A few months prior to the divorce but seeing it on the horizon, I had enrolled for 5 hours of graduate credit in order to renew my elementary school teaching certificate. Now I started graduate study in earnest. Seemingly, it was to earn an advanced credential, a new master's degree approved by the state of New Mexico for teaching English to speakers of other languages. It was indeed a matter of going to school as a way to earn a livelihood. But it was also going to school as a way to stay alive, a way to begin to feel again, just a bit, as though I might deserve to live.

My memory is that I walked around the entire first 2 years at the University of New Mexico with tears running down my face. Surely that's an exaggeration. But not by much. At the student union once, I overheard another student say to a friend of mine, "Carole Shuck? (my name then) No, I don't know her. Oh, maybe she's the one who's always crying." I felt viscerally the pain of such total rejection, the loss mixed with fury and humiliation. Emotionally stripped of any sense of being in charge of my life, I was eager, grateful even, to be taken in hand, cared for, told what to do. It was the language education professors at UNM who did that for me. They told me to apply for regular graduate student status instead of just taking 5 hours for recertification. I did. They told me to enroll in the TESOL master's degree program. I did. They persuaded me to accept a fellowship I hadn't applied for and that I was about to turn down (If I accepted it, I had to work on a Ph.D. but I was sure I wasn't smart enough). I accepted it. Sociolinguist Bernard Spolsky, a forbidding New Zealander who mumbled into his Talmudic-scholar beard and who would later lead me through my dissertation, asked me why I didn't take a course in sociolinguistics. I took his question as an order and obeyed him too.

The first day of that first course felt like a reunion; I had come home. Yes indeed! Who *did* say what to whom and why? What did they mean by *that*? And *then* what'd she say? Why'd they switch to Yiddish just when the story got good? My questions exactly! As I said before, it is probably more accurate to say that language education chose me, that I obediently went along with others' visions at a terrible time in my own life. After all, I was certainly used to obeying, used to having an authority figure who had more confidence in me than I had in myself. In more ways than one, graduate school was home. It wasn't until I began to work on my dissertation research that my professors' visions for me became my own, that I began to see that I might really be able to be a language educator/researcher and use the big general ideas I was learning.

And what ideas they were! On the one hand, they were radical and therefore frightening because they were unacceptable outside a very few circles. On the other, they were so obviously true and, once known, there was no going back to not knowing them. They represented a giant step onto territory I'd never been on before, yet at the same time it felt like I'd always known them. Clearly, the two immediate benefits of the divorce—graduate school and radicalization—were interconnected.

As far back as I can remember, my affinities had been for those who suffered unfairly at the hands of individuals or society (that injustice theme). By the mid-1960s, my voice had joined the chorus of those who sang and were moved by the lyrics of "We Shall Overcome." But I didn't quite get it. Despite the introduction Betty Friedan gave me in *The Feminine Mystique*, I hadn't been able to let myself see the implications of her thesis. Maybe I didn't have the right cothinkers—people willing to entertain such ideas with me. Maybe I smelled danger; really looking at the system of patriarchy would force me to look seriously at my marriage. Moreover, it might make me bite the hand that fed me—fee-for-service medicine in a capitalist society. The divorce both removed these constraints and, coinciding with the heating up of the anti-war movement and the women's movement, plunked me into a university community where people were caught up in just those ideas.

Even back then, it felt like my radicalization happened overnight. As an early subscriber to *Ms.* magazine, I read feminist writers who referred to clicks—sudden insights about how seemingly small slights are part of, stem from, support a huge system of oppression. That first year at UNM, the clicks were so frequent I could dance to them. With the help of long conversations with classmates/friends Nan Elsasser and Michael Colella, the discussions in classes taught by Steve Mann, and the talk in my women's group, I was finally able to understand that not just gender but race and class oppression are systemic, that injustice is built into the structure of systems, that it is not resolvable by individual acts of kindness or fairness no matter how welcome those are, that it is resolvable only through profound changes in structures and systems. For the rest of those graduate school years—and the years ever since—I have been trying to learn just how language and language education are implicated in systems of oppression and how, instead, they could contribute to struggles for liberation.

I have certainly had a lot to learn, considering the ideas I began with. For instance, until I started graduate work, I was certain that the way to teach reading was to teach students to sound out words. I remember standing in front of the refrigerator—4½-year-old Jay in a booster chair, Gail at 3 in the high chair, and Lynn in an infant seat in the kitchen—holding a carton, pointing to the word *milk* and saying "mmmmmmmilk." Not surprisingly, since views of reading and views of nonstandard language tend to go together, I was sure there was only one way to speak English (or any other language) and that my father's "he don't's" were clearly wrong.

I didn't learn on my own that I was the one who was wrong about reading and about nonstandard dialects, nor have I been by myself in puzzling out anything else about language education. The College of Education at the University of New Mexico from 1970 through 1974 offered an exhilarating curriculum. Its mission was to promote multiculturalism and more democracy in education. To these ends, it advocated compellingly for bilingual/bicultural education and open education. The teacher education program that was the home of my first university teaching job also advocated bilingual/bicultural education, but it did so within a competency-based teacher education model.

That experience confirmed that merely changing the language of instruction was insufficient. I began (and continue) to look for lectures, writings, classes, and conferences on language and language education that have a critical edge. Publications outside of language education have been fine teachers over the years: *The Nation, The Village Voice, Mother Jones, Tikkun, Women's Review of Books*, and *Rethinking Schools* have helped me locate what I've been learning about language in a larger arena. With dazzling writing—intellectually rich but stylistically graceful—these publications have also acted as my tutors on major concepts such as postmodernism and deconstruction.

I sought out the (written) company of Harold Rosen, Frank Smith, Ken and Yetta Goodman, and Dell Hymes during the first year of my job in the competency-based teacher education program. Though I didn't know them yet, I talked to them in the margins of their books, turning them into friends at a time of intense alienation. Real live friends were particularly influential teachers at key junctures. Cheris Kramarae helped me realize that the issue of gender and language went way beyond sex differences in language even as I was working on a dissertation on just that: sex differences in language. Bess Altwerger helped me really understand one of my most important current premises: Written language is language. It was in talks with Bess in the mid-1970s that I deepened my appreciation of the political importance of miscue analysis and that I became increasingly disaffected with open education—with its emphasis on process over all, its avoidance of the question of what's worth studying from the perspective of increasing equity in the world, and its general lack of attention to theoretical underpinnings of reading instruction. In recent years, Allan Luke has been instrumental in helping me understand just how thoroughly social, and therefore political and historical, every aspect of language is.

When did whole language come into the picture? I read a manuscript by Jerry Harste and Carolyn Burke (1977) comparing three different theoretical orientations to reading (phonics, skills, and whole language). At about the same time, at informal gatherings, I heard Ken and Yetta Goodman use the term *whole language, comprehension-centered view of reading* and experienced another one of those clicks. This new umbrella idea they were calling "whole language" strengthened, unified, and added to my own ideas (though *my own* really means what I'd learned and reinterpreted from Frank Smith [1971] and early Goodman works [e.g., 1969; Smith & Goodman, 1971]). I joined the group of people working in classrooms and writing about whole language, helping to shift it from a view of reading to a view of literacy education to a view (a theory-in-practice) of teaching and learning in general.

SO WHERE DO THE THEMES SHOW UP?

Justice, aesthetics, pretense, and marginality appear in my memories of long ago, as well as my memories of just yesterday. No wonder they jump out at me when I think about my own work. Some aspect of the implication of language and (in)justice has been part of all my work in classrooms and in writing in the past 25 years. Aesthetically pleasing language—the well-turned phrase—attracts me always as a reader (sometimes literally enchanting me so that I miss the substance); I try mightily to create it in writing. I've worked for years with various versions and implications of one notion: Pretense in language curricula ("reading" instead of reading, language exercises instead of language-in-use, language skills rather than learning skilled language use, learning reading instruction rather than learning to read) makes it harder for kids to learn written language, especially kids who have the most hurdles to jump over in school.

Whole language is a particularly apt harmonic for these recurrent themes. Heavy with progressive possibility, it fits my yearning for more justice and less hierarchy. But it does more. In eschewing stand-ins for language-in-use and even clever assignments that still turn out to be mere exercises, whole language also fits another of my themes: a dislike of pretense. And in encouraging play with words, tunes, and sound for the sheer joy of it, not as a cover for teaching word-attack skills or sound patterns, whole language resonates with my theme of tuning in to aesthetics (on some days, it almost makes up for abandoning my plans to go to art school). No wonder whole language has such appeal for me!

I've saved marginality for last in this summing-up. It's the theme that accounts for what I think people are really responding to when they accuse me of having whole language as my mission; it's the theme connected most directly, that is, to passion. Thus, we've come full circle, back to the beginning—although this isn't quite the end.

Being on the sidelines makes me ache with the pain of not belonging, not fitting in, not being quite acceptable. On the other hand, it is freeing. Because I am a perpetual outsider to academia on several counts (e.g., my class background, my gender, my politics, even my lack of professional lineage—I was never part of any professorial mentor's shop), no amount of good behavior will let me pass. So why try? Why use third person, passive voice academic discourse with its metamessage of neutral knowledge and cool, distant, uninvolved, technocratic knowers and its pretense of rationality and objectivity? Why not write with conviction about my convictions? Why not admit where I think I've been wrong in past publications and be explicit, in print, about how my thinking has changed? Why put up a front when I'll never be one of the guys anyway?

FORECAST: CHANGE

Contrary to the gossip in some quarters, there is no particular party line in whole language circles. There is tremendous variation in how whole language teachers teach and in what whole language educators write. Not only are there plenty of outside critics, there are also those who criticize whole language from the inside. I am one of them. Even here, within my chosen affiliation, I'm at the margin—either not quite in or else unable to give up the habit of standing outside to critically self-reflect. Though I believe whole language has the most potential for providing liberatory education, I also believe whole language educators do little to achieve that potential. Probably because so few of us know how. And so I criticize whole language from the inside—passionately (see, e.g., Edelsky, 1991, 1994).

Recently, I've been wrestling with some ideas put forth by James Gee (1990), Pam Gilbert (1989, 1991), and Ray McDermott (1992). Gee and Gilbert are persuading me that literacy is, above all, a set of discourse practices; McDermott is making me rethink my focus on the learner. Maybe, according to Ray, it's not that a person acquires a language; maybe a language (a discourse community) acquires (inducts) a person. I am intrigued by the twist. I'm also struggling with it. The problem is that I still think there are universal (yes, universal; even in these anti-essentialist times) underlying sociopsycholinguistic processes that occur when a person reads (in the sense of makes sense with/of) a text, and that it is important to look at how people learn and engage in those processes. But I'm finally beginning to understand the idea that there is no process without practice; that is, looking at process is itself a social practice. And I'm also finally beginning to appreciate the claim that a focus on underlying process prevents one from seeing the extent and power of the social practices that capture some people and reject others for membership in the literate community. I'm not so sure anymore of what I know (or knew) about (written) language and I don't yet know what I'll know if I ever resolve what is now a conflict for me between (sociopsycholinguistic) processes and (social) practices. Just be assured that whatever it is—continued conflict or resolution—I'll be using it for my mission (to struggle against injustice); I'll be watching out for pretention; I'll be trying to talk and write about it in a way that's put just right and conveyed with passion. In other words, look for me at the margins.

REFERENCES

Bereiter, C., & Engelmann, S. (1966). *Teaching disadvantaged children in the pre-school.* Englewood Cliffs, NJ: Prentice-Hall.

Edelsky, C. (1991). *With literacy and justice for all.* London and Bristol, PA: (Falmer Press) Taylor & Francis.

Edelsky, C. (1994). Education for democracy. *Language Arts, 71,* 252–257.

Friedan, B. (1963). *The feminine mystique.* New York: Dell.

Gee, J. (1990). *Social linguistics and literacies.* London and Bristol, PA: (Falmer Press) Taylor & Francis.

Gilbert, P. (1989). Personally (and passively) yours: Girls, literacy and education. *Oxford Review of Education, 15,* 257–265.

Gilbert, P. (1991). Writing pedagogy: Personal voices, truth telling and "real" texts. In C. Baker & A. Luke (Eds.), *Towards a critical sociology of reading pedagogy* (pp. 27–47). Amsterdam: John Benjamins.

Goodman, K. (1969). Analysis of oral reading miscues: Applied psycholinguistics. *Reading Research Quarterly, 5,* 9–30.

Harste, J., & Burke, C. (1977). A new hypothesis for reading teacher research: Both teaching and learning of reading are theoretically based. In P. D. Pearson (Ed.), *Reading: Theory and practice, 26th yearbook of the National Reading Conference* (pp. 32–40). St. Paul, MN: Mason.

McDermott, R. (1992). *Workshop.* Department of Language, Reading and Culture, University of Arizona.

Peller, G. (1987). Reason and the mob: The politics of representation. *Tikkun, 2*(3), 28–31, 92–95.

Smith, F. (1971). *Understanding reading.* New York: Holt, Rinehart & Winston.

Smith, F., & Goodman, K. (1971). On the psycholinguistic method of teaching reading. *Elementary School Journal, 71,* 177–181.

Stotsky, S. (1992). Conceptualizing writing as moral and civic thinking. *College English, 54,* 794–808.

What I Learned
in Catholic School

Michèle Foster
The Claremont Graduate School

For the past 25 years, I have been employed as a teacher. Some of this teaching occurred in urban elementary schools, some in an urban community college, but what these two settings had in common was that they were comprised primarily of African-American students. Later, I taught reading and writing to a predominantly working-class ethnically mixed student body in a large, urban state university. And for the past 10 years, I have taught master's- and doctoral-level education students at an Ivy League university, at a state university, and currently at a small elite graduate school of education. Each of the settings has its own distinctive features. In each context, however, one of my responsibilities has been inducting students into the norms of literacy; specifically, teaching them the reading and writing conventions of the communities they were preparing to enter. This was the case whether I was teaching reading to first, second, and third graders in a mixed-grade public school classroom in Boston, teaching English-as-a-second-language to pre-literate Haitian adults, helping students at the public university prepare to pass the reading and writing proficiency exam required to enroll in upper-division courses, or guiding graduate students as they learn to write a literature review.

I have no way of evaluating my successes or failures. I know from students' comments that some have liked my approach and learned from it; others, I am certain, have not. But enumerating my successes and failures with students is not the primary goal of this writing. Rather, my purpose is to state my ideas about teaching literacy and to consider the sources of those ideas and their influence on my teaching practice.

Throughout my elementary and secondary school years, my teachers had not only told me that I would make a wonderful teacher, but by assigning me to tutor other students, gave me many opportunities to practice the requisite skills. Despite their encouragement, this was not a profession I intended to pursue. Interested in becoming an interpreter, I studied French and English literature in college. Consequently, when I first began teaching as a substitute in the Boston public schools in the late 1960s, I had not had any training in teaching methods. Instead, I drew my ideas about literacy learning mainly from my own experiences as a student, and secondly from my immersion in the linguistic worlds of the African-American community. Although I was schooled in a variety of institutions—a small renowned liberal arts college in Massachusetts, a large urban state university, and an Ivy League Graduate School of Education—my ideas about literacy learning were conceived in Catholic school, and these ideas were leavened by my experiences in my family.

When I was 5, my mother, confident in my intellectual ability but convinced that public school teachers would have difficulty handling the energetic and determined child I was, sent me to Saint Antoine, the local parochial Catholic school staffed by the Sisters of Saint Anne, where I completed kindergarten and first grade. After completing first grade at Saint Antoine, I transferred to Académie Sainte Anne, a girls' academy, run by the same order of nuns, where I stayed until I completed the 12th grade. One of the distinctive features of Saint Antoine and Sainte Anne was that both institutions offered students a bilingual education. Instruction during our kindergarten year was entirely in French. Beginning in first grade and continuing through eighth grade, the curriculum was bilingual; in the morning, we were taught by a native French-speaking nun who conducted our classes in French; in the afternoon, a native-English-speaking nun instructed us in English. Most of the children who attended these schools were the children of immigrants from Francophone Canada; there were also a number of students from families of Haitian origin. When I entered kindergarten, however, I was a monolingual speaker of English. By the time we reached high school, these two modern languages were bolstered by the formal study of two ancient ones, Latin and Greek.

As my mother tells it, she chose to enroll me in the school because she believed the nuns would be more effective teachers for me than public school teachers. She saw them as possessed with a religious dedication that caused them to take seriously their responsibility to teach all of their pupils. In fact, she often commented that the nuns were ideal teachers because they believed they would go to Hell if their students failed to learn. Knowing that the nuns did not want to go to Hell convinced my mother that attending Catholic school would best ensure my academic success. The facts that I was usually the only African-American student in my classes and, moreover, that I was not Catholic did not concern her. On the contrary, my mother was not only aware of the nuns' missionary attitude toward African-Americans and non-Catholics, but she reasoned that these facts would induce the nuns to adopt a missionary attitude toward me that, if anything, would enhance my learning.

The nuns offered a rigorous college-preparatory curriculum that they expected all students to master. They used an explicit instructional method, one that made clear exactly what students were to learn and be able to do. In English classes, this method translated into a curriculum that emphasized memorizing spelling and vocabulary words, spending numerous hours diagramming sentences, analyzing parts of speech, and using various mnemonic devices in order to recall information. In French, this curriculum was actualized through taking dictation, conjugating and transforming verbs into different tenses and persons, parsing sentences, and writing answers to reading passages, always in complete sentences. The following dictation, dated May 13, 1959, from my sixth grade French copybook is typical of the kind of work we did at age 11.

> Voici le joli villa de M. et Mme Martin à la campagne. Ils prennent grand soin de leur magnifique jardin. Marie et Jean aide à l'entretien. Jean raze le gazon avec la tondeuse. Il aime que la pelouse paraisse propre. Marie aussi fait sa part. Elle se sert du boyau pour arroser les plates-bandes. Si Rover taquine trop Pussy, Marie arrosera Rover. Elle se sert quelquefois d'un arrosoir au lieu d'un boyau. Que ces tulipes son belles.[1]

Dictations such as these were designed to test our listening skills, our mastery of correct grammatical forms of verb tenses and masculine and feminine forms, and singular and plural forms of nouns and adjectives. Although great stress was placed on mastering grammatical rules, the nuns did adopt some pedagogical approaches that are linguistically defensible. For example, we did not begin the study of formal grammar either in English or French until third grade; that is, after we had a good command of both languages. We wrote weekly compositions, and occasionally there were even creative writing assignments. Although creative writing did not form the backbone of our written assignments, the nuns were appreciative of our creative instincts. I still remember one of these assignments—to write about an alarm clock—as well as the poem that I composed to execute it. It went like this.

---

[1]The translation for this dictation is: This is the pretty villa of Mr. and Mrs. Martin in the country. They take very good care of their magnificent garden. Mary and John help with the upkeep. John cuts the grass with the lawnmower. He likes the lawn to look good. Mary also does her part. She uses the garden hose to water the flower beds. If Rover teases Pussy too much, Mary will spray Rover. Sometimes she uses a watering can instead of a hose. Aren't these tulips pretty.

My Dear Little Alarm Clock,
Every day you are consulted,
A faithful friend indeed.
Ever moving never tiring
to serve man in his every need.
Two little hands and one little face
and twelve numbers large or small
sitting on the dresser or hung upon the wall.
Because of you men know when to toil.
Without you life would end in turmoil.
To eat, to sleep, to work, to play
One must know the time.
So my dear little alarm clock
to you I write this rhyme.

The nuns' feelings of self-efficacy were bolstered by their conviction of the usefulness of form and routines. They established explicit classroom procedures that extended to writing assignments. As with all compositions, this one was first drafted on newsprint and then corrected before being recopied into a bound copybook in which all of our finished compositions were kept. My sixth-grade copybook and several others still in my possession provide evidence of the form the nuns required—the day, date, and year on the first line, a skipped line, followed by the kind of assignment, all centered on the page. By today's standards, this pedagogical approach with its emphasis on form over function undoubtedly would be considered un-enlightened. Undergirding it, however, was a belief in routines, a focus on making explicit what students were expected to know, clear standards by which performance was to be evaluated, and most important, the conviction conveyed to us in every way that effort, not ability, produced achievement. On May 25, 1959, one of the grammar assignments in my sixth grade French copybook required us to transform the verbs in a sentence into the impera-tive, future simple, imperfect, present subjective, conditional present, and future anterior tenses. The sentence read, "J'étudie et je réussis" (I study and I succeed). The belief in persistence and effort, not ability, not only perme-ated the nuns' philosophy of education, but our grammar exercises as well.

As dedicated as the nuns were to making sure that we mastered the grammatical forms of French and English, they were ineffectual when it came to explaining the characteristics that made for a coherent written text, or explicitly teaching the various rhetorical forms of the essay, such as narration, description, and exposition. In comparison to the writing curricu-lum I encountered in Catholic school, the curriculum in my 1964 freshman composition class focused on the various rhetorical forms of the essay. Its pedagogy, standard at the time, consisted of having students read and then write essays on a variety of topics. The graduate students who conducted our classes never discussed the characteristics of the essays we had read, rarely explained what features made one essay better than another in their view, nor explicitly taught us how to produce the various kinds of essays. Somehow, we were expected to intuit the characteristics of the various kinds of prose from our reading and then mimic them in our writing. Unfortunately, I never did. Consequently, when I received an infrequent A on an essay I had written, it wasn't clear why I had been awarded that grade any more than it was when I received the more frequent C–. Compared to what I had learned about writing in Catholic school, what I inferred from my freshman English composition class was that some people were naturally talented writers and those of us who were not could never become proficient writers. The idea that good writing was inborn rather than learned was reinforced in graduate school, where I continued my uneven performance, sometimes receiving a mediocre grade, other times receiving an excellent grade and being publicly praised for my product, but never knowing why one product was substantially better than the next. Not until I took a writing course in graduate school in which the professor engaged students in discussing the characteristics of good writing, did I begin to develop some criteria to assess why some written products were better than others. Research on the writing process undertaken in the 1970s and 1980s, which I was exposed to in the graduate writing course, has been incorporated into and has undoubtedly improved the teaching of freshman composition. Consequently, the way I learned (or failed to learn) to write in my college English Composition course probably bears no resemblance to the way students enrolled in today's freshman composition classes learn to write.

Still, my experiences in college are worth the mention because they underscore how the valuable lessons I learned in my early schooling experience were undone in institutions that were ostensibly more enlightened. When I entered college, I was not proficient in writing various kinds of essays other than personal ones; I had little experience developing a thesis and supporting it by examples, logically developed arguments, or research materials. But I was competent with mechanical details and grammatical forms, practiced in turning out well-presented papers, and most significantly, I enjoyed writing and believed in my intellectual abilities. What is most disheartening about my college experience, and critical to this discussion, is that my strengths went unrecognized, and were not expanded on for almost 20 years.

There were other less explicit lessons about language that I absorbed in Catholic school. In an environment where languages coexisted, I realized without explicitly being told that all students could become fluent or at least reasonably competent in two languages, or three, depending on how you count. On the playground we slipped easily in and out of French, Canadian French, and English. It never struck us as that unusual that our daily Pledge of Allegiance to the flag of the United States was recited in French instead of English. We also thought it unremarkable that we would sometimes write the headings in our copybooks in French and then proceed to write our answers in English. Without being fully aware of it, we were developing a certain flexibility in our attitudes about language varieties, acquiring different ways of thinking about language and discovering the subtle ways in which different languages are never exactly comparable.

One of the highlights of my Catholic school years was the public performances that the nuns organized. Religious and secular choir concerts and student musical recitals occurred frequently during the school year. Elementary and high school graduation ceremonies, designed to be aesthetically pleasing, always included poetry and music. In addition, several times during year, the nuns mounted plays. These elaborate performances were staged to commemorate religious and secular holidays, as well as to mark the opening and closing of school.

Public performances had been part of my experience even before I entered school. My grandmother, an ex-showgirl who had danced in the Black Broadway Musicals of the 1920s, ran a dancing school in the town. Throughout my childhood, she had participated in summer stock and light opera performances. And desirous of a stage career for me, she inducted me into show business at an early age. At 12 months, I had donned dancing shoes and begun taking dancing lessons in her studio. By the time I began school, I had appeared in several summer stock performances, cut a record, been a featured performer at local policemen's balls, appeared on the Ted Mack Hour, been Miss Fire Prevention of Worcester, and had been interviewed on local radio programs. With its tradition of elaborate performances, St. Anne nurtured these experiences.

At home, my family and friends delighted in verbal performance. We frequently joked and teased each other, played the dozens, told elaborate and entertaining stories that were often laced with dialogue, embellished with fictional qualities, embroidered with exaggeration, and, using African-American discourse features of hyperbole, analogy, rhythmic delivery, challenged each other over various kinds of board and card games.

This assortment of multifaceted language experiences shaped my ideas about literacy. But it took a number of years before the creative and artistic view of language that surrounded me at home and the more static and structured approaches to language emphasized in school were blended into a satisfactory mélange of pedagogical techniques that I now employ and constantly reshape in my classrooms. When I began teaching in all-African-American urban classrooms, I instinctively drew upon the verbal traditions of that community. For instance, my penchant for public performance and my family's rich oral tradition drove me to include multiple opportunities for students to read their work out loud and to hear their own work, as well as that of others, read aloud.

Moreover, I also insisted that whoever was reading do so with expression. Over the years, I have found that reading in this way helps students extract more meaning from the text because the paralinguistic features of stress, pitch, and intonation provide cues beyond those available from the text alone. Out-loud readings introduce students at all levels to unfamiliar vocabulary, unusual sentence constructions, new discourse features, and different patterns of organization. Reading aloud helps students whose first language is African-American English to hear where the syntax needs to be transformed in order to conform to the conventions of Standard American English written text. Reading aloud helps graduate students hear sentences that are unclear, tangled, and that just plain don't make sense.

In addition to drawing on the verbal traditions of the African-American community, as a teacher I also instinctively drew on my experiences in Catholic school. As the nuns had done with us, I taught my students to use mnemonic devices to remember material. Nowadays, I rarely ask students to recall information. But over the years, I have transformed some of these mnemonic and metaphorical devices to make them more serviceable for the goals I want to accomplish. For graduate students, learning to write a literature review is a rite of passage, one that is often onerous, formidable, and perplexing. And despite its importance in graduate work, students are rarely explicitly taught how to write one. Some students learn to write literature reviews through an apprenticeship. Apprentices typically work as research assistants to faculty members, and in this role acquire the conventions and techniques of the genre. Other less fortunate graduate students never completely decipher the puzzle of the literature review, and I have heard faculty members routinely fault students for failing to acquire this particular textual form.

Although I have learned that acquiring the conventions of the literature review comes with practice, I do experiment with various metaphors to help students grasp both its purpose and form. The metaphor that I have found most useful is that of beachcombing for rocks. Imagine, I tell them, that you are walking along a beach, collecting rocks and depositing them in a sack. One approach is that as you are walking along the beach, you stop, pick up each rock, describe it, deposit it in the sack, and repeat the cycle. When you are finished, you have a description of each rock but not a description of the group of rocks. Adopting this approach will, I tell them, yield an inadequate literature review. Imagine, on the other hand, that as you are strolling along the beach, you gather the rocks, deposit them in the bag, and once you have gathered all of the rocks, sit on the beach and sort through the colection. As you compare the rocks, you look for patterns in the collection. Some characteristics for sorting them—shape, color, size—are immediately obvious. Other characteristics are not immediately obvious and will take more time to discern. By repeatedly revisiting the collection—reexamining, inspecting, looking over, and scrutinizing—other attributes, features, and properties that can serve as organizing schema will emerge. I tell them that the goal of the literature review is to describe such a collection of rocks, looking for patterns, themes, and motifs. The collection of rocks can be organized in a simplistic, commonplace, mundane, and uninteresting manner or in a complex, sophisticated, and unorthodox one. The great literature review aims for the latter. Although employing this metaphor does not render students immediately able to write the literature review, it does give them an image of the task that they can refer to as they write.

Given the emphasis placed on grammar in my Catholic schooling, it was unlikely for me to have eschewed it completely in my own teaching. Although I never taught formal grammar to my elementary students, each year that I taught community college, I was assigned to teach several sections of Developmental Writing I, a grammar course. I never considered grammar to be an end in itself; rather, I always understood grammar as only one set of tools to be used in the service of the larger goals of communicating through writing. At the same time, I have never been one of those people who considered having a rudimentary knowledge of grammar insignificant and who therefore has refrained from teaching it. My experiences have convinced me that the emphasis teachers, professors, and other gatekeepers place on grammatical correctness is inversely related to a student's status and to the perception of that student's intelligence; teachers are more likely to excuse grammar errors, and more prone to look past these errors to get at the intended meaning, when students are already perceived as intelligent or when they are from mainstream rather than from marginalized communities. African-American students at all levels of the educational system are all too frequently misjudged as less intelligent than other students, with various literacy tasks often used as a yardstick. Significantly, at postsecondary levels of education, students' writing is offered as the major piece of evidence to support such an appraisal. Because of these realities, I have always made it a point to acquaint students with standard rules of grammar. When discussing grammar rules, I not only present them as only one of several sets of writing tools that students can use to produce their written texts, but as a set of tools that, when skillfully manipulated, can mimic oral discourse features and thereby contribute to students developing distinctive written voices and styles within particular textual forms.

Unlike many pedagogues who appear to have achieved clarity about how best to teach students, I have not. I continually wrestle with my own ideas about teaching literacy—how much to emphasize form over function, how best to teach and help students understand the conventions of academic texts, how to help students effectively develop their individual writing voices and styles. As I struggle with these issues, I try new activities and modify my classroom practice to achieve my goals.

When I consider all of my educational experiences from kindergarten through graduate school, my education in Catholic school—founded on the conviction that all students would learn what was taught—was the most influential on the philosophy that undergirds my practice. The need to have high expectations for all students is a commonly accepted notion in contemporary educational circles. Only in Catholic school did such a notion hold sway; only in Catholic school was it consistently acted on.

Conversely, in too many educational contexts, one hears the goal of high expectations repeated as an empty slogan, while strategies for bringing to students' awareness the different forms that characterize the oral and written language repertoires of the empowered remain unelucidated and unexplored. *The road to Hell is paved with good intentions.* I confess I still delight in the image of the nuns going to Hell, although let me add that they won't wind up there on my account.

Luck, Fish Seeds, and Second-Language Learning

Lily Wong Fillmore
University of California at Berkeley

A person growing up in California's Pajaro Valley could hardly help being interested in language and language learning. In the 1940s, the Valley was much more linguistically diverse than it is now. It was then (and is now) a rich agricultural area—apple orchards, fields of lettuce and strawberries, truck farms growing everything from cauliflower to string beans. The people who transformed this coastal valley into the "nation's salad bowl," as the Chamber of Commerce liked to say, were mostly immigrant farmers and farmworkers from Yugoslavia, Portugal, Italy, the Philippines, China, Japan, and Mexico. The most recent of them, the dust bowl migrants, came from England, Scotland, and Ireland via Arkansas, Oklahoma, and Texas. They spoke as many varieties of English as the earlier immigrants did languages other than English.

When I started school, I spoke a Cantonese dialect but no English. An older brother dropped me off at my classroom and told me to stay there until he came for me at the end of the day. He also told me to stop crying.

My teacher assigned a classmate to teach me the color names of the crayons; from Billie Jo, formerly of Texarkana, I learned that the English term for the color red was a two-syllable word—*ray-yed*. I applied myself to the task of learning the names of the other seven colors in my crayon box as assiduously as my tutor applied herself to the task of teaching me English—in the half-hour or so of instruction she thought I needed. I was on my own after that. In those days, there was no special concession or help for children who did not speak the language of school. It was assumed that we would learn it out of necessity, and most of us eventually did.

There were many surprises that first year of school, even after I was able to understand a little English. For one thing, I thought everyone spoke English but me: I was the only person in the classroom who did not know what was happening. I was surprised when I discovered that there were at least six others in the class who did not understand English: María, Pablo, Pedro, Isabela (María's older sister), Eddie, and Luck. All of us had entered school with no English, although Isabela, who was doing the first grade over again, knew a little more than the rest of us at the beginning of the school year. Actually, it should not have surprised me because we were all seated together at the non-English-speakers' table in the back of the room, but it took me a while to discover the principle behind the seating arrangement.

Eddie and Luck both spoke more or less the same dialect of Cantonese as I. Thus, we might have talked to one another, and by talking, discover that we were all in the same linguistic boat. But we didn't. Eddie was so scared that he spent the year with eyes trained on the table and his lips pressed together. He said nothing in any language, so it was hard to know whether he understood or spoke any English. Luck, or Rotten Luck, as he was called by the other kids at school, was someone who did not waste his time talking with ordinary mortals.

His luck was anything but rotten. His name, in fact, was quite apt. Luck was the long-awaited, only son of older parents. To them, he was the second coming of Buddha himself—they pampered him, fed him with their own chopsticks, tolerated his peevish behavior and occasional tantrums, gave him everything he wanted—entire collections of comic books, bicycles, enough musical instruments to equip a marching band. Naturally, he was disdainful of the nobodies who sat at his table in school. He knew everything, or so he intimated. I assumed everything included English. It came as a real surprise that his English was as minimal as mine. He made fun of my attempts to use English, and he sneered at suggestions that his own English could use some improvement. The other children at our table—María, Isabela, Pablo, Pedro, and I—communicated with one another as well as we could. I thought we were speaking English, although I was not sure what English was. It did not occur to me at first that they were speaking a language that was altogether different than the one the teacher and the other students were using.

My first year in school was spent figuring out what we were supposed to be doing, what people were talking about, what things were called, and how to get people to understand what I was trying to communicate. I eventually learned that a person could sometimes figure out what people were saying by paying close attention to what was happening, and by guessing. Occasionally this strategy worked, but it was not foolproof, or so I discovered. A part of the problem initially was that I was taking my cues from the others at my table, but my tablemates were no better off than I. The first year was pretty much a bust, academically speaking—which is not to say it was not memorable. One event stands out.

The teacher had something to show us. She stood at the front of the room saying something I could not understand (she did not use any of the color terms which I had by then committed to memory). By her gestures, however, I guessed that what she was saying had something to do with what appeared to be a rectangular glass box—a tank—on the table at the front of the room. I was then, as I am now, near-sighted, so I couldn't see what was in the tank from where I was sitting at the rear of the room. Squinting, I could make out some green plants in it, but that was all. The teacher talked on for a few minutes—words that made little sense and sounded to my ears like, "Yes, and a gobble goobley is gobbling in the glopp, but gobbledy, googglug gobble gopped, okay?" And then she held up a small orange box for all to see, and she shook something from it into the tank. Smiling, she motioned for the children at the nearest table to come up to see what she had done. I waited impatiently as table after table went up, the children crowding around the tank, and oohhhing and aaaahhing before returning to their tables. Each group acted as if it had witnessed a miracle. The teacher had obviously done something pretty remarkable to the glass tank. Finally, it was my table's turn. My tablemates and I rushed up to the front of the room, pushing and shoving one another, each person trying to get directly in front of the tank. When I finally squeezed my way up close enough to see, I realized that the tank was filled with water. As I peered into it, I saw that not only were there water and plants, there were tiny silvery gray creatures darting around in the water. Fish! Where had they come from? I picked up the orange box I had seen the teacher shaking into the tank. I looked at the label, and sure enough there was a picture of a fish on it. I thought, "These are fish seeds; the teacher planted them in the water, and grew fish instantly!"

Never having seen live fish before, I was enchanted. I had to have some for myself: I would grow some too. I started by trying to reconstitute some tiny dried anchovies we had at home (it was an ingredient for a dish my family liked—pork flavored with soy sauce, the anchovies, some slivered ginger root, and scallions scattered over the meat and steamed). I sprinkled some dried fish into a jar of water. It didn't work. After a few days of soaking, the fish floated, but the only discernible movement in the jar came from the flies that were attracted by the rotting fish. I begged my mother to buy some real fish seeds, the kind I had seen the teacher using. My mother told me I was foolish to believe such things, but she eventually gave in and bought me some Hartz Mountain Goldfish Food. I sprinkled it liberally into a bowl of water. But no matter how many times I repeated this experiment, I could not get fish to sprout.

My failure to replicate the teacher's miraculous act was not kept as private as I might have wished. I had told Rotten and Eddie that I was in the process of cultivating fish, and was expecting to have enough to give away before long, so it was inevitable that everyone would hear how things turned out. Rotten saw to that, but fortunately for me, his English was so poor, no one except Eddie understood what he was saying, and Eddie was too shy to do more than smirk a little when he would look at me at all.

I learned to read in a similarly hit or miss fashion. That is, I listened closely to the sounds the other children made as they read, I mimicked them as well as I could, and tried to divine what meaning the noises we were making might have. I had a pretty good memory, so I was able to recall which nonsensical sequences of noises went with which squiggles on the pages of the books we were working on. My renditions must have been convincing enough to make the teacher think I knew what I was doing. Although I had no idea what I was reading, I was assigned the task of helping the other children at my table. The teacher told me I should help the others, and tell them what the words meant—I think. At any rate, I became the interpreter and reading tutor for the Mexican and Chinese children at my table. This, as one would guess, was not as successful an effort as it might have been, say, had I known Spanish—or English, for that matter.

I learned to read eventually (a year or two later). Once English made a little sense to me, the words on the printed page began to yield a bit of meaning here and there. What little I could understand was sufficiently intriguing to suggest that reading was a skill worth cultivating. The other children at my table were not as fortunate. María and Isabela were my best friends in school, once we had enough language in common to discover we liked each other. Both were open-hearted and generous, but they were more cautious than I in situations they did not fully understand. They did what the teacher asked when they were able to understand what she wanted, but otherwise they kept to themselves in class. We often went to the public library together after school, but they were afraid to take books home with them. Perhaps they didn't believe it really was free. Neither of them did as well in reading or in school as I did, although we were not all that different in ability, or so it seemed to me at the time. In fact, they often understood what was happening in class much better than I. Isabela dropped out of school in the fifth grade because she had to help her mother at home. María continued, but at the sixth grade, we were tracked into different levels, and we went off to different worlds in middle school: I ended up in the high track, she in the low one. I sometimes wonder what would have happened had we both been put in the high track—or the low one, for that matter.

Neither Rotten nor Eddie did much better than the other children at our non-English-speaking table. Eddie learned English after a time—actually, it was a long time before he said anything at all—but he remained inarticulate and non-expressive. He never became much of a reader as far as I could tell. He got through high school in the nonacademic track and graduated, but he didn't appear to be an enthusiastic student. Rotten bluffed and blustered his way through one year of high school, and then he left for San Francisco's Chinatown. He established himself as "Lucky" there and became a professional gambler. It was lucky indeed that the inauspicious nickname of his childhood did not follow him into adulthood, given the line of work he chose.

How did I decide to become a language researcher and educator? My first experience as a tutor to my non-English-speaking classmates was as unpromising a start in education as anyone could have. I did what I could and didn't worry much about it at the time, but there was little chance that I could have been very helpful to anyone: I was teaching skills I didn't have, in a language I didn't understand. Even if I could have understood the English spoken in the classroom, I had no means of communicating what was said to the other children at my table. I did not speak Spanish, and I wasn't even sure how to express in Cantonese what I thought people were probably saying in English. It would have taken much better developed language skills than I had at the time—trilingual skills, to be exact—to have done a credible job interpreting for the teacher and tutoring my fellow students. After that first experience as a teacher, one would think I should have avoided further involvement with either language or literacy education, and yet these two subjects have occupied my attention and thought for as long as I can remember. Did my early observations and reflections on my own language learning experiences lead me to study these subjects? Or was it restitution for my failed first attempts at helping my classmates learn to speak and read English? The truth is, my career choices have been anything but intentional. It was all fate and luck. It was my fate to become a language specialist, and luck that I got more than one chance to discover how satisfying it is to be a teacher.

Nonetheless, the insights on language education that have been the most useful to me came from my own early experiences as a second-language learner. For example, the practice of assigning children to serve as language tutors and buddies to newcomers is a strategy used by many teachers. It seems like such a sensible thing to do: Who can communicate more effectively with children than other children? What better way to insure that newcomers receive individual attention and meaningful practice than to link them up with a language partner? And for an English monolingual teacher, isn't it true that the only way to give every child access to the content is by having a bilingual student tell the non-English speakers what they should be doing and learning? My own early experiences with this practice cause me to question it: Does it really work, and how effective is it?

Billie Jo was my language tutor. To her credit, I did learn from her all of the English terms for the primary and secondary colors perfectly, and black and brown as well. She covered those words in a half hour of slightly impatient, off-handed instruction, and then she hurried back to her own friends. The two of us were not destined to be friends—we had little in common, and it was hard to sustain a relationship that was based entirely on shared color terms. For my part, I already knew the colors, although not in English, so it wasn't a subject that challenged me much. There were many activities happening in class that I wanted to participate in, materials lying around the classroom that I would have enjoyed using, and people there with whom I wanted to chat. Those were the reasons I wanted to learn English, and I think the other non-English speakers in my class were similarly motivated, although we never discussed such matters.

Some of these observations about motivation and opportunity for language learning proved to be useful, especially when I began to work in education. This was in another rural area in California, where I lived after high school. I lived in a town that doubled and sometimes tripled in population between spring and fall, with the arrival of seasonal farmworkers who worked in the fields and harvested the crops in the region. It was as a volunteer teacher for the children of these workers that I found a use for those early experiences and observations. In the mid-1950s and early 1960s, there were almost no special educational services for the children of the migrant workers. They began arriving in about March or April and some of them stayed in the area until late September or mid-October, when they returned to their home bases in Texas. The children would arrive at schools in the area in large numbers and the schools would accommodate them as well as they could without hiring any additional teachers. This usually meant that the children found themselves in bulging classrooms with teachers who did not have much experience, training, or materials to work with them. Most of the children spoke Spanish better than they did English, and few of the teachers knew more than just a few words of that language. They were grateful for any help they could get from volunteers, and because I had already established connections with many families in the camps, I was welcomed in the schools and in the labor camps as a teacher.

Me—a teacher. The problem was that I had no idea how to teach. I was a young housewife and mother with no college or teacher training. I assumed that teaching English and reading were the same thing, and I stepped fearlessly into the business of teaching children to read texts that were written in a language they did not understand. I bumbled my way through the first few efforts and was reminded of the futility of my own early experiences— learning to read in a language I didn't understand. It was clear that something else was needed. It obviously took more than good will and willingness to be a teacher. I read everything I could find at the the public library on reading, language teaching and learning, and teacher preparation. I experimented; I fumbled and bungled; I learned. The children I tutored endured my efforts with humor and forbearance. And they continued calling me *Maestra*—Teacher.

Over the next 10 years, I learned on the job. Perhaps the most useful things I learned came from observations of the many children I met who were learning English. There were considerable differences among them in how well they managed the task of learning a second language under non-supportive circumstances. There were differences, as well, in how they dealt with what could only be described as the educational neglect all of them encountered at school.

There was little coherence or structure in migrant children's schooling. Their movement from one state to another every few months as their families followed the crops meant that the children were not in school long enough to learn much before they had to move again. It also meant that the schools they attended seldom accepted responsibility for providing the children with more than desk space and activities to keep them occupied while they were in residence. Given those circumstances, the children needed instructional services that were quite different from those ordinarily offered children in the local schools.

And yet, some of these children nonetheless managed to learn English perfectly and to thrive academically when they were given some attention and meaningful instruction. It seemed to me that instruction and attention made all the difference to them—not just academically but linguistically, too. Language learning is probably the most social kind of learning there is. No one, I came to realize, learns a language without social support from people who already know and speak it. The support that learners need has got to be available and sustained over the years that it takes to learn a language. The migrant camps and schools I worked in as a volunteer teacher were quite different from the schools I attended as a language learner. There were just seven non-English speakers, and five or six limited-English speakers in my first grade class. The rest of the class were English speakers. They knew English well and could give access to that language to the dozen or so who needed to learn it. If Billie Jo wasn't inclined to socialize with someone with whom she could not communicate easily, there were others in the class who did not mind hanging around with that someone who had a pretty good sense of humor even if she didn't know English. These children proved to be an important source of English for me, and from them I learned what I could never have learned from textbooks or teachers. From them, I learned to schmooze and to defend myself in disputes and arguments with colorful invectives and effective put-downs.

In the classes and camps where I worked as a volunteer teacher, there were few children who knew English well enough to support the language-learning efforts of the many who were learners. At school, there were many children who knew English, but there was little social contact between them and the migrant children, who were treated as strangers and unwelcome guests in the classrooms. In the camps where the children lived, the residents were mostly Spanish speakers. Although many of them knew some English, they knew it imperfectly because they were in the process of learning it. Thus, the children's most frequent and dependable contact with people who spoke English at all was with learners like themselves, and it was not surprising that the variety of English they learned was heavily influenced by interlanguage forms. The process by which contextual factors in language learning resulted in the development of a new variety of English was a fascinating one to observe. It revealed much to me about the influence of social factors in language learning.

Probably some of the most important of the social factors I observed were related to the role of the primary language in the education of language minority students. In my own case, most of my education took place in what was to be my second language, English. Most, but not all. Each day after school (what we regarded as real school) I, along with most of the Chinese children in our community, would go across town to another school—Chinese School—which we attended from 6 to 9 p.m., or earlier, when the students were successful in exhausting our teacher's good will and tolerance in less time than that. During those three hours each day and all day on Saturdays, we were taught Chinese literacy and other subjects in Cantonese. Whatever else we managed to get from the experience, those of us who attended Chinese school learned that being a Chinese person entailed being an educated person, and that it was at least as necessary and important to develop and maintain the language of our heritage and home as it was to know English. As a result, many of the Chinese children in town had a bilingual education experience, divided though it was in schedule and setting.

There was nothing equivalent to that for the Spanish-speaking children who were in my class at school. As a result, there was nothing to neutralize the negative messages they were getting from school about their native language and about their ability to learn. What they learned at school was that Spanish was a handicapping condition: It stood in the way of participation and acceptance at school. They also learned that they lacked the ability to deal successful with academic pursuits—they had no aptitude for book learning.

Bilingual instruction, whereby children are taught to read in their native language while they are in the process of learning English as a second language, has been shown to be an effective approach to countering these negative messages for many children. However, bilingual education was not yet available as an option in the public schools in those days. And yet, it seemed reasonable to some of us working in the camps that if the children didn't speak English, literacy instruction in Spanish was not at all a bad idea. It was a reasonable alternative to confusion and frustration, which is what children experienced when they were taught in a language they didn't understand. Because the Spanish I knew had come largely from my Spanish-speaking classmates at school (it was pretty much the equivalent of the English I was learning from the other kids), I myself could hardly have taught anyone to read in Spanish (it would have meant teaching reading in yet another language I didn't know fully). It didn't matter, however, because many of the adults in the camps were literate in Spanish, having attended school in Mexico. They could serve as tutors for the children who wanted to learn to read in Spanish, if we could find reading materials in Spanish. In those days, there was little such material to be found in California. The only Spanish print material we could find came from the County Health Department and from a Pentecostal church group that was recruiting in the valley. Because we were volunteers, we were not concerned about maintaining a separation between church and state. Thus, our Spanish literacy program began with materials that discussed the dangers of parasitic infections that came from round worms, tape worms and pin worms; how to avoid enteric diseases like amoebic dysentery; and what kind of Hellfire and eternal damnation awaited those sinners who did not accept the salvation offered by the Church, or was it the County Health Department? Despite the heavy-handedness of our instructional materials, the children and the adults participated enthusiastically in our first Spanish literacy program, a response that convinced me of the importance of finding or developing appropriate instructional materials for language learners.

The years I spent in the camps were like that: There were many opportunities to try out new ideas and to experiment without fear of failure. If an idea didn't work, we abandoned it and tried something else. But each failure led to a close examination of why the thing we tried didn't work—and that almost always led to a new understanding of how kids learn language. Without a doubt, I learned more during those years than I taught. I learned enough to realize I needed to go back to school. I did not know enough about language or learning to do what I had been doing. I had to get some tools to investigate the many questions that surfaced as I worked with language learners. And so I went to the university. I started with an undergraduate degree program that focused on English linguistics, among other subjects, and that eventually led to a graduate degree program in linguistics.

It took that much schooling to gain the background and skills needed to address the questions that have framed my work ever since: When children find they have to learn a second language, how do they approach the problem, and what strategies do they follow in cracking the language code? What kind of social or instructional support do children need from others in order to learn a new language? What is the source of the considerable variation we find across individuals in how easily and quickly they manage the task of learning a new language? What happens to children's first languages when they learn a second one under the circumstances many of them encounter at school as immigrants? These questions are at the heart of both the theoretical problems of language learning and the pedagogical problems of language teaching. How do we explain how children acquire the complex linguistic and social knowledge that enables them to communicate effectively in a new language?

What have luck and fish seeds got to do with language learning? Teacher knowledge comes from many sources: From books and courses on teaching and learning, to be sure, but that kind of information is most useful when it augments and illuminates the real-life experiences we get by observing learners. There is much to be learned by observing children as they participate in instructional activities in the classroom, by trying to make sense of their behavior and responses to those activities, and by reflecting on our own role as teachers in what happens. It is part luck when things come together and begin to make sense, and it is as miraculous as seeds that sprout fish when our efforts at understanding the relationship between teaching and learning pay off and our students learn to swim on their own.

Between Scylla and Charybdis: Evolving Views on Literacy Education for Students With Hearing Impairment

Peter V. Paul

The Ohio State University

There are many phrases available that can be used to characterize my formative years and subsequent influences on my personal and professional development, specifically the development of a philosophy related to the teaching of language and literacy to deaf students. I have selected the phrase *Between Scylla and Charybdis,* based on a story from Greek mythology. The phrase *Between Scylla and Charybdis* is interpreted to mean that: when we avoid one evil, we fall into a greater one. The modern, common version that people use is: *Between a rock and a hard place.* Other related, modern variations are *Catch 22* and *Damned if you do; damned if you don't.*

Relative to my intent, Scylla is a metaphor for the English-speaking Hearing World and related aspects such as mainstream culture and values. On the other hand, Charybdis represents the American Sign Language-using Deaf World, as well as the accompanying culture, values, and belief systems. I recognize that dividing the American world into two—purportedly opposing—parts such as English–ASL and Hearing–Deaf is a gross oversimplification. It does not take into account the numerous subcultures within these two major divisions. Another problem is assigning the use of English only to the Hearing World and the use of ASL only to the Deaf World. In any case, these perspectives are common and representative of those held by many of my students and many professionals in the field of deafness.

As I chart my path through these two broad, amorphous worlds, I relate a past experience, bring it forward to a present or more recent point in time whenever relevant, and then return to the past experience and move forward.

Addressing the issues of these two amorphous worlds provides several either–or situations encountered throughout my formative years, and these continue into my present personal and professional lives. The evolution of my professional philosophy has been shaped by numerous events in my life: a progressive hearing loss, peer reactions to my hearing loss, my university education and experiences, my performance as a classroom teacher of children with severe to profound hearing impairment, my two marriages (the first to a hearing-impaired woman and the second to a hearing woman), the birth of my son with Down's syndrome, and a growing understanding of the interrelations of language, literacy, and literate thought.

ENCULTURATION INTO SCYLLA: BEGINNINGS

My family consisted of my parents, both of whom had normal hearing, and one older brother, who also had normal hearing but was in poor health. My father was the oldest of seven children reared by Italian-American parents with traditional Catholic values. At age 12, my father began his formal work life by toiling in the coal mines in Pennsylvania. This was one of numerous jobs and began a predictable pattern of a hard-working life for a man who had only completed an eighth-grade education. During a large portion of my formative years, my father took on various, unskilled jobs that resulted in his being away from home for long periods of time. He valued education for his children because he believed that it led to a better life than the one he had. Nevertheless, like most fathers during this time, he left it up to my mother to oversee my schooling experiences.

My mother's parents were both born in Albania. They fled before that country's doors were closed, until quite recently, to the rest of the world. She was the fifth child in a family of nine and was born between two boys named Vincent and Peter. They were her favorites and, consequently, these names became my middle and first name. My mother graduated from high school and wanted to continue into college. She seemed to be talented in the area of writing; nevertheless, she desired to become a teacher. Apparently, her story is that family finances dictated otherwise, so after graduation, she started working in a factory making buttons and stayed there until she married my father. My mother did not hold another job outside the home until she was in her 40s. Being of a strong, traditional bent, working was an unusual situation for her; however, our family finances dictated the need for a two-income household.

My mother's views of education were even stronger than my father's. For her, education was truly the way to the promised land of a successful life. She became very involved in my education from the beginning, and even more so after my brother decided to quit school during the ninth grade.

This involvement entailed making sure that I completed my homework and even asking questions about the reading selections in subjects such as reading, social studies, and science. She continued to be intensely involved until I reached high school. From this point on, she played a secondary, supportive role because what I was studying was "beyond her ken."

It might come as somewhat of a surprise that I viewed my older brother as a person with a major disability (congenital heart defect) and myself as one who had only a hearing problem. This personal interpretation of my hearing condition was influenced mostly by my family's reactions and adaptations. I was always told by my parents that my hearing problem was minor compared to my brother's problems and those of other members of the extended family. My nuclear family ensured that I was looking at them or touched me to get my attention before they said anything to me. Intuitively, I learned a few tricks of the trade. Reading people's lips was more tiresome during late afternoons and evenings; thus, it was best to have meaningful, deep discussions and interactions early in the day. Family members and the few friends that I had were reminded to keep their mouths free of food and other objects, which tended to interfere with my lip-reading skills (now called speech reading). There was no need to shout; just speak normally and be a little expressive with your face. The best tip of all: Find a room or a place that was relatively quiet and make sure the light source was behind you, not behind that person you were trying to lip-read. These are some of the strategies that helped me through my childhood.

Effects of Hearing Impairment: Personal and Professional Reflections

My hearing acuity was not formally evaluated and diagnosed during the first 11 years of my life. During most of this time, it was surmised that I had a prelinguistic, bilateral moderate hearing impairment, which meant about a 56 to 70 dB pure-tone average in both unaided ears across the speech frequencies. I say "most" because only later was it discovered that the loss was progressive, which meant it was gradually becoming worse and difficult to predict. To put this moderate loss in a practical perspective, some of my behaviors included turning the television up too loud for most normal-hearing people, cupping my right ear so I could hear the television and other people in the room, missing a ringing telephone 95% of the time, and not doing too well on the phone the other 5%. My parents' reluctance to acknowledge that something was seriously wrong (save for a small hearing problem) put off the dreaded medical diagnosis and the subsequent need to purchase a hearing aid. In any case, I continued to become withdrawn, to avoid large crowds—including family gatherings—and to dislike school because of the difficulty of communicating and interacting with teachers and other students in classes. I began also to resent and become jealous of my few friends and others with normal hearing ability.

I received my first medical diagnosis and hearing aid, for the left ear, at the age of 12. At this point, I was formally diagnosed as having a bilateral moderate-to-severe hearing impairment, described best as a prelinguistic, bilateral mild-to-moderate hearing loss until about age 12. Because the loss was progressive and was formally diagnosed at age 12, it can also be depicted as a postlinguistic, bilateral moderate-to-severe hearing impairment. Whatever the description, this degree of hearing impairment had pervasive effects on the development of some of my English language skills, on my socialization process, and on the shaping of my views concerning the Hearing–Deaf, English–ASL dichotomies.

During the early elementary grades, it became clear that my favorite course was arithmetic, courtesy of my early mathematical games and activities with my father, and my worst subject was anything that required a lot of reading or, in other words, the rest of the school subjects. This was disconcerting to my mother who felt, like many other mothers and educators, that reading and writing are extremely important skills for success during and after school. By the time I entered eighth grade at age 12, I was supposedly 3 years below the reading level for my age group, according to standardized reading tests. My mother's involvement with my education, at this stage and up to the high-school level, kept me from repeating a pattern established by both my father and brother, neither of whom had graduated from high school.

My difficulty with the acquisition of English was most noticeable in the domain of semantics; that is, meaning in language, and in some aspects of phonology; that is, the articulation of some speech sounds. This is fairly typical for most individuals with progressive, postlinguistic hearing losses up to the moderate to severe levels. Again, generalizations need to be made with caution. It is not uncommon to find that two or more individuals with the same degree and age at onset of hearing impairment have different profiles relative to English speech and language problems.

Relative to articulation errors, I had difficulty perceiving and producing some affricates (e.g., *ch* as in *chop*) and many fricatives (e.g., *s* as in *sit; sh* as in *ship*, and *z* as in *azure* and *Wednesday*), which are high-frequency sounds that are typically beyond the auditory perception ability of most individuals with severe to profound hearing impairment. I attempted to keep my speech errors to a minimum by substituting words that were easier for me to pronounce. For example, *orchestra* was a very difficult word, so it was replaced with the word *band.* Interestingly, I did not take speech therapy until college and can remark that not engaging in speech therapy earlier was one of the biggest mistakes in my educational life.

I can make this statement now in light of the growing awareness that the connection between speech development and literacy in English is often overlooked by many current speech and language pathologists. Many of these professionals have little or no education in or understanding of the process of English literacy. Thus, a great deal of attention in speech and language therapy for deaf students in their formative educational years is placed on producing intelligible speech. There is no question that intelligible speech is desirable and convenient; however, it is becoming clear that cognitive knowledge of speech sounds, particularly as it relates to the alphabet system of English, is a critical factor for the development of literacy skills. Deficiencies in the morphophonological system of English have a pervasive impact on the acquisition of subsequent English literacy skills. What is even more revealing is that this is true for almost all poor readers—children with hearing impairment, learning disability, and developmental disability.

As an individual with professional and personal ties to deafness, I certainly understand the difficulties of the sound system of English. However, this understanding hit even closer to home, deepening greatly, when I became the father of a child with Down's syndrome. At 6 years of age, my son has great delays in the development of both his receptive and expressive language abilities. It was somewhat of a surprise for me to learn that he has something in common with all poor readers and writers (for different reasons, of course): a general deficiency in the phonological component of a spoken language.

Looking back on my difficulty with speech, I can surmise that this difficulty with phonology impeded the development of adequate word identification skills and word meaning (i.e., vocabulary) growth. Nevertheless, it provided a personal perspective for my current understanding of the problem of developing phonology and morphology in many deaf students. Of course, there is more to English literacy than knowledge of the sound system; however, this knowledge is considered the foundation of literacy because it enables individuals to develop a working understanding of the alphabet system, the system on which English literacy is based. Because of this area of difficulty, the field of deafness is ensnared in a current, contentious debate on whether English literacy proficiency is a realistic goal for most students with prelinguistic, bilateral severe to profound hearing impairment. I will return to this issue later.

It is not easy, however, to cover your errors with vocabulary, especially if you have had limited experiences with the use of certain words and with figurative language. I encountered the word *journalist*, and for some reason, kept insisting that it meant a person who travels. Not a bad guess, if you use your eyes and see that the word is almost (well, almost) spelled like *journey*. And then, you notice that the ending looks like something we use to mark nouns, as in words such as *elitist*. I should have received an award for creativity, but not much else. I should remark that this personal example has been etched deeply in my memory because of another similar association (or rather semantic, in this case) example from one of my deaf students during my teaching years. I asked the class for a definition or sentence for the word *percolate* (typical procedure in my time), and I informed them I did not want anything about coffee making (wails of protest in signing ensued). So, one student raised his hand and signed *My dad's car percolate* [sic] *down the street.* Creative, even poetic.

In any case, the metaphorical uses and devices of English caused me the worst nightmares. I had the same problems in this area as many of my deaf students did during my school-teaching years. I was amazed that one could *cleave* a tree and *cleave* onto a person. The fact that a word could have several meanings was a nuisance. Words, and their meanings, are indeed slippery customers. It required tremendous effort on my part to learn new words and, at least, single meanings. It was difficult and mind-boggling to deal with those other, albeit important, nuances and usages. As I was to discover later, this is a common problem often associated with many poor readers, including students with severe to profound hearing impairment; it has been referred to as *word rigidity* or *word meaning rigidity.*

Multimeaning words become even more interesting and confusing when they are part of idiomatic or figurative expressions. For example, I realized that *bank* was a place where one could save items such as money, clothes, food, and sperm, but the phrase *You can bank on that* seems silly. I preferred *You can count on that* (which, of course, I had learned to use rather well). Even more troublesome were phrases you could not say. For example, although *The head of the class* was okay, *The foot of the class* was not. On the other hand, *The foot of the mountain* was acceptable, but *The head of the mountain* was not. And, I really understood how my deaf students must have felt when they encountered phrases such as *a pride of lions* and *a school of fish.* English is, indeed, strange when lions can be proud and fish can go to school, perhaps even obtaining an advanced degree.

CHARYBDIS: CONSIDERING A SCHOOL FOR THE DEAF

If Scylla was daunting during the first 11 years, she became downright intimidating after I received my first hearing aid. Although wearing eyeglasses has become chic, wearing hearing aids has never been and is usually perceived as a weakness of the body. Strange as it seems, the wearing of hearing aids contributed even more to my feelings of isolation and difference. The ability to receive additional information (most of the time) was offset by what seemed to be incessant ridiculing by my classmates. Consequently, I convinced my parents to allow me to grow my hair longer to cover up part of my ears, especially the hearing aid. In the middle 1960s, this practice was becoming common, much to my father's chagrin.

In any case, I had had enough, and in the eighth grade, I tearfully related to my mother the desire to quit school. Fearing that I would repeat the pattern of my brother, she and my father began the first of several discussions of alternative schools, especially for children with hearing impairment. Years later, I understood that their debate focused on the school up North, which favored the use of sign language (in retrospect, mostly English-based signing, but American Sign Language (ASL) was an option) and the school down South, which favored the use of speech (or oralism). My father wanted the school down South, and my mother did not care as long as I was happy. I liked the idea of attending a special school for students with hearing impairment. Neither my parents nor I fully realized the implications of either choice.

My father's remarks and feelings reflected the ongoing, current debate on the use of signs or speech for children with hearing impairment. For example, he forbade anyone to call me deaf; I merely had a hearing problem. He also felt that I should not use my hands to speak; there was nothing wrong with my voice. In effect, he was a big proponent of spoken English, especially as used by members of the mainstream culture. His remarks are acceptable to the present-day oralists; that is, proponents of oralism, who favor the use of speech, speech reading, and residual hearing. More important, his remarks reflect what can now be called a clinical view of deafness. Proponents of this view focus on the prevention and cure of deafness. The goal is to enable the deaf person to function like a typical, hearing, non-disabled person in the mainstream of society. In essence, there is a focus on improving the English speech, language, and literacy problems of students with hearing impairment. The clinical view has been broadened to include English-based signing (in addition to oral training), but more on this later.

In one sense, my father's remarks are really appropriate for individuals who are considered to be hard-of-hearing. Typically, it is possible for the individual who is hard of hearing to develop language and communication skills via the use of residual hearing (i.e., remaining, usable hearing) with or without the use of amplification such as hearing aids. There is the popular and scholarly perception that individuals who are hard of hearing have more in common with normal-hearing individuals than they do with deaf individuals.

The major problem with some generalizations—as most parents of children with severe to profound hearing impairment eventually discover—is that they do not always apply to each and every child. With all due respect to my father, I did not feel predominantly like a hard-of-hearing person; that is, an individual who could mingle mostly and comfortably with members of the so-called Hearing World. And my struggles with English, particularly English literacy skills, certainly added to my anxiety and distrust of hearing people.

On the other hand, I did not feel predominantly like a deaf person either; in this case, a person who needed to join the world of signs, which I did not know much about anyway. I knew nothing about the presence of a different culture or even a different language, such as ASL. I had no idea that, within the growing development of the cultural paradigm, deafness is considered a natural sociological condition, not a disease or disability. The role model for deaf students is said to be the typical, well-adjusted Deaf adult who is a member of the American Deaf culture. This adult is one who knows and prefers ASL as the major means of communication and who has attended a residential school, the bastion of Deaf culture and the Deaf World.

Of course, I had misconceptions about this world of the deaf. I imagined that it was a place where everything was visual and made visible; something that I could accept, and, perhaps, enjoy. However, I also thought that it was a world totally devoid of sound, full of eerie silence. This would be problematic for me. I did (and still do) enjoy certain sounds immensely, such as music, the calls of some animals, and the low whistle of moving trains. I also wanted very much to communicate with hearing individuals via the use of my speech and lip-reading skills. The desire to use this mode was most comfortable and natural for me; it has an intimate quality to it. Yet, the difficulty of understanding spoken communication caused me to feel less than human—frustrated, confused, and unconnected.

There was a feeling of being in the middle without embracing or understanding either side wholeheartedly. Is it possible to be in the middle? What exactly is the middle? Is it appropriate to be a part of either side at various times, depending on your ability and preference? Why did one have to choose only one side or the other? Why should this be construed as an either-or situation? Can an individual wear one hat at one time and the other at another time, and occasionally put on a third, different hat?

What was missing then and, for many cases, now was the recognition that individuals in a particular culture (or cultures) varied greatly in their use of and proficiency in a particular language. Eventually, I became convinced that either-or situations tend to oversimplify the complexity of human interactions and abilities. Clearly, there is a range of abilities and preferences in individuals with hearing impairment; indeed, in all individuals. Some individuals with hearing impairment might choose to interact solely or more frequently with the Deaf World or with the Hearing World. Others manage to shuttle back and forth between the two so-called bipolar extremes. What I gained from this experience is that it is much more important to have a choice than it is to make one or to think one has to choose only one path.

Returning to the problem of school choice, my parents could not make a decision, or I should say that their indecision produced a decision. So I remained where I was—in the local public school—with the stipulation that my mother would remain involved and help me as much as possible. This strategy was, for the most part, efficient and effective. Despite my continued struggles with socialization and literacy issues, I graduated seventh in a class of 249 high-school students. I should add that I had only a few friends and spent most of my time alone. I went to a community college, did very well there, and along the way, I lost more hearing, mostly via an accident (fell off the top of a car, courtesy of a trick played by a few normal-hearing friends). I now had a bilateral severe-to-profound hearing impairment, and my career goal, after much deliberation, was to become a teacher of the deaf with an emphasis on teaching English language and literacy. Perhaps, I should add that this career goal found or selected me—almost like a calling, due to the degree of my hearing loss and the resultant self-perceptions. I did have a desire to become a teacher (like my mother did), but my interests, originally and for most of my high-school period, were in the areas of mathematics and history.

UNIVERSITY AND PROFESSIONAL EXPERIENCES: EVOLVING VIEWS OF LITERACY

I received a Bachelor of Arts in Elementary Education in 1974. Obtaining a degree in Elementary Education for general education students (i.e., for hearing students) provided experiences that have influenced my professional views on the teaching of language and literacy, especially to deaf children and adolescents. More important, I became convinced that it was necessary to understand the typical development of nondisabled students as well as the development of students with specific conditions, such as deafness or hearing impairment.

My most influential course was the one on reading methods. In addition to discussing various methods for the teaching of reading, the instructor was imbued with the implications of the great debate; that is, the debate between whole word (or look-say) and phonics approaches. In essence, he favored the phonics approach, although he opined that there might be instances when one can and should use the whole word approach, at least for a short period of time. Furthermore, this professor argued that reading was basically the same for everyone—that is, everyone needed the basic, foundational skills, which were often interpreted as word recognition (word identification) skills.

Fascinated by these remarks, I struck up a friendship with the professor, eventually beating him badly in a tennis game. Not much later, I asked two $64,000 questions—*Is phonics important or necessary for deaf children, especially for the development of word recognition skills?* and *Is it possible to develop adequate word identification skills with the whole word approach alone?* I noticed that he was uncomfortable with the questions so he side-stepped them for a moment by asking me: "Do many deaf children become good readers?" I replied: "I don't really know," and, like a good professor, he encouraged me to do some research and find out.

I missed the opportunity to use my personal experiences, in part, to address these academic questions. I was still having difficulties with reading, although I found reading textbooks to be much easier (and much more boring) than reading magazines, newspapers, and the few novels that I attempted. I understood something about the sound system of English; however, I really could not hear the vowels and consonants very well, even with the use of my hearing aids. In any case, if I had done my homework, I could have provided this professor with what is now considered to be an unchanging, enduring classic description of the English language and literacy development of deaf students: Most students with severe to profound hearing impairment graduate from high school reading on only a fourth- or fifth-grade level. This level of achievement has not changed significantly since the beginning of formal testing in the early 1900s.

Even more interesting was my growing realization that the development of English language and literacy of deaf students was qualitatively similar (i.e., manner, strategies, errors), albeit quantitatively slower, when compared to that of their hearing counterparts. That is, the English language process is developmental in which deaf students proceed through stages, produce errors, and use strategies that are essentially similar to those of hearing students learning English as a first language.

I reasoned that, indirectly, this means that phonics and other word identification skills are important for all readers. Or, could it mean that the knowledge of the sound system was important? I also wondered: Is knowledge and use of the sound system critical for reading comprehension? For me, as a virtual hard-of-hearing person (analogous to virtual reality), I must have received sufficient information through my ears peripherally during meaningful social interactions to internalize most of the English language, particularly its morphophonological system. But, what about deaf students with very little residual hearing or limited speech reading skills? Is hearing that critical for acquiring a spoken language such as English? Would not the use of the whole word approach (or, to use today's metaphor—whole language) be just as sufficient? What else is necessary for the understanding of reading? What about information or knowledge of topics in the head? What about strategies that are used to figure out the meaning of words and concepts in the story? Isn't reading a strategic, thinking activity? Surely, there must be levels of reading, proceeding from reading the back of a cereal box to *The New York Times* to *Moby-Dick*. What exactly is reading anyway?

A deeper—still evolving—understanding of the literacy process did not emerge for me until the 1990s. Despite the controversies regarding the teaching of phonics, I was beginning to accept the fact that the development of literacy skills was dependent on a working knowledge of letters, spelling patterns, and words and their phonological equivalents. It also helps to have some knowledge of the topic that one is reading, or what is often called *prior knowledge experiences*. I found that I often used my prior knowledge background to figure out the meaning of some words and to attempt to understand the meaning of the text, especially texts that contain rather difficult and esoteric information such as my texts on literacy. Sometimes my prior knowledge got in the way of understanding; sort of like having preconceived notions that make it difficult to pay close attention to the details. The details in this case are the words and ideas being expressed on the page.

Because of the either–or debate of phonics versus whole words, I had overlooked (as had others) the contributions of knowledge of letter–sound relations (e.g., the alphabetic system) to understanding and improving a sight-word vocabulary (e.g., the orthographic system). It was astonishing— and somewhat disheartening—to review studies on typical hearing students that show that it is possible to see the influences of letter–sound knowledge on reading sight words if children have understood letters (i.e., names and sounds) and can read some words in isolation. I say *disheartening* because many teachers of deaf students, myself included, always felt that the sight-word approach, combined with good signing skills, was the way to the comprehension promised land of reading for deaf students. We would have never suspected that knowledge of the sound system plays an important and efficient role in a sight-word approach for many words. This is assuming, of course, that the research on hearing children can be applied to deaf children, of which I had become convinced.

Throughout graduate school, I came across several ingenious methods that were used to assess knowledge and use of a sound system, particularly one associated with a phonetic language such as English. The focus was on measuring the relationship of the use of a mediating system to overall reading comprehension. Mediation refers to the thinking and reasoning processes that individuals use as an interloper between two entities—in this case, print and meaning.

I reached the conclusion that deaf students who mediate in or use pre-dominantly a phonological-based (i.e., speech- or sound-based) code tend to be better readers than other deaf students who depend predominantly on a nonphonological-based code. It appears that the use of a phonological code (basically, the conversion of print to sound equivalents) is more efficient for handling the verbosequential information of a phonetic language such as English. The use of a nonphonological-based code places heavy demands on memory processes, and this, in turn, prevents or interrupts the use of higher-level cognitive skills for comprehending larger units such as syntax and connected discourse structures.

In essence, I had realized, as suggested by several scholars, that one of the major goals of phonics was to enable students to develop (on a cognitive level) an awareness of the alphabet system—that is, the relationship between phonemes and graphemes. Still, it was (and still is) not clear how one can teach phonics or other aspects of the sound system to individuals who have limited or no usable contact with the world of sound. This begs the question: Is English literacy a realistic goal for most students with severe to profound hearing impairment? My insights on this question did not emerge until just a few years ago. These insights have been influenced by my previous experiences with members of the Deaf community and attempts to teach English literacy skills as a classroom teacher.

During my graduate programs, several important personal experiences seemed to call into question the heavy focus on the teaching of only English literacy skills to deaf children and adolescents. I learned to sign (requirement of the program), and this enabled me to interact with members of the Deaf community, especially at the local Deaf clubs. Hitherto, this was my first real-life contact with the Deaf World. It was an intimidating, overwhelming experience as I struggled to make sense of the multitude of hands dancing all over the place. It was amazing that one could carry on conversations from across the room; in fact, there were several long-distance conversations occurring simultaneously with no difficulty. This would be quite difficult for hearing people via the use of a spoken language. One would have to shout, and that would interfere with other conversations.

What amazed me further was the revelation that this language of signs was not based on English. In fact, 6 to 7 years later, several texts appeared on the scene documenting the grammar and legitimacy of this language—American Sign Language. Despite the fact that ASL has no written, literacy form, I learned that it still is a complex symbol system, capable of meeting the needs of its users. It was a shock for me to learn also that most of these individuals at the Deaf club could not read and write English well, but were able to solve complex, thinking problems and live fairly typical lives. Given my personal struggles with English, perhaps, I should not have been surprised at all.

Although I accepted the idea of a cultural choice, I was still adamant that it was absolutely necessary to learn English. Spoken English would be convenient; however, reading and writing skills were essential. I was also convinced that one of the best ways to teach English was through the use of signing—particularly English-based signing, not ASL. Because ASL had a grammar that was different from both English and from the English-based signed systems, which are still based on English, I felt, as did many others at the time, that there was little value in using ASL. (Obviously, many of us had no education in or exposure to bilingualism or second-language learning.) For example, I asked myself: How could deaf students learn idiomatic expressions such as *It's raining cats and dogs* or *I ran into a friend the other day* if they did not see every word in a certain word order specific to English. I also reasoned that using ASL would be like using French—it has nothing (or little) to do with English. Consequently, I was intent on using English-based signing to teach both word identification and comprehension skills, even possibly to explain the sound system of English.

This heavy emphasis on the use of English-based signing is now considered to be related to the dominant view of the education of deaf students, the clinical view. This view dominated my experiences as a classroom teacher of deaf students and continued to influence my thinking for the first 5 years of my university professorship. However, I must admit my difficulties in teaching English (assuming that we really do teach this language) to deaf students provided the catalyst for a paradigm shift, and then later, paradigm oscillation (i.e., going back and forth between two paradigms) on the issue of English literacy.

Armed with a knowledge of an English-based signing system (*Signing Exact English*), I was determined to solve the English language problems of the deaf students in my classroom. The schools at which I worked did not particularly care how we signed to the students, just as long as we signed well. I spent my first year teaching at the elementary level, the next 3 years at the high school level, and the last year back at the elementary level (1975 through 1980).

The three high-school years were rather depressing because my students seemed to be stuck at the deaf plateau; that is, the fourth-grade literacy level that I mentioned previously. Although they exhibited low proficiency levels in English-based signing, I noticed that several of them were able to sign up a storm using a form of signing that I conjectured was ASL. Unfortunately, because of my inexperience in the use of ASL, I could not capitalize on this situation. I might have missed some opportunities to convey academic knowledge in a system in which several of them were proficient. My insistence that English-based signing was the only appropriate method kept me from exploring other options. Besides, I was good at this type of signing and thought ASL might be too difficult for me to learn.

At this point in my career, I asked myself a serious question: How can deaf students learn about history, science, or any other content area if I or other teachers present this information in a language in which they have little or no command? One analogy would be to use English to teach history to French-speaking students who have little or no knowledge of English.

More questions emerged during my subsequent doctorate program a few years later. One of the most critical was: Is ASL sufficient for teaching English literacy skills? During the doctoral program, I had become familiar with the notion of teaching ASL as a first language to deaf students and to use this knowledge to teach English as a second language. This notion was gaining attention in the field of deafness.

LITERACY, LITERATE THOUGHT, AND DEAFNESS

During my professorial years at the Ohio State University, my understanding of literacy and deafness has continued to evolve. This process has also been influenced by the birth of my son with Down's syndrome, particularly my reflections on the implications of his difficulty with the English language. In other words, I am struggling with the possibility of his illiteracy and the effects on his future life. In putting this struggle and the struggles of other students with literacy difficulties (e.g., deaf students) in perspective, I have encountered yet another either-or situation. At the risk of oversimplifying, I am labeling the two bipolar views reading-comprehension and literary-critical. For most of my educational career, I have seen issues in literacy only through the reading-comprehension lenses; more recently, I have tried on the literary-critical lenses.

Developing the most accurate theory and effective practice within the reading-comprehension perspective is important if the goal is to foster the acquisition of adequate English literacy skills. If I put on my reading-comprehension glasses, I am mostly concerned with both decoding and comprehension aspects of literacy. I want to know the manner in which children and adolescents learn these aspects, and also why some of them have difficulty. The ultimate practical goal of this understanding is to improve the literacy levels of students. There is also the belief that it is possible to improve the literacy skills of most individuals up to a reasonable literate level.

Seeing the world from this perspective, I have also become convinced that the link between the conversational and written forms of English is important for students learning English as a second language. This is, indeed, a surprising—perhaps unacceptable—finding for most proponents of ASL-English bilingual programs. I believe that it is possible for second-language learners to learn about English culture for the purpose of reading via the use of their native language by classroom instructors. However, I have found no compelling evidence in my research syntheses that second-language students can learn to read adequately in English via exposure to the print of this language with only explanations in their native or first language. The assumption here is that students do not have to learn to manipulate or use the conversational form of the language of print. According to the major tenets of reading-comprehension theories, this is an incorrect assumption. It seems to me that we need to find more effective methods (technological and educational) to assist deaf students, and other poor readers and writers, in learning the connections between the phonemes of speech and the graphemes of print.

If I wear my reading-comprehension glasses (i.e., my Scylla glasses), my whole focus is on the development of adequate literacy skills, specifically the ability to read and write English. Most educators, indeed, most people in the mainstream think that this is the most desirable set of skills to display for success in society. There is no question that literacy skills are important. But what happens if we are unsuccessful after 12 to 15 years of instruction with deaf students? What will happen to my son if he cannot develop the ability to read and write well? Does this also mean that he, as well as other poor readers and writers, will not develop the ability to think and reason well? The big question: Is literacy absolutely critical for success in our society? What if my son and others can develop the ability to think critically and reflectively in the conversational mode (speaking and/or signing)?

By placing an inordinate amount of emphasis on English language and literacy, I was (and still am) faced with the fact that many deaf students might acquire a low level of proficiency in English (the only language) by the time they graduate high school. At least two points come to mind here. One, educators and researchers (including me) have failed to capitalize on the growing understanding of the advantages of possessing a bona fide language system at as early an age as possible. Two—a painful reminder of my classroom teaching days—how is it possible to teach school subjects such as science and social studies to students who have neither communicative or academic proficiency in the language of instruction?

These concerns have led me to examine another group of literacy perspectives, which have been influenced by critical theories. Critical theorists are mainly concerned with concepts such as accessibility, enlightenment, and empowerment. In general, when I see these issues through my literary-critical lenses (i.e., my Charybdis glasses), I am not really interested in the improvement of literacy. I am attempting to understand how literacy is used and valued by groups of individuals within a particular context or situation.

In this view, being literate entails the ability to read or write as one mode of literate thought. Thus, the emphasis should be on developing literate thought—the ability to engage in critical and reflective thinking processes. Individuals might have varying levels of proficiency in one or more of the variety of modes of literate thought (e.g., via conversational language form, text-based literacy, computer, mathematics, etc.). Literate thought, itself, is dependent on the acquisition of a first language (especially the conversational form) at as early an age as possible.

It might be important for all language educators to consider experimenting with a literary-critical perspective. For example, suppose that the acquisition of print-based literacy skills is extremely difficult, perhaps impossible, for most individuals with severe to profound hearing impairment. This does not mean that these individuals cannot attain a high level of thought through an accessible form (perhaps, a sign language such as ASL). Nevertheless, a focus on one mode or language can lead to an impoverished development of cognition or subject these individuals to what can be called second-class citizenship, mainly because they cannot obtain a high level of text-based literacy (i.e., reading and writing skills). Thus, if text-based English literacy is the major requirement for graduation credentials (e.g., high school and colleges) and also for access into, for example, the learned professions (e.g., medicine, law, university), it can be argued that this requirement represents an oppressive situation for many deaf students. And, I will add, it will become an oppressive situation for my son.

A FINAL WORD

Despite the radical implications of the literary critical perspective, I do not mean to imply that I should surrender my attempts to teach reading and writing skills to deaf students. Similar to the clinical-cultural paradigms, I do not think it is necessary or prudent to select one permanent way of seeing literacy issues—that is, reading-comprehension or literary-critical. However, the bigger question is: Are both views acceptable to the larger society? From my perspective, the answer should be Yes.

To put this another way: Why should some individuals, who can develop high-level thinking skills either via spoken English only, or via the conversation forms of other languages such as ASL and other international languages, be denied access and opportunity in the United States? Is the presence of text-based literacy skills a prerequisite for an advanced civilization? Or, is it merely a coincidence? Is the real benchmark the ability to think creatively and critically?

The question of which stances to adopt initially—clinical or cultural; ASL or English; reading-comprehension or literary-critical—should not be answered only by me or any other language educator. I have learned that this question must be ultimately addressed by the informed decision of either parents or their children (especially on reaching the legal adult age). That is, parents of children and adolescents with disabilities should bear the major responsibility for this decision-making process with input from a variety of professionals. As the father of a son with Down's syndrome and an individual involved with deafness personally and professionally, I can attest that this is a difficult—albeit important—process.

As a language educator and scholar, I recognize that no decision can be final. Indeed, it feels like I am jumping from one frying pan to another in an either-or continuum, as in the theme for this essay—between Scylla and Charybdis. But, I feel that the situation should not be construed as either-or; the movement between the two bipolar posts should be based on a periodic evaluation of goals by parents and professionals. In some cases, it might be necessary to develop another perspective. These revisions of goals are contingent on the growing, evolving interrelationships among educators, parents, and children with disabilities.

English literacy is often considered to be a critical educational goal for success in school and society. Nevertheless, parents (and language educators) might need to decide if and when this goal becomes unrealistic for the particular deaf child. At this time, I am convinced that the development of a first language at as early an age as possible should be of paramount importance. This is essential for the subsequent development of literate thought, which, for this language educator, is the most important goal in the education of all children.

FURTHER READINGS

Adams, M. (1990). *Beginning to read: Thinking and learning about print.* Cambridge, MA: MIT Press.

Baker, C., & Cokely, D. (1980). *American Sign Language: A teacher's resource text on grammar and culture.* Silver Spring, MD: T. J. Publishers.

Gibson, R. (1986). *Critical theory and education.* London: Hodder & Stoughton.

Hanson, V. (1989). Phonology and reading: Evidence from profoundly deaf readers. In D. Shankweiler, & I. Liberman (Eds.), *Phonology and reading disability: Solving the reading puzzle* (pp. 69–89). Ann Arbor: University of Michigan Press.

Klima, E., & Bellugi, U. (1979). *The signs of language.* Cambridge, MA: Harvard University.

Levine, E. (1981). *The ecology of early deafness: Guides to fashioning environments and psychological assessments.* New York: Columbia University Press.

Liddell, S. (1980). *American Sign Language syntax.* The Hague: Mouton.

Meyerhoff, W. (1986). *Disorders of hearing.* Austin, TX: PRO-ED.

Olson, D. (1989). Literate thought. In C. K. Leong, & B. Randhawa (Eds.), *Understanding literacy and cognition* (pp. 3–15). New York: Plenum.

Paul, P., & Jackson, D. (1993). *Toward a psychology of deafness: Theoretical and empirical perspectives.* Boston: Allyn & Bacon.

Paul, P., & Quigley, S. (1994). *Language and deafness* (2nd ed.). San Diego, CA: Singular Publishing Group.

Reagan, T. (1990). Cultural considerations in the education of deaf children. In D. Moores, & K. Meadow-Orlans (Eds.), *Educational and developmental aspects of deafness* (pp. 73–84). Washington, DC: Gallaudet University Press.

Stokoe, W. (1960). *Sign language structure: An outline of the visual communication systems of the American deaf.* Studies in Linguistics Occasional Papers No. 8. Washington, DC: Gallaudet University Press.

Wilbur, R. (1987). *American Sign Language: Linguistics and applied dimensions* (2nd ed.). Boston: Little, Brown.

Echoes From the Past: Stepping Stones Toward a Personal Critical Literacy

Jim Cummins
Ontario Institute for Studies in Education

Literacy is dangerous and has always been so regarded. It naturally breaks down barriers of time, space, and culture. It threatens one's original identity by broadening it through vicarious experiencing and the incorporation of somebody else's hearth and ethos. So we feel profoundly ambiguous about literacy. Looking at it as a means of transmitting our culture to our children, we give it priority in education, but recognizing the threat of its backfiring we make it so tiresome and personally unrewarding that youngsters won't want to do it on their own, which is of course when it becomes dangerous. They will read only when big people make them—a teacher or some other boss down the line. The net effect of this ambivalence is to give literacy with one hand and take it back with the other, in keeping with our contradictory wish for youngsters to learn to think but only about what we already have in mind for them.

—James Moffett (1989, p. 85)

When I look at the issues I have attempted to address in my professional work, I hear distant echoes from my childhood and adolescent experience. Issues related to the acquisition of conversational and academic proficiency in a second language, the efficacy or otherwise of immersion and bilingual education, and the historical legacy of centuries of oppression at the hands of a more powerful nation all formed part of my personal learning experiences growing up in Ireland in the 1950s and 1960s. These issues were also the subjects of frequent media attention and, at times, acrimonious public

57

discussion. Policies designed to revitalize the Irish language (Gaelic), the decline of which had accelerated dramatically as a result of the famine in the mid-1880s, were tolerated uneasily by much of the population. These policies were instituted after Ireland gained its independence from Britain in 1921 (with the exception of six northern counties that remained part of the United Kingdom) and involved both incentives and penalties, as most language planning policies do.

Among the incentives to learn and maintain Irish were the following:

- Students who opted to sit the Leaving Certificate examination (required for secondary school graduation) through the medium of Irish were given a 5% bonus on the grounds that taking the examination in content areas through Irish was more challenging than taking these exams in English;
- Families in Irish-speaking areas (*Gaeltacht*) who used Irish at home were granted a small yearly stipend;
- Jobs in public school teaching and in the civil service required fluency in Irish, although English was the usual language of communication in the civil service.

At the more punitive end of the language planning spectrum were policies that made the teaching of Irish compulsory in all schools at all grade levels. In addition, a passing grade in Irish was required for secondary school graduation. In other words, failure in the Irish examination resulted in no formal credit being granted for any other subjects in the Leaving Certificate examination that the student did pass.

This policy touched my family directly insofar as my younger brother failed Irish despite having studied it for more than 12 years. As a result, he received no formal recognition for the five subjects he did pass in the Leaving Certificate. An irony is that one of the subjects he passed was German, which he had never studied formally at school but had picked up during a summer spent in Germany staying with a German pen pal. A few days before the examination, he phoned a friend who had taken the German Leaving Certificate course during the previous 2 years to get the gist of the German literature texts that were prescribed for the examination. Experiences such as this have made Stephen Krashen's (1981) constructs of learning versus acquisition and the importance of the affective filter very convincing to many people in spite of some degree of skepticism among academics.

Not surprisingly, Irish revival policies generated considerable controversy and social divisiveness. The approximately 95% of the population who spoke English as a first language were potentially disadvantaged by policies that privileged competence in Irish in a variety of social spheres. A large majority of the population favored the revival of the language in principle, but were ambivalent or even hostile to policies that they saw as being coercive. Divisiveness was exacerbated by the militancy of strong supporters of the language, sometimes referred to sarcastically as *Fior Gaels* (true Irish) by their equally militant opponents. These militant supporters of language revival argued that national identity was vacuous in the absence of a national language, thereby implying that those whose competence in the language was limited were somehow less Irish than those who spoke it fluently. The phrase *Gan teanga, gan tir* (literally, "Without a language, without a country" [i.e., national identity]) was frequently invoked to suggest that independence from Britain was illusory while the English language still dominated private and public discourse.

During the 1960s, opposition to policies of compulsory Irish in the schools and elsewhere coalesced into the self-styled Language Freedom Movement and large-scale research on language attitudes was conducted to assess the national mood. A consequence was the modification of language policies during the 1970s to remove some of the more contentious provisions while maintaining the overall thrust to revive the language.

Thus, I grew up in a context where debates about language policies and revival of an endangered national language were passionate and often heated. My involvement in, and understanding of, these debates was naturally minimal, although my educational experience reflected a variety of practices that derived from these policies. Irish was taught as a subject at the equivalent of pre-kindergarten and kindergarten levels, but my first intensive experience in learning the language came at the Grade 1 level when I attended an all-Irish school. Today in a North American context, this would probably be labeled a two-way bilingual immersion program insofar as students included some who spoke Irish as their home language and the majority, such as myself, whose home language was English. About 80% of the instruction was through the medium of Irish with only English language arts taught through English.

My parents' motivation in sending me to the all-Irish school had little to do with any significant interest in or commitment to broader policies of language revival. My older brother attended a nearby school and it was convenient to send me to the closest school to his so that we could travel by bus together. There was no space available in my brother's school until the following year.

I recollect no particular difficulty in picking up fairly fluent Irish during that year; I recall speaking it with friends going home in the bus and the process appeared largely automatic. My standing in the class went from 13th at Christmas to near the top by the end of the year.

In Grade 2, I went to the school that I attended for the next 11 years until secondary school graduation. There Irish was taught as a subject for 40 minutes a day. The focus was on the structure of the language itself;

vocabulary and grammar were taught out of context; there was no communicative context that would encourage active use of either oral or written language. As my peers and I grew older, we became increasingly conscious of the fact that there were very few authentic communicative contexts anywhere in Ireland (or elsewhere in the world) where the language could be used in a functional way. The bulk of Irish cultural endeavor (music, literature, sports, etc.) was transacted in English with the result that there were virtually no domains of language use unique to Irish. Appeals to nationalistic duty fell on deaf ears for most adolescents who were taught Irish as a subject. Motivation to learn the language was almost entirely extrinsic rather than intrinsic. Not surprisingly, I was much less fluent in Irish at the age of 18 than I had been at 8, despite countless hours of study of the language in the intervening decade. I did very well in formal examinations in Irish, but my fluency was limited. I regained some degree of fluency when I carried out research on the effects of bilingualism in all-Irish schools almost a decade later as a result of having opportunities to use the language with teachers and students in those schools.

The experience of students who attended all-Irish schools for much of their schooling was very different from mine. For them the language was functional and fluency and literacy were unproblematic. The vast majority of Irish adults who are really fluent in Irish today attended such schools.

Although my own experience of learning Irish emerges from memory when I look back from the vantage point of 20 years of research on language learning issues, it was not in any sense a cause or catalyst for my getting into this academic area. I went to Canada to pursue graduate work in Educational Psychology at the University of Alberta with no expectation of carrying out research on bilingualism or bilingual education. I was interested in issues related to language and cognition, but bilingualism entered the picture only when I received a graduate assistantship to work with Professor Metro Gulutsan. Metro, himself fluent in at least six languages, had started teaching graduate and undergraduate courses on the topic of bilingualism. This issue had been prominent in Canadian national policy discussions for a number of years as a result of the work of the Royal Commission on Bilingualism and Biculturalism in the late 1960s. I experienced my own form of submersion as a teaching assistant for an undergraduate course about which I knew virtually nothing. I ended up carrying out my dissertation research on the topic, working in a two-way French-English bilingual immersion program in Edmonton.

In 1974, I returned to Ireland for 2 years, during which time I had the opportunity to carry out a survey of all-Irish schools outside the *Gaeltacht* (Irish-speaking areas) and also to examine the effects of Irish-English bilingualism and bilingual education. The Canadian research on bilingualism and French immersion that had begun to emerge in the late 1960s and early

1970s (to which I had contributed through my dissertation) showed clearly that such programs were viable and effective. Yet, in Ireland, educators and the general public harbored considerable doubt about the wisdom of educating children through their second language. The number of all-Irish schools in English-speaking areas peaked at close to 300 in the late 1930s and had declined to less than 20 by the time I carried out my survey in the mid-1970s. They have since climbed to around 80, largely as a result of parent demands rather than through government interest or incentives.[1]

In my more recent work, I have integrated a focus on psycholinguistic and psychoeducational factors in bilingual education and language learning with an examination of how societal power relations affect educational outcomes for subordinated groups. I have suggested that students who experience profound and persistent educational underachievement across generations tend to come from social groups that have been subjected to long-term devaluation of their identities in both the wider society and in schools. These coercive relations of power are at the root of academic failure.

I have frequently been asked why a White male from a relatively privileged middle-class background should be concerned about power and status relations. Perhaps the historical oppression that Ireland has experienced over centuries and the current power struggles in Northern Ireland have contributed to my focus on issues of intergroup power relations? Maybe so. I suspect, however, that two other sets of influences are more directly relevant. First is the discourse of religious control as it has been practiced for generations within Irish Catholicism, and second is the work of the Scottish psychiatrist R. D. Laing.

Ireland is frequently described as a Catholic country and this characterization was even more true in the 1950s and 1960s, prior to the spread of television and other forms of mass media, than it is today. The Church dominated both personal and political life. The choice between Heaven and

---

[1]The Irish language planning experience evokes in me a sense of sadness at the opportunities lost. Currently, the Irish language is on life support, kept alive artificially through the largely passive knowledge transmitted to students in primary and secondary schools. Yet, we know from both the Irish experience itself and the results of countless international studies that teaching content areas through the medium of the target language in some form of bilingual education is highly effective in promoting target language proficiency. This strategy was pursued by the government after independence in 1921, but in the 1950s, the government expended considerable resources developing an audiolingual program for teaching the language as a subject based on the predominant learning theory of the time that derived from behaviorist psychology. Had some of these resources been expended in researching the outcomes of all-Irish and bilingual models and refining their implementation, the Irish language would likely be considerably more vibrant today. Instead, policy makers and many in the general public assumed that teaching through Irish would entail academic costs to students; those fervent for language revival argued that any costs to individual students were justified in order to revitalize the language; most of the population didn't buy this argument and so the number of such schools declined (see Cummins, 1977, 1978, 1988).

Hell preoccupied the psyche from a very young age. Indoctrination and social control were ensured by means of vivid descriptions from the pulpit, contrasting the indescribable joys of eternal salvation with the equally indescribable agonies of eternal damnation.[2]

If the Church's focus had remained theological, it would not have been particularly objectionable to me when I reflected on it during the 1970s and 1980s. However, in the Irish context, the Church has legitimized its consistent blocking of progressive social reform on the grounds that it alone has privileged access to God's intentions on matters such as birth control and divorce, both of which were banned in Ireland until very recently. The fact that God does not appear to have expressed Him- or Herself clearly enough for the rest of humanity to arrive at the same interpretations appears simply to have reinforced the Church's self-image as the chosen people and its institutions as God's instruments on earth. I think of the many Irish women trapped in abusive relationships, with children appearing every year, and I feel not only anger at the flagrant abuse of power but also a desire to challenge all forms of political, religious, and cultural indoctrination that robs people of their ability and responsibility to think and act for the common good.

My first awareness of how the Church used its power over people's minds to limit social programs of which it disapproved came in relation to a policy initiative of the early 1950s known as the Mother and Child Scheme. Strong opposition from the Church doomed this progressive policy that would have guaranteed minimal prenatal and postnatal care for all mothers and infants. The policy was introduced by a left-wing government Minister (Dr. Noel Brown, a psychiatrist) in a short-lived coalition government. The Church labeled the proposed program Communistic and Noel Brown himself an atheist, and the program died.

Although I myself was little more than an infant at the time, the incident was frequently discussed in the 1960s at a time when much more ambitious social programs were the norm with no dissent from the Church. I remember discussing the Church's destruction of this policy with my mother (a devout Catholic) and asking her why the Church would have opposed a program that was so much in line with its concern for helping the poor. She replied

---

[2]By coincidence, I attended the same secondary school that James Joyce describes in his *Portrait of the Artist as a Young Man*. When I read this book as a 1st-year university student in Dublin, I was particularly struck by his description of the sermon on the horrors of Hell. During the 1960s, I never heard anything quite as graphic as what Joyce describes (e.g., "and the damned are so utterly bound and helpless that, as a blessed saint, saint Anselm, writes in his book on similitudes, they are not even able to remove from the eye a worm that gnaws it"; 1916/1968, pp. 119–120). However, what I did hear about Hell, albeit more subtle than Joyce's description, did not lack for vividness. In fact, the intent of the message was identical in its attempt to control thought and behavior. Ironically, in my early teens, I remember asking my mother who James Joyce was. She replied that he was a writer who had gone against the Church and was forced to leave Ireland and died as a result of being eaten by worms in Europe.

to the effect that "Noel Brown may have been well-intentioned but he was ahead of his time." Her unwillingness and perhaps inability to criticize the Church reflected her total identification with its mission and the subordination of her own thought processes to the superior wisdom of the Church's authority.

Long before I read any of Noam Chomsky's (1987, 1995) political writings, incidents like this made me intuitively aware of how consent could be manufactured through discourse by establishing Us versus Them categories where moral superiority and eternal salvation belonged only to the chosen people (the Us). In the case of the Church, complete abdication of intellect to the Church's authority was a necessary condition for salvation. One of the rhetorical loops we zoomed around frequently in high school religious knowledge class was the fact that the Church did allow that people could follow their conscience (i.e., do what they considered right) but on condition that their conscience was an informed conscience. You ensured that your conscience was informed by exposing it only to writings approved by the Church (in other words, those that had the bishop's imprimatur, or seal of approval, stamped on them).

Those who stepped outside this zone of spiritual development, or who were unfortunate enough not to be exposed to it through baptism into the Church, were the Them (or the Other) against whom We defined our identity. The Them were regarded as morally inferior and somehow deserving of their inevitable destiny and ultimate destination in either Limbo or Hell. I could never work out whether they would experience the agonies of eternal damnation in spite of God's infinite mercy or because of it. However, if God was/is all-powerful and infinitely merciful, it did seem to me that She or He should have been able to figure out some better solution.

When contradictions such as this were raised in my adolescence, the invariable response was that these were mysteries and we had to have faith to appreciate them. The unspoken implication was that those who did not have faith were walking the tightrope between Heaven and Hell.

The contradictions in this discourse were not just abstract. As a very young child, I remember my mother talking about a retired English doctor (a relative of her brother's wife) who had settled in the village in Co. Cork, where she was born and grew up. She said: "You know, it's very sad about Dr. XXX; he's such a lovely man." I asked what there was to be sad about and she replied: "Well, he's a Protestant and that means he can never get to Heaven." God the all-merciful didn't seem to care about the fact that he was a lovely man. In retrospect, I realize that it wasn't my mother I was hearing; it was a discourse that reflected the form of cultural invasion (Freire, 1970/1981) that she had experienced from an early age.

This form of psychologically and sociologically coercive religious discourse is totally at variance with the genuine spiritual commitment of many religious persons throughout the globe. Irish Catholicism as it was (and to some extent still is) practiced is not typical of religious sentiment elsewhere.

However, the intrinsic devaluation of other belief systems that I experienced echoes, in a more subtle form, the xenophobic rantings of zealots who inhabit the fundamentalist fringes of major religious groups today; it also echoes the paranoia about immigrants and cultural diversity that afflicts much of contemporary Europe and North America. The imperatives of Us versus Them discourse also form the deep structure of debates about the merits of bilingual education in the United States or of heritage language programs in Canada.

A final note on my experience of religious discourse and its influence on my work: The revelations of widespread sexual abuse of children by clergy that have emerged during the past decade in countries such as Canada, Ireland, and the United States suggest the complexity of oppressive relationships and the victimization process. Many of these clergy are/were themselves victims of the same coercive discourse that they then imposed on others. The fact that this sad and ugly reality is now out in the open in Ireland has somewhat exorcised the control that the Church has traditionally imposed on people's minds and lives. It has also created a severe identity crisis for the large majority of committed clergy who have dedicated their lives to helping people both materially and spiritually, but who may not have fully realized the coercive potential built into the Church as an institution.

A major influence in helping me articulate and make sense of my experience of religious discourse was the work of the late Scottish psychiatrist, R. D. Laing (1961, 1967, 1969). I came across Laing's writings in 1970–1971 in the course of pursuing a 1-year post-graduate diploma in Applied Psychology at University College Dublin. The diploma involved courses in a variety of Applied Psychological areas (e.g., industrial psychology, school psychology, clinical psychology, etc.). One of our lecturers was a psychiatrist who invariably dressed in a three-piece suit and who came across to my peers and me as insufferably arrogant. We delighted in using Laing's theories to challenge his mechanistic descriptions of psychiatric conditions, each of which had its own drug or electric shock therapy.

In a series of books written in the 1960s, Laing had proposed an experiential and social interpretation of schizophrenia. He argued that schizophrenia should not be seen as a pathological condition within the individual but as an attempt to work through and break out of double-bind situations in which the individual had been positioned in the course of family interactions. The pathology originated in the familial social nexus and was perpetuated and exacerbated by psychiatric categorizations and interventions. To the intense anger of many conventional psychiatrists, Laing suggested that anyone who became the object of psychiatric scrutiny had a right to be paranoid, and he argued convincingly that notions of sanity and insanity are socially constructed. For example, he asked provocatively why we should regard someone who believes he or she is someone else and who acts in a somewhat peculiar but harmless way as insane while considering the normal people who have slaughtered at least 100 million of their fellow human beings over the past 50 years as sane? My mind returned to this contrast many times during the Nixon and Reagan administrations of the 1970s and 1980s. For example, few people questioned the sanity of Richard Nixon and Henry Kissinger, who bombed hundreds of thousands of innocent Cambodian men, women, and children into oblivion for highly obscure reasons related to the global chess game they imagined they were playing. For Laing, madness was a way of trying to cope with the pathology embedded within the society and its institutions. Conventional psychiatrists responded by accusing Laing himself of being schizophrenic.[3]

For several of us in that course, Laing's influence was profound because he highlighted how power relations operated interpersonally and between groups, and how discourse was used in the service of these power relations to define, pathologize, and victimize. My interest in Laing's work continued through my graduate studies at the University of Alberta and on several occasions in the early 1970s, I visited and stayed with a friend who had become a community member in one of the therapeutic communities in London established under the influence of Laing's work.

While Laing's work strongly influenced my personal belief system, I did not initially connect it with my academic interests that were focused on what to me at the time were abstract, academic issues related to language and cognition. However, gradually during the late 1970s and 1980s, issues of social justice became much more closely connected with my academic concerns, and Laing's insights on how discourse is used to construct and locate pathology and define identities began to exert an influence on how I saw language policy questions.

The process that Laing described operates very clearly at both the macro social level between dominant and subordinated groups and at the micro level in the interactions between educators and culturally diverse students. For example, in research I carried out on psychological assessment, it was clear that for many psychologists, their professional identity was very much dependent on the power that IQ tests gave them to define and locate academic pathology within students. The fact that these IQ tests were being

---

[3]One film that appeared around that time that was clearly influenced by Laing's work was *The Ruling Class* in which Peter O'Toole played a young English aristocrat who believed that he was Jesus to the extent of sleeping upright on a cross that he had erected in his castle. The film somewhat crudely transforms this benign eccentric into a serial killer as a result of psychiatric intervention. However, a wonderful line from the early part of the film comes when Peter O'Toole (Jesus) is asked why he believes that he is God; he responds: "Because everytime I pray, I find I'm talking to myself."

administered in bilingual students' second (or third) language and reflected cultural knowledge that students had minimal opportunity to acquire was not permitted to obstruct the process of identifying the deficits that could explain students' poor academic performance (Cummins, 1984).

A similar process of social definition operating to constrict the educational opportunities and life chances of bilingual children is evident in the writings on multiculturalism and bilingual education of neo-conservative intellectuals in the United States. For example, when Arthur Schlesinger, Jr. (1991) says in his book, *The Disuniting of America*, that "bilingualism shuts doors" and "monolingual education opens doors to the wider world" (pp. 108–109) and this absurd message is picked up by the media and spewed into the minds of educators, policy-makers, and the general public, we are observing how a socially pathological discourse legitimates the constriction of identity options for bilingual children.

My concern with social justice issues and with how coercive power was wielded in the international arena was strong during the 1970s but operated independently of what I focused on academically. Trying to work out theoretical issues related to the effects of bilingualism and the relationships between first- and second-language proficiency was very much like an intriguing puzzle that had very little to do with either my personal life or my broader political concerns. Thus, I was able to insulate academic issues from my dismay and anger at the CIA-inspired coup that overthrew Salvador Allende's democratically elected government in Chile and that resulted in the torture and murder of countless people; or my later disgust at U.S. support for brutal military dictatorships in Central and South America (painfully and brilliantly captured in Oliver Stone's film *Salvador*).

Gradually, however, I integrated these two spheres of academic and personal/political as the sociopolitical debate on bilingual education escalated in the United States, and it became very clear to me that similar forms of discourse were being mobilized to legitimate coercive relations of power in domestic and international arenas. Noam Chomsky's political writings were a major influence in highlighting to me how public consent was (and is) manufactured for policies and practices that are diametrically opposed to the overt democratic and egalitarian ideals of the nation.

My recent work (e.g., *Negotiating Identities: Education for Empowerment in a Diverse Society*, 1996) reflects this dual concern with interpersonal negotiation of identity between educators and students (Laing) and how this process relates to the broader operation of power relations in the society as a whole (Chomsky). It also attempts to integrate in a more complete way the relationship between the academic issues of language acquisition, bilingual development, and the like, and my personal and political commitment to challenging coercive relations of power and the discourse that legitimates their operation.

To conclude, it is clear that I, like others, define my identity along a variety of dimensions, and that we all argue in interpersonal and social arenas for our beliefs. This is natural and unproblematic when the discourse does not violate the human rights of others. Discourse becomes coercive when it mobilizes power to the detriment of other individuals or groups by violating their basic human rights. In Us versus Them discourse, whether the Us is defined by religious, nationalistic, political, cultural, linguistic, class, racial, or sexual orientation categories, it inevitably entails a coercive definitional process in relation to the Them.

I find this coercive discoursal process reprehensible and much of what I have written in relation to bilingual education and the education of culturally diverse students generally is intended to identify empirical and logical contradictions in this discourse, thereby making its coercive intent visible. This perspective also underpins my concern that collaborative critical inquiry should become the dominant pedagogical orientation in schools with the development of critical literacy as its primary goal.

REFERENCES

Chomsky, N. (1987). The manufacture of consent. In J. Peck (Ed.), *The Chomsky reader* (pp. 121–136). New York: Pantheon.

Chomsky, N. (1995). A dialogue with Noam Chomsky. *Harvard Educational Review, 65,* 127–144.

Cummins, J. (1977). Immersion education in Ireland: A critical review of Macnamara's findings. *Working Papers on Bilingualism, 13,* 121–129.

Cummins, J. (1978). Immersion programmes: The Irish experience. *International Review of Education, 24,* 273–282.

Cummins, J. (1984). *Bilingualism and special education: Issues of pedagogy and assessment.* Clevedon, England: Multilingual Matters.

Cummins, J. (1988). Review of P. O'Riagain (Ed.), *Language planning in Ireland. Language, Culture and Curriculum, 1,* 303–308.

Cummins, J. (1996). *Negotiating identities: Education for empowerment in a diverse society.* Ontario, CA: California Association for Bilingual Education.

Freire, P. (1970/1981). *Pedagogy of the oppressed.* New York: Continuum.

Joyce, J. (1916/1968). *A portrait of the artist as a young man.* New York: Viking.

Krashen, S. (1981). *Second language acquisition and second language learning.* London: Pergamon Press.

Laing, R. D. (1961). *The divided self.* London: Tavistock Publications.

Laing, R. D. (1967). *The politics of experience and the bird of paradise.* Harmondsworth, England: Penguin.

Laing, R. D. (1969). *Self and others.* Harmondsworth, England: Penguin.

Moffett, J. (1989). Censorship and spiritual education. *English Education, 21,* 70–87.

Schlesinger, A., Jr. (1991). *The disuniting of America.* New York: Norton.

Explorations for Part One:
Evolving a Philosophy

1. Carole Edelsky talks about both the alienating and liberating mindsets associated with, in her words, her "marginalization," that is, her position outside the mainstream of academic endeavor in her field. What criteria does she appear to rely on or defer to in asserting a marginalized status? Do you share the view that she is an outsider?

2. Michèle Foster describes an early education experience characterized by an emphasis on explicit criteria and procedures and on adherence to routine. She contrasts this formative experience with that acquired during her years as a college undergraduate, where she was "expected to intuit the characteristics" of the models she and her fellow students were responsible for critiquing and emulating. Foster is clear that the latter orientation was considerably less successful for her learning than was the former. To what extent do you share her reasoning for this preference? As a student, were you exposed to significantly different approaches to the instruction of similar subject matter? How do you articulate the distinction between those approaches, and how did you respond to each?

3. Over the years, both Edelsky's and Foster's agendas as pedagogues have been motivated by social concerns with issues of educational access. Yet the women diverge in their framing of the central problem and in their views of the kinds of pedagogic strategies, particularly where language is concerned, required to correct the inequities they both identify. With one or more colleagues, take the position of each woman, either as a reflection of your own position or as an exercise in alternative perspective-taking, and argue the rationales, merits, and implications of both views.

4. Lily Wong Fillmore gives a number of examples of how she developed beliefs about second-language learning and teaching from her hands-on experiences as a young learner and teacher. Yet she suggests in the conclusion of her essay that her advanced university education has helped her understand these experiences in ways that first-hand experience alone could not have. What do you think that Wong Fillmore's university education contributed to her philosophical positions on second-language education that her own experiences as a learner and teacher could not do alone?

5. Undergirding Peter Paul's essay are the following premises: All humans need to acquire a fully developed language by a certain age in order to ensure full cognitive development, and children who are severely hearing impaired from birth or early childhood do not automatically or easily learn to speak, read, and write in what should be their mother tongues. What previous assumptions and preconceptions about the linguistic and cognitive development of children with hearing impairment have you or your colleagues held? What literature and/or first-hand experiences have you encountered that pertain to these issues?

6. Paul speaks out as a strong advocate for a phonics-style approach within an interactive theoretical framework (both bottom-up and top-down rather than a whole language approach such as that advocated by Edelsky) to help hearing-impaired students become literate in English. Do you find his arguments convincing? How have your assumptions about literacy education for hearing-impaired children changed after reading Paul's piece?

7. Jim Cummins asks himself in his essay why a "privileged White male" might have evolved such passionately held views on the relations among language, power, and status. What are your thoughts on his explanations? To what extent do you believe that the privileged can come to understand and speak with or for those whom they perceive as less privileged? In examining the evolution of your own philosophical stance within your educational specialty, what similar contradictions and influences do you find, if any?

8. In considering the very different stances taken by Foster and Cummins on the subject of religion, what are your views on the influences of religious practices on the evolution of your own beliefs about language education?

9. Cummins and Paul both discuss the development of their views on language and education in ways that suggest direct links between their past experiences and their current positions. Edelsky, Foster, and Wong Fillmore, on the other hand, seem to perceive these links in more nuanced terms. What is your view on how the authors in this section characterize these links? How clearly can you identify causal links between your formative experiences and your path of professional development?

10. Several of the authors in this section suggest that their careers and philosophical outlooks chose them, rather than the other way around. If you have a sense of this having happened in your own professional devel-

opment, share the details of this evolution with colleagues. How do you characterize the forces, and the interactions among them, that have shaped (and continue to shape) your career and your educational philosophy?

FURTHER EXPLORATIONS

1. If you are currently teaching, examine your own classroom behaviors by keeping a journal for several weeks in which you record, as accurately as possible, the dozens of daily decisions you make as a regular part of your job. Later, with peers, try to determine why you made the decisions you did. To what extent do your decisions reflect your beliefs about language education? If you do not find clear connections, consider what other factors motivated your decisions.

2. Discuss with colleagues how you conceptualize the interaction between your early first-hand experiences of learning/teaching and your university education. Does one or the other seem to have played a more important role in the development of your beliefs about language learning and teaching? Interview several established professionals in your field about this question and compare the responses you get with those your colleagues get from their interviews, as well as with your own views.

3. If there are any hearing-impaired students or teachers on your campus, or if any of your friends are hearing impaired, query them about the questions that Peter Paul has been struggling with on literacy education. If possible, discuss these questions with more than one person because opinions vary among hearing-impaired individuals themselves. Share your findings, and your own views if you yourself are hearing impaired, with your colleagues.

4. With a colleague, assume the perspectives of a father and mother of a severely hearing-impaired child who are discussing how to educate your child to become fully literate. Be sure to consider the roles of speaking and signing, and in signing, the roles of a non-English language system such as American Sign Language (ASL) versus a sign language system based on English. Consider also the relation in English between speaking and writing. Construct a second role play about literacy education between immigrant parents of a young child being raised in a second-language environment, taking into account the various hotly debated approaches to literacy (some of which are reflected in the essays by Edelsky, Foster, and Cummins).

5. To what extent do you believe that your philosophy about language education is motivated by the theory and findings in your field? Who are the major figures and personalities who have influenced your thinking, and what do they say? Explain and compare your views with those of your colleagues.

PART TWO

Introduction:
Identity Dilemmas

It is probable that conflict of some sort characterizes the struggles that most of us have in establishing our identities as professionals. Much of this conflict may be played out internally, as images we hold of ourselves as language educators shift with major or minor career changes, as concerns with our work and professions evolve, and even as colleagues' perceptions of our professional personae begin to contrast with our own.

Such changes can be interpreted as growth, and professional growth, of course, is thought to be a good thing for all the reasons we have discussed. However, we ofttimes are unsettled by the doubts and uncertainties that accompany these discontinuities, our socialization having somewhere along the line inculcated in us the belief that our maturity is signified by a stable, centered identity. On the surface and in the public eye, then, we tend to hide the fact that our self-definitions are in flux. The resulting disjuncture between our public and private personae may cause us to question the sincerity of our motives and the authenticity of our actions (McIntosh, 1989).

There are times, too, when identities, refracted through the filter of one's own consciousness, simply do not fit comfortably. Rather, they poke and chafe, drawing attention to themselves and away from the goals they are intended to facilitate until eventually such discontinuities are too distracting, or even too obstructive, to be ignored. Equally important are issues that arise as a result of the ways in which we are perceived by others, especially when these perceptions are at odds with our own. Such issues may have to do with dilemmas over the agendas that others' perceptions of our professional selves tend to further, and with the rights and prerogatives that others associate with the identities they have assigned us.

We see the authors in this section making efforts to understand these identity dilemmas and how they relate to their work as language educators. Although they struggle along very different paths toward resolution, the accounts of their efforts toward self-knowledge reveal several common characteristics: Each writer has chosen to confront the problem that has arisen in conjunction with the evolution of their professional identity, each demonstrates an appreciation of the complexity and nuances of the issue, and each understands well the responsibility both to make choices and to assume ownership of the choices that they make. Some of these choices involve relinquishing an outmoded self-concept for a newer, more useful one. Most, however, entail processes of catharsis and synthesis as the authors come to terms with their need to accommodate more than one professional vision and to acquire the strength of character to live with the stresses and conflicts of multiple identities. We do not see many resolutions. On the contrary, the authors leave us with a sense of wonder and curiosity about how these identity dilemmas will influence their work in the coming years.

Norma González takes us "home" to the Mexican barrios in the Southwestern United States where she grew up. There, as part of her dissertation research in anthropology, she sought to identify language socialization practices of Mexican-American families. But having acquired the objectivist, rationalistic rhetoric of the academy during graduate school, she struggles to reenter her community in her new persona, growing increasingly convinced of the connections among language, knowledge, power, and human emotion. David Shea recounts the anguish he went through during his dissertation research as he tried to make sense of a serious intellectual conflict between him and an advisor—"the struggle that goes on under tutelage"—to determine ownership of intellectual property. How should control over a student's work be partitioned? And how do our beliefs about the respective roles of student and teacher shift when we complete our formal education or training and take on our own students? Sandra Schecter traces the evolution of her professional persona from teacher, with "insider" expertise in the teaching and learning of language in the context of specific classrooms, to researcher, with "outsider" expertise in the theory and design associated with the study of classroom language-learning issues. She reflects on the boundaries of moral authority normally associated with each role, and speculates on how these boundaries constrain important societal conversations about language education.

REFERENCE

McIntosh, P. (1989). *Feeling like a fraud: Part II.* Work in Progress # 37, The Stone Center. Wellesley College, Wellesley, MA.

Blurred Voices:
Who Speaks for the Subaltern?

Norma González
University of Arizona

a person occupying
a subordinate
position

I was not taught about language. It was simply there. "Nothing worth learning can be taught," Oscar Wilde is said to have once observed. My own lack of consciousness about language in my childhood is illustrated by an offhand remark I overheard referring to the fact that my great-grandmother, Yaya, could not speak English. "Well, of course she speaks English," I had insisted. "I understand her and she talks to me, and I understand English." I was convinced that what was intelligible to me was intelligible to her because somehow we understood and communicated. Languages had blurred and it was difficult to disentangle where one left off and another began. There was no boundedness to language, no readily identifiable edges that could be marked off. There was only communication, however and whenever it took place. How often have I heard of Latino adults who as children were admonished to speak only English in the schoolgrounds, and their unspoken dread that somehow they would not be able to tell the difference. As languages blur, the contexts that they evoke intermingle and blend.

Although I was aware that language use with Yaya was fraught with the seductive pull of her *cuentos* and the sublime narratives of her childhood, I could not fathom that she did not speak English. Even in my immature state, I could discern that a person who did not speak English was invisible. He or she did not exist. English was the currency of exchange for securing personhood.

Yet my Yaya existed, and the world that she created for me through her crafting of language often bore little resemblance to the world that I then

75

inhabited. I became aware of the legacy of bilingual children everywhere: the arbitrariness of the sign. When she drank *cafecito*, it was more milk than coffee, sugary and served in a glass. It was not the same as coffee, which was dark and bitter and always in a cup. A *vaso de leche* was milk warmed to just before boiling and was drunk with *pan de huevo*. A glass of milk, on the other hand, was cold and drunk with cookies.

I learned that the world was not carved into discrete and knowable chunks that were simply labeled differently in different languages. When she spoke of the *sierra*, of the smoky campsites of Mexican miners on their treks to mining camps, the images that she conjured could not be mapped onto any English equivalents. Ineffably, I knew that the dimensions of Spanish were far different from the dimensions of English. They did not feel the same, taste the same, nor sound the same. Spanish was the language of family, of food, of music, of ritual; in short, of identity. It was the language of endearments to children. It was the language of dressing in white in long processions in dark churches. It was the language of tinkling music on Saturday morning. English was for arithmetic, for the doctor's office, for the teacher. English was the newspaper and television. Even though we mixed languages effortlessly, the underlying symbolism was correspondingly parallel: Home and hearth were woven with Spanish; out there was constructed with English.

In the course of my schooling, I initially and unquestioningly accepted the division between English as productive currency and Spanish as the discourse of connection. This demarcation further extended to English as objective and scientific, and Spanish as subjective and evocative. As a fledgling academic, it became easy to hide behind the cloak of objectivity because it rendered messy topics distant and impersonal. Once shrouded in academese, racism, poverty and other facile constructs became sanitized and anaesthetized. By objectifying the researched, by assuming an impersonal stance toward the data, I could validate my academic credentials as a social scientist. And so, it became possible to talk about language patterns without reference to the relations of symbolic domination that surround those patterns. Language contact could be bandied about with no reference to the devaluation and denigration of one language to another. The intersection of social class and language could be confined to a discrete variable subject to quantification. In short, the use of the phenomenally multiplex medium of language could be stripped to its phonetic, morphemic, and syntactic carcass.

Of course, it is only now in retrospect, having been fitted with academic lenses, that I can label the then-familiar world with theoretical constructs. But it has been a treacherous journey, replete with detours, often ricocheting from one side of the academic fence to the other, while pushing forth to forge an identity, both personal and academic. It is only now in retracing and reflecting on this experience that I can label the dilemmas with which I struggled. Because academic language use and its attendant ideology had distanced me in some ways from my own community, I struggled with voicing that which was experiential.

As an aftermath of grappling with these issues, the validity of reflection on one's personal experiences as a source of social theory took on for me an intensely revelatory dimension. As discourses seek to redefine theoretical perspectives that can be constructed only from the insider's point of view, *emic* as natives begin to talk back, the voices that are heard may be neither unified nor cohesive. There are levels and intersections of shared subjectivities. Mexican-origin adolescents, born and reared in the United States, often find little in common with newly immigrated youth, and minority discourse is inherently imbued with multiple perspectives. Contradiction and ambiguity are not to be thrust away as confounding variables, but as the essence of analysis. As I have continued as a researcher within my own community, I have found that the integrated and cohesive pictures of culture, which did not always mesh with my own experience, were not always forthcoming. Further, I have found that in studying language with predigested structures, we can often defeat the creative forces that it unleashes.

I had been drawn to the study of language in context partly because of the magnetic sway of the assemblages linguists had fashioned for phenomena that I had implicitly accepted as everyday occurrences. To learn that there was a term like *code-switching* for what was a commonplace household discourse pattern was to somehow validate and elevate the practice to the realm of That Which Is Worthy Of Study. Yet, these same constructs did not always resonate with my own experience. The conclusion I drew was that my own experience was somehow nonstandard, that my subjectivity clouded the clearer interpretations of others who were more adept than I at fashioning theory. But because knowledge and power are intimately bound up with each other, I could not have the knowledge of my experience without the power to assert that knowledge. Like my great-grandmother, I too was invisible because I did not control the discourse.

When I began anthropological fieldwork investigating language socialization practices in my home community, it became impossible to disassociate the interminglings of language with the larger contexts in which people played out their lives. During the course of my fieldwork, the sting of race and class distinctions, unemployment and underemployment, lack of health care, divorce, death, alcoholism and drug abuse; all were touched on in one form or another in the interviews on language use that I conducted. But if all of these elements coincided in their barbs, so did the soothing balsam of warm and supportive networks of kinship and friendship, and multiple strands of complementary and mutual affiliations and relationships. The study of language use in the community became, in a sense, a study of oppositions: the opposition of being both insider and outsider, of objectivity and subjectivity, of language solidarity and language schism, of language as private, personal domain, and language as publicly constituted discourse.

As an anthropologist, I was not the detached and disinterested social scientist. I became a participant/observer, not in an exotic or unknown land, as anthropologists usually do, learning the language for the first time, but within my own intimate circles, where the nuances were well-known, and hence, less salient to the insider. I recalled a graduate school conversation with the only other two Latinos in my department at the time. One had been advised that doing fieldwork in one's own community was not as valid as working in a foreign setting. The anthropological cliché of fish being the last to discover water was tossed about. Could I truly make the familiar strange? Was my linguistic subjectivity an entree into the inner realms of the insider's point of view, or was it a filter that obscured the emergence of patterns visible only to the outsider?

Because the neighborhoods where I worked were nonexotic to me, the angst of dealing with the anthropological rite of passage of immersion in an alien population was absent. I couldn't help but wonder how non-Mexicans, driving through these streets, would picture the lifestyles of the people within these homes. I had observed women from other areas of the city discreetly lock their car doors as they entered into the South-side quadrant, and police presence was never far away. What of everyday life, though, as it hummed along in these neighborhoods? What happens within the walls of these homes that is not reported in the mass media, and is the genesis for the transmission of intergenerational knowledge? Is the concept of otherness really that marked within the emic conceptualization of the community? Or was it a construct from without, an etic formulation to explain away discontinuities?

Yet another dilemma remained: Somewhere out there, there had to be households that fit the traditional markers of U.S. Mexican ethnicity, that combined the essence of what it is to be Mexican. Academic discourse had constructed a picture of a normative culture out there somewhere. If I could only objectify the data, its rationality would emerge as it had in the academic literature. Even though I implicitly knew that the households within my own circles of kinship and friendship were nonstandard in some way, somewhere it must be possible to study households that would truly represent the population. Because my experience with the community was subjective, I felt it could not be accurate, and that even though I knew that all Spanish, or *barrios,* or levels of poverty, or degrees of Catholicism, are not created equal, I searched for canons of cultural practices. I knew that the straddling of two cultural systems impelled a surge toward identification, definition, and redefinition. I knew that music (romantic, nostalgic, gripping, seductive, throbbing, Mexican music) was a formative force in molding identity. I knew that joking and teasing and verbal play were integral parts of linguistic context: that the best teasers were never alone. I knew how subtle shifts in discourse marked qualitatively significant shifts in cueing speech events: that people slipped in and out of speaking styles effortlessly and glibly, crafting intricate verbal art that would drive sociolinguists berserk. I knew that the children of the members of my age cohort had felt the linguistic homogenization of Sesame Street and other such shows. Who better than an insider could grasp the complexities of language use?

THE DISCARDING OF PARADIGM

One anecdote in my early fieldwork experience illustrates how I came to discard notions of quantification and objectivity and rely more heavily on the shared subjectivity of self-reflection.

I began my first study on language use with a particular notion of how anthropological research should be done in general, and language socialization research in particular. I first started out with ideas of coding linguistic exchanges with categories focusing on participant structures, child's turns at talk, types of interactions sanctioned, turn-taking, child-initiated speech, and so on. I tinkered endlessly with methodological models, trying to interject a quantifiable (and hence more valid) dimension. I labored under the assumption that identifiable patterns would emerge under these prepackaged constructs that would readily explicate the sources and content of variation in language use in households. I soon came to a halt in the research process because language practices I encountered were not content to be boxed into the prefabricated niches that had been molded. For a while, I insisted that I simply had to search harder, to tinker longer with the scenarios I was presented, and that somehow the refined, orderly, and cohesive picture that other language socialization studies described would emerge. This did not happen. Instead, I was jolted out of the frames that I had complacently embraced. I came uncomfortably face to face with contradiction, ambiguity, and the blurring of boundaries between categories.

On my first ethnographic interview, Marina Escobedo sat at her small dining room table as she spoke rapidly. Her voice belied her impassioned hope that her children never get involved in drugs:

> . . . I mean, I've seen families where people will go into the home, and a father and a mother, or an aunt or an uncle, will come, will walk in, and will roll up a joint and smoke it, like it's a cigarette, with the kids around. Then the first time they have difficulty with their child, if they catch the teenage kids with it, and they say, 'Why are you doing this?' And the kid retaliates by

saying, 'Look, you do it.' . . . There was a situation recently . . . there was a family where there were two teen-age boys, OK? Aunts and uncles, everybody in the family smoked it. Their parents are both in jail because of it, OK? These kids have grown up with marijuana and drugs as a normal thing in the family life, OK? Normal, completely. I mean they have never passed a day when it was not in their normal everyday activities, where somebody wasn't rolling it, somebody wasn't selling it, somebody wasn't doing something, it was normal. OK, and they all went out on a picnic. Unfortunately, the kids stole the stuff from a couple of their aunts, and went off to the corner . . . and got caught doing it. And the aunts ANGRILY, I mean really indignant confronted them and asked them, well WHY did you do this. You know, 'why are you doing this?' And the kids say, well YOU do it. 'But you have to have some respect.' And the kids go, 'well, you don't'. And they get all upset. They came and they were talking to their brother, and [   ] said, well, what do you expect from these children? You do it in front of them, you're their role model to them, they look up to you.

I cringed inwardly as she detailed the picnic scene, as I always feel a pang of distress whenever the subject of Hispanic kids and drugs surfaces. My intent was to provide an ethnographic description of the processes of language socialization within Tucson U.S. Mexican households. It was not to feed stereotypes of drugs, gangs, and violence. It was a contradiction that is played out in the many images of "Mexican-ness." The community I know is a nurturing web of familial alliances and friendship, of an interweaving of connections from a shared and inherited Mexican Tucson where the past slips effortlessly into the present, as omnipresent as the Santa Cruz River, and as omniferous as the Sonoran desert from whose soils it has flourished and blossomed.

It is a community in the true sense of a fellowship of shared commonalities in an arid and parched ecosystem into which its early Mexican settlers sowed the seeds of *compadrazgo* and *confianza* from which their descendants now reap the fruits. The unwelcome intrusion of drugs onto my panglossian best of all possible worlds is both disturbing and irritating. Yet, the contradiction surfaces surreptitiously on my first interview in the field.

I mull over the word respect, so often bandied about by social scientists in discussing Mexican children. An ironic permutation of the word inspires drug users to accuse their young nephews of not having respect because they use marijuana. The concept seemed somehow anachronistic. Respect, *respeto*, conjured up presences of Spanish dons and doñas, of devoted mothers and stalwart fathers, of priests and peons, all entwined by the consolidating laces of mutual respect. It was not a hallmark of drug use.

I gratefully mused on what a stroke of luck it was that I had encountered such an articulate and open informant on my first foray into the field. Who could have predicted that I would stumble onto a veritable torrent of mores, strategies, and ideology within her tiny, easily overlooked house. Her home conveyed the struggle of a family aching to make ends meet. The furnishings were sparse, even spartan. It was difficult to imagine a family of six crowded into the confined quarters. The interior was unremarkable except for one thing—books. As one entered the small frame house, the eye rested on an antiquated set of encyclopedias within a modest bookcase. Her conversation was punctuated by sporadic bursts to the bookcase, from which she would retrieve some book or other and which she would eagerly display for my perusal.

Marina was unabashedly outspoken. She chatted candidly about her distress in dealing with her oldest child, born with a birth defect. She spoke of her tireless efforts to shield her children from profanity, from alcohol abuse, and her undeviating involvement in her sons' classrooms and school work. She intrigued me. As I scrupulously tried to record the outpouring of discourse she directed toward me, a small red warning flag of social science methodology went off in my head. Granted, this woman was extraordinarily astute and articulate. She was an outstanding informant. But, I wondered, how typical is she of the neighborhood I was attempting to personify?

I was unsettled by what I perceived to be the unrepresentativeness of Marina. Marina did not fit the demographic profile of the neighborhood. She lived smack in the middle of it, her income level was consistent with it, but somehow, she didn't fit. She had been raised on the far east side of Tucson. She had attended a local Community College for a year, and she had been in the military and in law enforcement. How many other mothers in the neighborhood liked martial arts and guns?

I soon discovered that every other household I encountered had characteristics that complicated a comparative sample. I had ostensibly set out to do a microethnography of language practices within the home, using traditional sociolinguistic methods, and focusing on such publishable constructs as participant structures, turn-taking, and the allocation of communicative resources. Instead, I was being furnished with a methodologically discomforting reality: the nonuniformity of the field. The categories that I had tried to identify were in a constant state of flux. I had tried to capture the heterogeneity of the population by dividing the sample according to some notion of naturally occurring divisions within the community. I had opted for a residential variable, that is, comparing families from *barrio* settings with families from non-*barrio* settings. This had proved problematic. Marina, originally tied to her *barrio* street, during the course of my fieldwork, moved to the eastside non-*barrio* home of her parents. A second family moved from their home to the wife's parents' southside home, and then again to a north-side, working-class, non-*barrio* area. Other variables confounded a neat delineation of the households. Rosalba, chosen for the study based on her enrollment in a class for 4-year-olds who were at risk, was cared for by her grandmother who lived in the *barrio*, but Rosalba actually lived on an acre of land with ducks, chickens, and rabbits. Additionally, her mother turned out to have a degree from the University of Arizona, even though she worked as a cashier at a small southside grocery store. Where could I classify her family? I had also hoped to get a fair number of Spanish-dominant households from the *barrio* sample. I had only one. The emergence of language patterns within the homes that was predicated on an infusion of evangelical Christian tapes, books, and discourse patterns was a further deviation. This was not the data set that I had hoped for. Yet, was it really so different from what I already knew?

I obviously had known of an influx of proselytizing among Latinos. I was well aware of high levels of English dominance among children in the local schools. I had long rejected ideas of a monolithic community or of a simplistic two-dimensional analysis based on class, education, or residential pattern. But because I needed a comparable set of household data, I had stripped my own subjectivity of any validity. I had begun to view the processes of everyday life as getting in the way of analyses, rather than being the heart of analyses. My primary question remained. Are there identifiable processes by which children are socialized through language in U.S. Mexican households? The next question that inevitably followed was more enigmatic: How can these processes be elucidated taking into account the smorgasbord of households I was encountering?

As I contemplated the disjointed scenario before me, I attempted to come to grips with all of the facets I felt were involved. How could I devise neat theoretical constructs when the continuum of everyday life kept getting in my way? I was unaware at the time that it was precisely because of the fluidity of the field I was observing that I would glean one of my most significant insights.

I had come full circle in constructing a theoretical perspective. Alarmed that my subjectivity and in-member status was an impediment to unbiased research, I had opted to reject variation from the socially defined norm. Yet, my objective analysis had led me back to my original starting point: faced with the multiple perspectives of subordinated discourses.

I came away from my fieldwork experience changed in a fundamental way. I had experienced first-hand the fracturing of subjectivities, inter- and intra-personally. I had begun by stripping away my own life experiences in the quest for social science objectivism. I had found that objectivity was a facile construct, predicated on the dismissal of the nonnormative. Most important was the insight that I had gained about language. In studying language with predigested structures, we defeat the creative forces that it unleashes. Language reflects the ineffability of our being. Through language we define, and are defined by, ourselves and others. The recognition of raw effect of emotion on language, and of language on emotion, was one legacy of doing fieldwork in my own backyard.

I gleaned a second insight at the level of communicating with the households I interviewed. Because these households were mediated by intersections of class, gender, religion, and other constructs, I found that language use crafted multiple identities. Our identity is not fixed and immutable, but is malleable and subject to our own choice. Language choice is often a marker of the particular identity we choose to adopt. Language is not simply something that stands outside of experience and refers to it; rather, we use language to create a particular order. The world we live in is built on the linguistic beliefs and practices of social groups and language builds our social identities. As Gloria Anzaldúa (1987) noted, "So, if you want to really hurt me, talk badly about my language. Ethnic identity is twin skin to linguistic identity—I am my language" (p. 59).

I also came away convinced that the affective dimension of language use must not be relegated to the unknowable and therefore discarded. Although the connection between language and affect has been referenced, it is often relegated to either grammatical markers of affect or to classroom techniques for producing language learners. The ineffable creative force of language to construct social worlds and personhood is a dimension that cannot be overlooked.

As a researcher who works with language, I need to remind myself regularly never to fall into the labyrinth of equating language with grammar, or with phonology, or as simply a means of getting things done with words. As I reflected on my earliest language experiences, I became aware that much of communication is extralinguistic . . . that communication involves much more than words. As I continue the process of self-reflection, I have come to accept self-questioning as an integral part of the development of a researcher. Because I work in my own community, I am aware that there is no one or correct interpretation to language data. Questioning the data, questioning the informants, questioning the methodology, and questioning oneself are not often represented in published sources. Data do not always neatly fall into place, and objective discourse often obscures the very processes we are attempting to document.

As I continue to straddle two systems as both language researcher and language producer, I have come full circle to my first and most basic insights on language: that its most powerful use is as a creative force—a creator of personhood, of domain, and of identity. These insights were wrested in opposition to academic and positivistic traditions that deprivilege experience, emotion, and subjectivity, and that cannot be extirpated from learning about language.

REFERENCE

Anzaldúa, G. (1987). *Borderlands-la frontera: The new mestiza*. San Franciso: Aunt Lute Books.

In Search of Gender Bias

David P. Shea
Heisei International University, Saitama, Japan

One of the stories generated in the process of writing my PhD dissertation relates to a contentious struggle with a member of my doctoral committee and how, in order to get approval to carry out the research necessary for my thesis, I had to agree with the professor's injunction to go in search of gender bias. Generally, the story concerns authority, but it relates particularly to the struggle over academic writing: Who was to define the scope and direction of what I considered my research. In one respect, the struggle was resolved in my unexpected discovery within the give-and-take of conversational interaction and my realization about where (and how) I stand in relation to the dynamics of that activity. In another respect, the struggle still continues today.

I began the search for gender bias rather reluctantly at first, and proceeded with general indifference until I unexpectedly stumbled upon it (at least a closely related variety) quite by chance. I was dismayed to find, however, that the bias in question was far more incriminating than I ever imagined. Although I can't conclude that the professor who insisted I go on the search in the first place was entirely right, neither can I claim he was wrong. And I end up with the unsettling realization that my original resistance wasn't entirely correct, either.

There are theoretical aspects of the story that are related to the reproduction of gendered relations in conversation. There are methodological details concerning the role of unquestioned assumptions that shape whatever the research is supposed to uncover, but the story concerns principally the struggle that goes on under tutelage, and how the political impinges upon the pedagogic when teachers, who maintain certain academic standards and theoretical principles, attempt to impose them on students who are trying to articulate their own standards and principles, which aren't necessarily in complete accord. The tension can pose a very real threat to a student's career, given the unequal power relations in which most interaction between teachers and students is set, with the teacher invariably standing on more secure institutional ground.

People sometimes say that writing a dissertation is like giving birth, producing an intellectual child. But in many ways, writing a dissertation is also like growing up, akin to going through academic puberty and enduring the maturation process that generates fundamental conflicts that scar one's identity with ugly, distressing pimples. As I struggled with my dissertation, I vowed that I would never treat my own students the way I'd been treated by my professor, and I wouldn't make them endure what I'd been through. Now that I'm done, I think the discipline was probably good for me.

I also think that perhaps I resemble my professor more than I could have imagined at the time, in the discomfort of my academic adolescence, as I struggled with my dissertation and rebelled against him. Ironically, the sense of identity associated with the search is one of the more important discoveries of my dissertation. The narrative has informed my subsequent career as a teacher and the pedagogic relationship I have developed (or try to develop) with my own students.

THE FIGHT AND THE POWER

It is often thought, even to the point of being taken for granted, that people from different cultures find it difficult to communicate because they follow different customs and ways of speech. It seems reasonable to make this assumption because people grow up in separate communities and hold dissimilar expectations about what is polite, persuasive, and appropriate in conversation. The crucial question, however, is how these differences are actually enacted in cross-cultural conversation. And it might also be more profitably asked what can be done to maximize the success and minimize the friction that does occur. As a student of language education, I had a theoretical interest in these questions. As a nonnative speaker of Japanese, I also felt a compelling personal interest to explore the issue further, so I designed a qualitative research study for my dissertation that would allow me to collect and analyze data on the interactional dynamics of everyday conversation between Japanese nonnative speakers of English and their American friends, colleagues, and professors at the university. In planning the study, I had the support of my committee (I thought) and felt fairly confident that my research proposal would be accepted when I walked into the prospectus defense. That is when the matter of gender bias arose, and where this story begins.

Jason (not his real name) is a critical theorist, a committed progressive who believes that American society is unjustly structured and unfairly biased against people of color, against the poor and working classes, and against women. Jason believes that, without recognizing the categories of race, class, and gender, it is difficult if not impossible to understand the dynamics of American society and the character of language acquisition that takes place within it. Jason argues that, even where there is little overt or obvious discrimination (such as when the KKK marches down Main Street), the voices of minorities are nevertheless ignored and their experiences marginalized in ways that people from White middle-class backgrounds characteristically fail to recognize. Jason addresses these issues in his own academic work, and he passionately and compellingly encourages his students to do the same in theirs.

I agreed strongly with Jason. In my program of studies, I had taken his seminars, where I wrote papers on related issues and participated enthusiastically in class discussions. I subscribed to some of the same political magazines as he and, during most of the time I was in the department, I would often stop by his office to talk about the latest policy outrage of the conservatives controlling the U.S. government. I also felt personally close to Jason, so when time came to form a dissertation advisory committee, I asked if he would serve on it, even though I knew neither intercultural communication nor qualitative research methodology was his field. Nonetheless, I thought Jason would provide positive theoretical support as well as encouragement not to forget my critical roots.

In the prospectus defense, Jason was the last to speak after I had made my proposal. "I don't see how you're addressing gender bias in this study," he said.

I asked what he meant.

Jason explained that because in American society, women are so clearly marginalized and male privilege is so obviously saturated in everyday activity, gender bias was bound to affect the way men and women talk in conversation.

"I'm not dealing with gender bias," I answered defensively, "on purpose. Not because I'm avoiding the issue, but it's just not part of the study." I explained that, while I agree women clearly face unfair structural barriers in such terms as discriminatory patterns of employment, restricted access to political power, and unequal treatment in social institutions (including marriage), it's impossible to expect these broad, macrosocial factors, which are always calculated in statistical terms of aggregate norms, to appear in an interpersonal study involving only four individual informants talking to their friends and teachers. I argued that there are certainly situations where women face unfair discriminatory treatment because of their gender, but such bias doesn't necessarily apply to every man and woman in every conversation all the time. In fact, in some situations, women might, in fact, do the reverse and treat men unfairly. To argue that because women face discrimination on the societal level, they therefore face it in interpersonal interactions is deterministic. It implicitly assumes women are incapable of equal treatment and are inherently less powerful than men. It's tantamount to arguing that women don't receive equal consideration because of their lower social status.

"No," countered Jason. "I don't see how you can argue that. It's obvious gender plays a role in conversation. It influences every aspect of social life, even though we don't recognize it." He cited a colleague who recently did a study on gender discrimination. She had told him of her results, how men dominate conversation at professional conferences, interrupting women when they speak, monopolizing the floor, ignoring their comments, demeaning their opinions. Jason said that he now goes to conferences with his eyes open. He now sees that men dominate panel discussions and committee sessions. "It's amazing," he said. "I'd been going to academic meetings all those years and never noticed it before." Jason insisted that I include gender bias within the scope of my study. I couldn't do otherwise, he said. He wouldn't accept a dissertation that claimed to deal with the social aspects of language without accounting for such a fundamental category.

Another member of the committee spoke up, agreeing with Jason. She suggested that because I recognized gender as a crucial category on the societal level, I should include it for consideration, and the rest of the committee went along with the recommendation. When the meeting came to an end, I was in search of gender bias whether I wanted to be or not.

I walked out of the conference room overwhelmed by a sense of helplessness. I felt as if I'd been physically attacked. I also felt that I'd lost control over my own research, that I couldn't decide what questions were to be asked, how they were to be pursued, and possibly even what answers I could come up with. I resented the usurpation of what I considered my intellectual property and I seethed with frustration that I'd lost the right to define my own subject of inquiry.

"What happened to academic freedom?" I thought. "Jason's upholding standards he feels strongly about, but he's imposing those standards on me. He's asking me to think like him, to agree with foregone conclusions. What right does he have to tell me what to say in my dissertation? Where's the personal respect we'd developed (or I thought we'd developed) over the past 2 years?" I was angry and resented Jason's attitude. As I recall, I bought some beer on the way home and took the night off.

The next day, I sat down at the computer and wrote a bitter letter to Jason (which I never sent). I accused him of telling me to "do as I say, not as I do." He had admitted that he didn't address gender in his own dissertation research but now he was imposing the obligation on me. He talked about broad, structurally biased racism in schools, but he certainly wouldn't argue that every school teacher was racist or unaware of racial bias around them. I said Jason was failing to make an important distinction between individual and social behavior. He was assuming a deterministic Marxism that reduced individual behavior to the reproduction of social structure.

I wrote that Jason was denigrating what he didn't understand. He called the research studies I cited (arguing that gender discrimination is not automatically displayed in conversation) esoteric, a criticism that reflected a bias against empirical research. Put bluntly, I wrote, "Jason doesn't care about the way things are, but the way he thinks they ought to be, which is the bias not only of a critical theorist who doesn't want to be bogged down in the complicating details of what actually happens in the world, but also of someone not trained in empirical research."

I also criticized Jason's authoritarian style. He insisted that I define the term *social* his way, even though there are sociolinguists writing in academic journals who define it differently. My dissertation was for that audience, not critical theorists like Jason. It didn't seem to bother him that the insistence on his definition was a prime example of power dynamics not related to gender. What better way to demonstrate problems of inequality than the way the teacher holds authority over the student?

What if, I wondered, I were to incorporate gender bias into my study, but use a definition that didn't match his. Would he insist that it was unacceptable? Would I have to write the way he wants, produce findings he thinks right?

The letter went on, but it didn't help much. It didn't alleviate the sense of alienation or bitterness I felt inside, and the next day I went to my major professor and asked if I could drop Jason from the committee. She told me that I could but shouldn't. She said it would only make things worse and create misunderstanding and dissension. She recommended that I stick with the committee I'd chosen, and everything would probably work out all right.

I put on a friendly face because there was not much else to do. I couldn't oppose Jason. I was a graduate student with the political power of a mosquito, and he was a full professor with the weight of a major research institution behind him. I could only harbor a smoldering sense of injustice until everything was over when, if I survived the experience, I could express my anger somehow. So I hid my resentment and carried it inside me the afternoon I went into Jason's office and said, "I'm sorry. You're right. I'll consider gender bias." I wasn't really telling the truth, but I couldn't have him working against me. Basically, I was scared.

I was also torn by principle, between doing what I thought in my mind was right and what others were telling me was important. On one side stood my ideals, bolstered by my wounded sense of pride, and on the other side stood the practical considerations of supporting a family, where the bank balance was becoming a matter of concern. There wasn't much money left in the savings account, and the monthly bills reminded me with disturbing regularity that I needed to get a real job and start earning an income.

I thought I was right but I didn't have enough power (or courage) to act on that certainty. I decided to go in search of gender bias. I would simply find some and write about it, although I wasn't exactly sure where or how I would do that. One doesn't walk up to a couple engaged in conversation and ask the man, "Are you mistreating this woman conversationally?" And then ask the woman, "Is he interrupting you, denying you the floor, demeaning your opinions? I mean, do you feel the exclusion your gender dictates?"

I wanted to walk out of Jason's office and end our relationship. I wanted to forget gender bias. It was my research, and I should be in charge.

I was soon to discover how wrong I could be.

THE ENEMY AND ME

With data collection beginning the next week, I didn't have much time to worry. I also partially avoided the problem by completely avoiding Jason. I didn't stop for a friendly chat about the latest politics. I slipped in and out the department back door instead of walking past his office. And I busied myself with the technical details of recording conversation, which were far more complex and time consuming than I had imagined. But my predicament was soon solved.

It was in the latter stages of data collection. After 3 months, I hadn't come across anything I could really call gender bias, except perhaps a short-tempered academic advisor (a woman) who treated Jiro, one of my informants (a man) rather imperiously in an advisement session, but I didn't think that was the kind of bias Jason was looking for. I had collected some friendly and very cooperative conversations between another informant, Kazuko, and her colleagues, but the speakers were all women and there was little, if any, interruption or unfairness evident in their talk. I had little beside these two examples, and I wasn't sure they would count.

It didn't seem to have anything to do with gender, but I was in special need of interaction between Jiro and his friends because every conversation of his I had recorded up to that point was rather formal interaction with professors and advisors. I needed to observe the way he ordinarily talked among friends.

Catching Jiro had been difficult. He often ate lunch with friends in the cafeteria, but the room was always too noisy or the group was too large, or I arrived when everyone was leaving, or no one showed up the day I did. But one afternoon, I found Jiro with a friend, Neil, sitting at a quiet corner table. George, an older Graduate Teaching Assistant who liked to give English conversation lessons to Asian coeds, was also at the table, talking to Emiko, a Japanese exchange student. "Now there's an example of gender bias," I thought as I sat down with the tape recorder running.

I noted with some disappointment that Emiko soon left, taking with her, I supposed, the potential for unfair and unequal interaction. Then, I continued the conversation with Jiro, Neil, and George, and went home to begin transcription. It wasn't until I started the analysis a couple of days later that I realized what had happened.

The methodological principle of my research was to impose as little of myself as possible on the conversation, to let my informants talk so I could observe what was going on. As a participant, I would gain access to the group, but as a detached observer, I would be able to more objectively evaluate the interactional dynamics of the talk, recognizing where and how cultural differences might block successful communication and cause misunderstanding. I realized that I had to justify being present in the first place because people don't normally go around silently observing other people's conversations, a notepad and whirring tape recorder in hand, without generating some degree of self-consciousness and invariably ruining the natural flavor of what is going on. Nevertheless, my basic idea was to stand back and watch from the sidelines. Until I analyzed the recorded transcript of the conversation with Jiro, Neil, and George, I thought I had been doing that.

The three of us were talking about traveling in Asia, and Neil mentioned that he had heard Japan has dirty water, especially Tokyo. He asked Jiro if that was right. Jiro began to answer when I interrupted. "Probably cleaner than the U.S.," I replied.

Jiro tried to explain, "I mean if they clean up—"

But George talked over his answer. "Seriously? Like New York?" he asked me.

"I heard it's kinda brown," remarked Neil.

At this point, Jiro commented that, though the taste isn't very good, Tokyo water isn't harmful, but no one was listening. The native speakers, George, Neil, and I, were already discussing chlorine in the water supply, the effects of the runoff from chemical pollution, how to get safe water in Asia, and so on. We never noticed (at least I didn't) that Jiro was being left out and ignored, his opinions bouncing off a well of excited native-speaker babble, unheard.

Most of the conversation developed like this. In fact, I left the cafeteria with the impression that Jiro hadn't participated very actively in the conversation. It was only after analyzing the transcript that I realized, to my horror and dismay, that Jiro had indeed been talking. I just hadn't been listening. None of us had. Jiro, rather than me, was on the sidelines of the interaction.

The talk wasn't at all contentious. The conversation was animated, pleasant, and friendly. The other speakers, including Jiro, seemed to enjoy themselves and later made no comment about anything out of the ordinary. An outside observer passing by would probably not have noticed anything amiss, and may have even thought that Jiro was fully involved in the exchange, listening intently. Nevertheless, I had effectively worked to exclude Jiro, preventing him from participating in the group—at least participating as an equal member. Interrupting his sentences, talking over his comments, ignoring his opinions, I helped to reduce his position in the conversation to someone with secondary status whose main role was to listen appreciatively to the more privileged voices of authority. What Jiro said wasn't as important as what I said, in spite of the fact I was supposed to be listening to him. He was sufficiently knowledgeable, but I didn't grant him the position to articulate that knowledge. Isn't that what gender bias is also about?

If I had this attitude in my own head, if I were acting on unstated assumptions that gave my voice privilege over people like Jiro, then I was no longer in search of bias. I had discovered it in my own view of the world. I'd found the enemy and he was me.

ASSUMPTIONS ABOUT PRIVILEGE

In spite of my best intentions and training as a researcher, I was insensitive to the person I was supposed to be listening to, squashing the very data I was trying to elicit. Indeed, after nearly four months of observing and analyzing conversation, I'd changed very little about my own behavior in interaction, and this realization brought me to a screeching halt. It made me stop and think first-hand about the problem of empirical research and how easy it is to see what we anticipate seeing, and how different it is to recognize what we don't expect. More importantly, I began to understand how my behavior had been (and still is, actually) based on implicit, unnoticed assumptions about interactional authority in conversation, grounded in what I thought were natural ways to talk, and associated with judgments about whose opinion is more significant, whose turns should be longer, and whose voice is supposed to be heard. I had adopted an unfair, discriminatory attitude, assuming that I held more interactional rights to talk than Jiro and what I had to say was more important.

The dynamics of Jiro's exclusion strike me as similar to the gender bias women face in conversation. In the implicit attitudes and taken-for-granted presumptions that underlie interaction, a man's experience is considered more important, more central than a woman's. Male voices carry a good deal of authority and "deserve" to be heard first, while female voices carry less authority and prestige, requiring justification for their expression. In the cafeteria conversation, I didn't see a prototypic example of a man dominating a woman in conversation (which is what I expected of gender bias and, in fact, how I had defined it in conversation), but what I did see demonstrated not only how gender bias takes place, but also how it can indeed be described as part of every conversation.

I began to see that communicative processes of personal interaction are grounded in broad social attitudes, in a prevailing common sense that is connected to widely shared assumptions of prerogative, even if outward behavior doesn't always explicitly or consistently display those beliefs. Where Jason had equated (or I thought he'd equated) social attitudes and personal bias, I had separated them, imagining that people carry an independent set of political beliefs inside their heads that could be consciously articulated like a consonant political platform, with clear cut alternatives between us and them. Where Jason had assumed (or I thought he'd assumed) men would behave in a certain manner because they were men, I had assumed that liberals who subscribed to a progressive outlook would avoid bias, as if they were immune to its influence. I had put ideology inside the individual, a function of personal politics over which we could exercise as much conscious control as our vote. What I failed to see was that interaction is neither that individualistic nor that transparent. The issue is not a dichotomous choice between societal or individual levels of analyses, but rather a dialogic interplay between the two, set within a reciprocal, sometimes discordant interpenetration of broad social attitudes into the individual consciousness, thus mediating (not determining) behavior. After realizing the extent of my own tendency to assume priority in conversation, I'm more willing to recognize gender bias not simply as an issue limited to the level of individual expression, with authoritarian or receptive men and assertive or submissive women, but as something inherent in the social fabric in which all interaction and all individual beliefs are woven. If we look at individuals, we can expect to see only occasional snatches of the ideologies that are unthinkingly accepted.

I didn't find what Jason wanted me to find, at least not the way he phrased it. I didn't find men dominating women in conversation because, as I predicted, I found individual men in certain contexts who didn't, and women in other contexts who did. But I did find bias informing conversational interaction as he predicted, working according to ultimately discriminatory assumptions about position and prestige. Although the locus of discovery wasn't a conversation between a man and a woman, I realized that the basis on which I interact with other people (and conduct research) is fundamentally related to the privileged and gendered position from which I see the world. My understanding of interaction began to change, and not only did I see cross cultural interaction in a new light, I also saw gender bias where I didn't see it before.

I'd always thought discrimination was something other people did—extreme people like the KKK. When I realized that I, too, was implicated in constructing a society of unequal access, perhaps as guilty as the most imperious discourse bully I had recorded in my data, I began to think about Jason and his imposition on my research. He'd been imperious but, in a sense, he'd also been right and I had to go about the hard task of admitting it.

I struggled against Jason's injunction and resented his control, but were it not for his insistence that I look for gender bias in the first place, I might never have recognized the character of ideological bias and how it plays out in conversation. Without Jason's influence, I might not have synthesized my analysis the way I did, and my dissertation would likely have turned out with a very different focus. It was a painful process of discovery, but the product has a critical edge that I'm glad is there. I was able to integrate this critical dimension into my research that, in planning the project, I didn't expect I would be able to incorporate.

TOWARD A RECOGNITION OF DIALOGUE

The conversation with Jiro was an embarrassing shock to my research pride but my dismay was tempered by a certain relief. At least I had a reply to Jason to present in my dissertation defense. I had found bloody gore and conflict in conversation that I thought might satisfy his critical thirst for depicting relations of authority and the discriminatory processes of marginalization in conversation. But would he buy the argument as an example of gender bias? There were no women actually present in the conversation, so how could I have gender bias without women? My analysis seemed to be as much a challenge to, as compliance with, Jason's injunction.

I went into the defense tense and uncertain about the outcome. Would Jason accept my interpretation, or would he insist on a more traditional analysis and mount another crushing attack? He did neither, actually. After listening to the discussion among other committee members, he finally spoke up. "We often talk about voice in this department," he said, "but it's important that we appreciate it when we see it." He proceeded to say that he thought my voice came through my research and he felt satisfied with the result. "It's easy to say what's not included or what we disagree with, but we should recognize what's here.

"A dissertation is supposed to be a beginning. I think you need to develop some of your ideas, particularly the connection between gender bias and conversation further," he said. "But this is a start."

For a second, I wondered if he'd forgotten about the prospectus meeting. On reflection, though, I found that I agreed with him. I hadn't catalogued the deterministic gender bias he expected (or I thought he expected), but I also hadn't fully addressed the implications of ideology (and gender bias) in the dynamics of conversation either. (That, in part, is what I'm trying to do here, in this essay.)

I also heard (I think I heard) Jason saying something different.[1] Instead of, "You have to find gender bias," he now seemed to be saying, "You need to think about this issue." I could accept that injunction. While it retained an evaluative tone, it was closer to dialogue than foregone conclusion and went far to affirm my sense of control over the direction of my research.

To make a long story short, I passed the defense. I had to make some revisions that, given the alternatives, I was willing to do. So Jason gave me his official stamp of approval, and I was admitted through the ivory-walled gate of the academically approved. When I left the conference room, I felt relieved, stronger in a sense, more aware of myself and the issues of ideo-logical reproduction, and better prepared as a language teacher and re-searcher. Or so I thought.

My narrative might end with a satisfying conclusion if it were to stop here, on the one hand offering a positive resolution of the contention be-tween opposing orientations to academic research and, on the other hand, affirming the integrity and inviolability of student voice against the domina-tion of authoritarian teachers who savage student identities with impunity. But like life after the dissertation, the story about my search for gender bias continues. It has a sequel where Jason returns to haunt me, like those horror movies where, just when you think the monster's dead, he reappears to terrify the townsfolk and everyone shrieks, "He's baaaaack."

The secret is that I'm really Jason.

Well, not exactly, but in the sense that I've adopted his character and begun delivering his lines, the irony of the identification is as fitting as it is dismaying.

ENGAGEMENT AND IDENTITY

I had been teaching English classes for ESL students at a well-known Japa-nese university for nearly a year when Kanako, a friendly and pleasant young woman, stood up and dropped a bombshell on my professional demeanor. I had assigned an informal presentation on the last day of class, asking students to talk about what they'd learned over the course of the semester. When Kanako's turn came, she announced in her characteristically cheerful style, "In my journal, I've been afraid to write what I really thought in this class, because I didn't think it was what you wanted me to say."

I was stunned.

---

[1]Maybe Jason was saying something different because I had changed. Perhaps I've taken liberties with Jason in order to tell this narrative. Although the story really happened as I tell it, what you're getting is the way it exists in my head, what I felt, and how I saw it. Which means, of course, that others close to the situation (including Jason) will likely recall things differently and tell their own version of events. But I promise: This is the story I experienced.

Kanako explained that, in her response essays to the films and short stories we used as texts, she felt compelled to articulate interpretations similar to the opinions I had expressed in class. She felt constrained and intimidated to write in my voice, not hers.

It took me a few seconds to reply. "I've had a similar experience," I said and explained that I tried to read and respond to her essays not on the basis of what she said, but how she said it and the kind of effort she made expressing her ideas. Even if I disagreed with her opinion, I wanted her to write her ideas in her own style, articulating a unique response. Journal essays were her compositions, not mine. My job as a language teacher was to respond to ideas not squash them, and I certainly hoped that she would challenge my interpretations as a first step in her own response.

I thought I'd made it clear to the students they were supposed to write what they honestly felt, without worrying about my evaluation. I thought they knew I wouldn't force my opinions on them, telling them what to think or write about. Obviously, though, Kanako didn't think so. She had her own voice and a different sense of interpretation, and she thought I hadn't allowed her to articulate what she felt was important and wanted to say.

All of a sudden, I was back at the dissertation defense, except that my students were sitting across the table and I was insisting they find the kind of answers to the questions I thought they should ask. Now I was the authoritarian teacher suppressing student voice, standing at the ivory walls of the academic gate, deciding who could enter and who had to go in search of gender bias. I was Jason, imposing political standards on the pedagogic, trying to make students understand more than they might be willing to recognize and deal with issues they might not want to address.

I've thought a good deal about what Kanako told me that day, especially in light of essays other students have written for my English classes, expressing opinions that I've found myself unable to agree with. One student, I remember, made a pretentious argument for a repeal of the international moratorium on whaling because he thought whale meat a necessary part of traditional Japanese culture. Another wrote a response to the movie *Gandhi*, arguing that nonviolence was an old-fashioned concept and that Japan needed to strengthen its military in order to use force again on the international scale. Then another expressed her skepticism about an article on Columbus that talked about the resultant massacre of Native American Indians: "From my viewpoint, the victims are necessary for human progress because we could never make any progress if all the nations were equally wealthy."

How am I supposed to ignore ideology when I read these essays? Can I honestly, realistically separate style from substance, reading solely for grammatical correctness or fluency of expression when I find the ideas disagreeable, even repugnant? Do I praise students who make a fluent argument for racial discrimination? Do I accept a regressive defense of gender bias? Do I limit the scope of my responsibilities as a teacher to the technical elements of style, excluding the broader ethical and social implications of ideas? Jason couldn't accept my research on conversation that avoided the ideologically charged valences of gender. In much the same way, I find that I can't accept a content approach to English composition that fails to consider the ethical implications of interpretations generated in class discussion and student writing. In other words, I have to amend my instinctual reassurance to Kanako that it's okay to write whatever she honestly feels in her essays. What I mean is that, in one respect, it is okay, but in another respect, something more is called for.

I certainly don't think teachers should tell students what to write or how to interpret literary and cultural texts. At the same time, I don't think responsible teachers can celebrate everything students think and feel because, as my search for gender bias disastrously demonstrates, people make implicit assumptions about the social world, unquestioningly accepting tacit common sense notions as right and natural that are actually quite biased and artificial products of socially constructed interpretations.

Perhaps students like Kanako are resisting me with as much anger and frustration as I resisted Jason, and I certainly need to listen to them with as much attention as I expected Jason to listen to me, not to mention with far more engagement than I showed to Jiro. But my self-assured indignation at Jason's usurpation of my intellectual property was seriously undermined by the cafeteria conversation, and my vow to treat students with more respect than I was treated strikes me now as an oversimplification of the complex dynamics of intellectual development, located within the dialogic engagement between teachers and students.

Perhaps Jason was too quick to cut me off, too slow to recognize my voice, too reluctant to amplify my response through supportive response. Perhaps Jason too easily assumed that because he was older, more experienced, more fluent, he had the authority to assert his knowledge vis-à-vis mine. But I know that, based on my own experience in the cafeteria conversation with Jiro, this is an assumption that is easy to make.

There is no simple, dichotomous choice between affirming student voice by letting students take charge of their writing to investigate topics they want to explore, and telling students what is important to know, where to search, and how to interpret the significance of what they find. The teacher is inevitably bound to do both, and to do both at the same time, to challenge and support, to assert and respond, in a back-and-forth contrapuntal balance of dialogue. To deny either side of this collaborative equation would slight the complexity of the responsive engagement between teacher and student.

Looking back on my dissertation, I don't resent Jason for insisting that I search for gender bias. His influence turned out to be the catalyst that pushed me to successfully synthesize the central theme that emerged from my research. It was a painful process but in an important sense, it was necessary and even positive.

The search for gender bias has changed my identity as a teacher, as I've realized that part of me is Jason. His concern for gender bias, I've come to understand, is also my concern. I've reached a point of integration (which is where I think I need to be) that incorporates Jason's position within my own. I see the dialogue that recognizes the logic and justice not only of one's own participation, but also that of the other person's as well. From this point of view, I have to get my students to listen to me as much as I had to listen to Jason, and I have to listen to my students as much as I wanted Jason to listen to me. It's not a solution as much as a perspective or an orientation, a commitment to respond in an engaged way, without relinquishing personal beliefs but at the same time recognizing that the bias we dismiss may not be as distant and unrelated as we might imagine.

CONCLUSION: SHARED INQUIRY

When I showed a draft of this essay to Jason, he expressed surprise at how painful the dissertation search for gender bias had been for me (because I hadn't told him about it), but he also reaffirmed his belief in the ultimate authority of the teacher to guide the student. "Admit it," he said. "The teacher is older and knows more than the student. The teacher gives the grade at the end of the term. You can't disguise that authority."

Jason's comment made me think about two things in relation to the interactional politics that are inherent in any response. First, I thought about my 4-year-old son, who himself becomes quite intent sometimes about articulating his opinion, such as when he's screaming in protest at something I've told him to do, or shrieking in excitement at the prospects of doing something he wants to do. As a parent, I want to affirm my son's voice and his right to express his emotions, but I can't responsibly say that anything goes, especially when it disturbs the neighbors who live far too close to provoke without the risk of becoming a local object of censure.

I also thought about Christine and Sandra, the editors of this volume, who read earlier drafts of my essay in varying stages of critical agitation and insisted that I rethink and revise my ideas in a manner that met their concerns for appropriate scope and consistency of argument. In a sense, their respect for my authorial voice reproduced Jason's concern for gender bias. My control over the topic I'd chosen to write about was mediated by their attention to its resonance, and this attention worked to elicit a more coherent, more persuasive essay. Were it not for their suggestions that I go beyond what I'd already written, this essay would have never appeared in this collection.

Christine and Sandra as editors, Jason as dissertation advisor, me as teacher and parent: We're all involved in the educational activity of jointly and interactively articulating interpretations of the world around us. We're committed to the same dialogic process in which the key point is not simply responding to students' preformed opinions, but collaboratively working to construct those opinions through our supportive response and extending engagement. In my case, as a student, the political impinged on the pedagogic, painfully so, but that's the way it has to be. The issue is the character of that political response, and what I see as the progressive, transformative alternative is not a smooth, painless choice. It's a matter of struggle and engagement to which, as a teacher, I'm committed as a means of learning in a Freirean sense to read the world. There is no certainty, there are no definite answers, and the road is fraught with students like me who are resistant, often resentful, and typically full of a wide variety of biases.

If I were to do it again, I think I'd give a different answer to Kanako than the one I gave the day she protested that my comments precluded her from articulating her own opinion. I would probably add to what I said before: "I also think it very important to consider certain issues and ideas which you might not at first recognize as significant or find familiar. It's difficult to deal with politically charged social issues like gender bias, because they often go against the grain of what you've always accepted as given and just. But I believe they are critically important and essential not only to writing a good essay, but to learning about the world in which you're living."

And I would also try to stress that we're engaged in the inquiry together.

see p. 236

My Professional Transformation

Sandra R. Schecter
York University, Ontario

I knew I would be a teacher from the time I was really little. My earliest memories are of assembling my dolls—my captive audience—in linear arrangements on my bed, then proceeding to lecture them for hours on end while pacing the room. I have no idea what these primal teachings were about. They anteceded my earliest experience of formal schooling, and there were no teacher role-model types in my immediate or extended family (although I vaguely recall mining my older cousins for information about what school was like). I find it somewhat disconcerting that direct instruction appears to have been my default teaching method—that I was preprogrammed to be didactic. Thankfully, socialization has exercised a moderating effect.

I realize that being born to teaching, as it were, doesn't have nearly the grandiose ring as being born to play the violin or to be a world-class skater, to cite some contrastingly impressive examples. Still, although I have at times flirted with other career options, I have never regretted my calling.

I began my formal career in 1970, following in the footsteps of Alan Strand (see later, this volume) who, in eastern Canadian teaching circles was well on his way to becoming legendary. Immediately out of the university, I obtained a salaried position—or, as my Québecois friends would say, *un job steady*—teaching English-language arts and French as a second language to every student enrolled in a small, anglophone high school in rural Québec.

English had been my undergraduate major and my primary subject for my teaching credential. What attracted me most about teaching language arts was the developmental and ideational aspects. Of course, like other conscientious high school English teachers, I was aware of my responsibility to facilitate students' access to the structural features and rhetorical devices of the language, but these concerns were decidedly secondary to creating a literate environment where kids were reading and writing and all over a text in the interest of self-actualization.

I had a male friend in a far-off town who was accessible only on weekends—a good thing, too, for he caused me enough grief to necessitate a strategy for distraction on weeknights. And so I started teaching English as a second language in the evenings to adult francophones and immigrant minorities in the region. Initially, I regarded such opportunities as less inviting than teaching English-language arts, but my biases soon dissipated. I found the experience of teaching adult, nonnative speakers gratifying in the most immediate ways. Twelve weeks after the start of your Beginners ESL class, your students are palpably more fluent, more grammatical, and more articulate than they were when you first encountered them. Like many colleagues involved in second-language education, I acquired the zeal of one embarking on a mission.

There were other advantages as well. My nonnative-speaking students appreciated my efforts to bring received forms of language to their attention more than students in my English-language arts classes did. And by approaching it from the perspective of the nonnative speaker, I actually learned quite a bit about my native language. I discovered, for example, that no matter what the textbooks would have us believe, the use of prepositions in English is highly arbitrary. We have a lot of them, and indeed it often makes no sense whatsoever which we use when.

Several years later, armed with something of a reputation as an inventive teacher, I decided to devote myself to the introduction of French Immersion in a seventh-grade classroom in a suburban school across the St. Lawrence River from the island of Montréal. Those were the early days of French Immersion, when bilingual education was still considered risky business and when school and university personnel committed to change in this direction moved with caution and a sense of gravity in identifying the conditions and resources needed for the enterprise to succeed. In the fretful sleeps that followed the grueling days of intensive advance training for that first school day in September, I had visions of myself in a spacesuit, the first female astronaut to command a spaceship to Planet Bilingual Education.

That year, I had my first experience of sustained contact with university researchers in education, for they were in my classroom almost every day. Most of the researchers were from McGill University in Montréal, then home to Wallace Lambert and Elizabeth Peal, but there were also some from Concordia University, and others from Université de Montréal, I think. I didn't attempt to keep track of their many comings and goings; I had too much work to do. On the whole, I found them pleasant, even somewhat deferential, as they stood or sat, their bodies tightening at my approach so as not to impede my access to their subjects. I did not question the need for these people to be in my classroom. We were experimenting with an educational innovation that had never been tried before, at least not on this scale with dominant-culture, majority-language children. The venture needed to be closely tracked and its outcomes assessed for the benefit of future generations of learners.

I remember remarking to a friend that not one of the university people returned to tell me what they had found, as though I were not a critical consumer of these concepts. However, I didn't find it odd at the time that none of the visitors bothered to ask me what I thought. Notwithstanding that I and every member of my cohort talked with anyone who would listen about issues to do with bilingualism, both individual and societal, and also notwithstanding that ideas were the measure that defined us both individually in relation to one another and as a group in relation to the rest of the world, I noted no incongruity. In the environs in which I earned my livelihood, inside schools, I was an able teacher, not a person with ideas. It was only later that I would come to have a different perspective on these university researchers' lack of interest in my ideas, in my agency as a theory builder.

Eventually, I obtained a master's degree, which proved enough to secure a faculty position at a provincial university serving a largely rural population. My primary mission in this role entailed summoning the skills I had acquired through my diverse teaching experiences and advanced book learning to the task of preparing first- and second-language educators enrolled in pre- and in-service programs. It was not long into my first semester that I discovered that I was not up to the challenge. Nothing in my background or history had prepared me for the dearth of study skills and aversion to text that characterized the mostly middle-aged, mostly female, mostly practicing teachers in my language teaching methods classes.

I don't remember much about the Christmas break that followed that first horrible teaching semester, except that I was ill throughout with a high fever. Coupled with the fear and loathing I felt in anticipation of my return to the workplace, it had an effect that kept me pretty well confined to the WC for the duration. As the winter progressed, however, the resilient side of my nature gained the upper hand.

I credit my salvation in large part to changed work circumstances that now had me teaching courses in the preservice program to a group of young, aggressive credential candidates who had sent their previous instructor, a tenured professor, to premature retirement with a nervous breakdown. I don't know what motivated my department chair, Roger, to propose this change of venue. Subsequently, I would only half-jokingly accuse him of seeking to cut his losses early by getting me to fold sooner rather than later.

In fact, however, the change had more or less the reverse effect. While I had felt sympathy for the recalcitrant older female learners, many of whom had not had occasion to read a book in more than 20 years, I would be damned if I was going to let these impudent upstarts who questioned every homework assignment and contested every grade drive the final nail into my coffin.

Over the 6 years that I remained at this watch, I acquired some skills for working with diverse groups of learners differentially prepared for the literacy demands of university coursework. My agency as a pedagogue remained central to my identity, and on that basis, I got involved with various educational reform efforts at the local, national, and international levels. I revamped the second-language teacher preparation programs for the universities serving western Québec; I was active in the university teachers' union, helping to negotiate advantageous maternity leave benefits for Canadian teachers; and I served on the Canadian Commission for UNESCO, where I became knowledgeable about, and active in, issues of universal access.

Notwithstanding my heavy teaching and marking load and other professional obligations, not to mention my demanding social life, I also did some writing and publishing during this period. My appointed editors—friends who would correct my spelling, grammar, and punctuation for free—were mostly journalists, and so my writing tended toward this genre. I also tried my hand at scholarly writing. Most of these pieces were rejected, and the reviewers' comments were so mean-spirited and caustic that I began to view the university research community in oppositional terms to the professional context with which I identified. Even though I, too, was technically a university worker, at professional meetings, I could be overheard muttering about the inaccessibility of academic presentational forms and dismissing university types as too disconnected from the day-to-day issues confronting real teachers in real-life classroom situations to be up to anything really useful. Sometimes I would even challenge their assertions, citing my personal research to counter an argument advanced from the podium. I hear a daunting echo of the intonation I used in these interventions when my young son Zachary invokes "my dog Spikey" in an effort to wrest the spotlight from a bona fide dog-owning 4-year-old. Zachary doesn't have a dog.

In 1981, I took a leave from my position to begin a doctoral studies program at Stanford University. The province of Québec had issued both a carrot and an ultimatum to anyone still teaching at the university level with nothing higher than a master's degree. I left with the blessing and financial support of my employer, and with an institutional understanding that I would return.

Fourteen years, one PhD, one wedding (relevant, also, in that my husband's interests constrain my movements geographically), and two young children later, I currently earn a living by helping to direct a federally sponsored research center housed in a prominent American university. The normal duties associated with my position are administration, dissemination, and some independent research activity.

For a while, I also taught courses to candidates enrolled in various second-language teacher certification programs associated with the university; however, I have since discontinued this practice. Teaching was extra and with two new little faces on the scene, I couldn't afford the additional time. I also discovered that, as perceived by those who carried moral authority in the teaching community, teaching university-level courses at a major research institution neither enhanced nor detracted from my status as a teacher—it made absolutely no difference whatsoever. It was as if I, like other colleagues working in similar institutional contexts, had become severed from the real issues confronting real teachers in real-life classroom situations.

In my early post-PhD existence, I was perplexed by this change in the identity I was assigned. Teaching seemed as central to my life as it always had been. When at a professional meeting I would reunite with cohorts from my doctoral program, many of whom had gone on to occupy university teaching positions, the conversation would inevitably turn to issues and dilemmas that arose in conjunction with classes, students, and teaching. One close colleague—who insiders in the teaching community would think of as a university researcher—responded to my inquiry about her summer by saying that it had been miserable because her teaching had gone poorly. Another acquaintance works in the same building as I do, and everyone in the workplace is aware of her teaching schedule. Normally funny and spirited, on her teaching days she is terse and dismissive, unable to attend to even the smallest detail in the hours before her impending class. After a good class, she is observed walking around the building briskly for hours—she's so psyched that she feels a need to come down before driving home. After a bad class, she heads directly to her vehicle, drives maniacally home, and buries her head in her pillow in a vain attempt to contemplate oblivion. Just the usual, really.

Over time, there were increasing indications of my disenfranchisement as a teacher, someone with insider expertise in the teaching and learning of language in the context of specific classrooms. In contrast, I acquired a respectable identity as a university-based researcher, someone with outsider expertise in the theory and design associated with the study of classroom and extra-classroom language-learning and socialization issues. I gained some insight into this professional transformation through my participation in a group of teacher-researchers for whom I had been active in obtaining funding. Neither my status as a fellow group participant nor my extensive experience teaching English, ESL, and bilingual education at the elementary, middle, high school, and adult education levels figured strongly in my relationship with the group or with individual members. Instead, whatever authority I enjoyed derived primarily from my status as a university researcher (Schecter & Parkhurst, 1993).

The previous observation was by now predictable for me. But what was new in this experience was a coming to terms with the persona I had been assigned: an acceptance that things were as they should be. Participants knew that I would be writing about the group's functioning, and they understood, correctly, that the role I embodied as researcher, rather than as teacher, was crucial to the perspective I would develop. It would shape the way I would organize my observations, the narrative forms I would use to represent them, and the interpretive methodologies through which I would understand them (Grumet, 1988; Miller, 1990). Although I was not unconflicted about my professional identity, I could accept that university researcher was the identity that made most sense to the interpretive community comprising my colleagues in the group.

I am not exactly barred from expressing my views in the company of practitioners or from challenging assumptions underlying pedagogic practice. I have, in fact, developed sophisticated accommodation strategies in order to accomplish those acts regardless of audience composition. In the presence of educators concerned primarily with issues of teacher empowerment, for example, I have learned (after considerable trial and error) to append my point to an argument someone has already made that I essentially agree with or at least don't disagree with, citing a research study or two in support of their position. In short, I hitch my wagon to an insider.

Unlike some who are fearful of dissonance, I find creativity and some social importance in the tensions between university-based researchers and school-based practitioners. Such positionings, after all, are in the nature of all hegemonic relationships. My problem is not so much with the tensions as with the reductionist language we use to characterize the work of the other, which constrains important societal conversations that we could be having about language education.

I am happy, as a university researcher, to be associated with theory building, but I don't agree that all university-based researchers engage in this activity, and I certainly don't agree that the stratum of expertise of classroom teachers is adequately represented by the term *practice*. I tire of hearing that outstanding teachers are characterized by their reserves of practical knowledge; I may be more accepting of this epithet when practical knowledge ceases to connote abilities such as those entailed in negotiating a child's snowsuit. I accept that teachers' work conditions are far from ideal, that they aren't given enough time to reflect, collaborate, observe, and develop theories, curriculum, and materials—in sum, to engage in what Mark Clarke (1994) called thoughtful work (cf. Schecter & Ramirez, 1992). At the same time, I also want to make clear that the elementary and secondary school teachers I hung out with in Canada while I was teaching elementary and secondary school related what they were doing in the classroom to important societal issues and the human condition as a matter of course.

They understood that the educational process is inherently complex and holistic in nature.

I had wanted to have this piece finished by the end of the summer, before leaving on vacation. For the last 3 years, we have rented a cabin in the lake country of northern Michigan, driving distance from where my increasingly incapacitated mother-in-law lives. It's difficult to locate something decent to rent in these parts: At our site, the rates are reasonable and the vacationers loyal. Last year, the best we could arrange was a week in late June; this year, the best availability was late August and early September.

Our site comprises a row of cabins managed by a local middle-aged couple of German origin, Mr. and Mrs. Faulhafer (we've kept things on a last-name basis). I've developed a certain fondness for them, especially Mrs. Faulhafer who, in addition to possessing the kind of pragmatic problem-solving skills that evoke appreciative sentiments from decision-weary summer patrons, is a high-school English teacher. I enjoy trading notes with her about the state of literate thinking among youth attending North American high schools: I find her insightful. For example, when recently I described to her my work with Mexican-origin families, noting how the power balance can shift dramatically as children become literate in English and acculturate to mainstream society, she launched into her theory of literacy attrition among White, middle-class families, pointing out that most of the youngsters who she saw on a regular basis engaged significantly less often with print, in less varied environments, than did their parents.

But this morning I have a more mundane reason for climbing the hill to the Faulhafers' home overlooking the row of vacationers' waterfront cabins. I need to inform them that our kitchen sink has stopped up and ask whether they wish to deal with this situation or whether we should just borrow a plunger and some Drano. Mrs. Faulhafer, normally attentive and focused, appears distracted, harried. I notice that her hair is wound tighter than usual and that she has on a red plaid skirt and an long-sleeved, ivory, buttoned-down blouse. She also is wearing nylons, which look unnatural on her tanned, muscled legs, and black pumps. (I didn't know she owned a pair of heels; I can't imagine her actually walking in them.) Apparently preoccupied with locating her car keys, which she believes are to be found in the large black rectangular double-strapped leather bag she is rooting about in, she excuses herself, explaining that this is the first day of class and she needs to be on her way. She will tend to the problem, she says, just as soon as she gets back. From school.

From her front porch, I can see the sparkle of the whole lake. Somehow the image, normally soothing, is unsettling, incongruous. What am I doing here, in shorts, on vacation? It's autumn. Averting my eyes from the panorama, I move closer toward the threshold of the doorway where she stands, clutching her car keys and a large red-manila-covered lesson-plan book with unfrayed, autumn-crisp corners. At once, I am overwhelmed by my self-deception. My carefully constructed edifice of rationalizations has crumbled to dust. "Take me with you," an inner voice, an old friend, stirs from the ruins. "I want to go where you're going."

REFERENCES

Clarke, M. (1994). The dysfunctions of the theory/practice discourse. *Tesol Quarterly, 28*(1), 9–26.

Grumet, M. (1988). *Bitter milk: Women and teaching.* Amherst: University of Massachusetts Press.

Miller, J. L. (1990). *Creating spaces and finding voices: Teachers collaborating for empowerment.* New York: State University of New York Press.

Schecter, S. R., & Parkhurst, S. (1993). Ideological divergences in a teacher research group. *American Educational Research Journal, 30*(4), 771–798.

Schecter, S. R., & Ramirez, R. (1992). A teacher-research group in action. In D. Nunan (Ed.), *Collaborative language learning and teaching.* New York: Cambridge University Press.

Explorations for Part Two:
Identity Dilemmas

1. How do you respond to the quote from Oscar Wilde—"Nothing worth learning can be taught"—which Norma González uses in the first paragraph of her piece? How does this quote square with your notion of what a teacher is and does?

2. At the beginning of her essay, González describes how, growing up, she learned to associate different domains with the Spanish and English languages. Do you associate different language varieties with distinct identities or value systems? Have you encountered this phenomenon—a duality of experience expressed through language alternation—in the course of relating with students? (See also Casanave's essay in Part Four.)

3. In her research odyssey, González discovers that life in the *barrio* does not reflect the categories and classification systems that the academic literature had taught her to look for. She writes: "I had begun to view the processes of everyday life as getting in the way of analyses, rather than being the heart of analyses." What discrepancies do you notice, if any, between the language and/or issues you encounter in your academic setting and those you encounter in the real world as a practitioner?

4. At the beginning of his story, David Shea poses a number of important questions. Who is in charge of a student's work? What is the role of a teacher in guiding students' thinking? When does advice become coercion? What is your thinking on these issues?

5. How would you have handled Shea's problem with Jason? With his student Kanako?

6. In her teacher persona, over a number of years of gratifying teaching experiences and interactions with her cohorts, Sandra Schecter notes that not she herself, nor her practitioner colleagues, nor the researchers who visited her classes, viewed her as someone "with ideas" or as a "builder of theories." This was in spite of her engaged intellectual life at the time. What is your position on her view that an anti-intellectualism pervades the teaching field in North America?

7. Schecter is clearly distressed by the stratification of expertise, and the corresponding moral authority, associated with the teacher and researcher roles. Do you feel that there are boundaries or bifurcations associated with the knowledge that you are presumed to have in your current professional role? If so, to what extent do you believe that these divisions constrain your ability to express opinions and to advocate?

8. Both González and Schecter appear to believe that there are qualities or attributes routinely assigned to people, such as *Mexican, teacher, researcher,* and moreover, that such labels create stereotypes that function to constrain perceptions (held both by self and others) of one's personhood. Can you illustrate such stereotyping with an example from your own professional experience? Schecter goes on to talk about a "coming to terms" with her assigned persona, and both González and Shea also pick up on this theme. How do you relate to the very different ways in which each writer accommodated to the framework of others' perceptions of their roles?

FURTHER EXPLORATIONS

1. Try this for fun. Take a few minutes and design a business card for yourself that describes several of your primary attributes as a professional (e.g., peacemaker, role model, disciplinarian, . . .). (Alternatively, list as many attributes as come to you in 3 minutes.) If this task turns out to be difficult for you, consider why, in discussion with others. Do your labels suggest there is a conflict in your image(s) of yourself as a language educator? In further discussion, explore where these conflicting (or consistent) images came from. How have they changed over the years?

2. Consider an interaction that you have had with a colleague or student in which it was apparent that the other person perceived or defined you in a way that did not fit your own self-perception at that time. Did you do anything to resolve this dissonance? If so, what action did you take? If not, what could you have done?

3. Assume the perspective of someone in your professional life who you are currently interacting with and with whom you are having some difficulties. In the guise of this person, either write a letter to yourself, in which you learn in detail that person's perception of you; or write a letter from

that person to someone else in which those perceptions are revealed. Do not write a response to this letter to defend what may seem like misrepresentations of yourself, but share the letter, if you wish, with a colleague. In what ways has seeing yourself from the perspective of this person influenced your understanding of the conflict you are experiencing?

4. What do you do when confronted with a situation where students express ideas or opinions with which you strongly disagree, or even find morally repugnant? How do you characterize your professional identity in such a situation? How do you believe your students characterize you?

5. To what extent do your home and professional identities blend or bifurcate? Is the blend or bifurcation a conscious choice on your part?

PART THREE

Introduction:
Lessons From Teachings
and Learnings

The work of a language educator is situated in a world full of people—students, colleagues, teachers, and mentors, as well as friends and family. Often the interactions and contextual stimuli that characterize our work environments become so routine that our sensitivity to their importance in our lives may dull over time. Without periodic jolts and surprises, self- or other-instigated, we lose the ability to fully respond to the voices of colleagues and to our own voices and intuitions. However, a key characteristic of the profession is that the predominant activity of our work occurs between a single adult and a group of students in a closed area. This fact contributes further to the process of spiritual numbing. Many teachers report a sense of isolation from other colleagues and alienation from the larger professional community. They see this problem as endemic, and bemoan the absence of time and contexts for extensive, substantive interactions with colleagues and for conversations with students.

We are further blinded to potential insights from our work environments by narrow conceptualizations of what teaching involves that exclude teachers in the role of learners. In reconceptualizing ourselves as learners, we confront society's stereotypical notions of what teachers are supposed to know and do. Indeed, in spite of recent trends to the contrary, traditional expectations thrive that teachers know and teach, and that students don't know and learn. Paolo Freire's banking concept of education is alive and well.

These obstacles notwithstanding, many of the events that are credited with precipitating change in a professional course or way of understanding come to be associated with the human faces and voices we encounter in our activities of teaching and learning. Both inside and outside the classroom, lessons are there to be learned, meanings there to be constructed, if we provide ourselves with opportunities to reflect, to observe from perspectives outside the frequently frantic buzz and bustle of our daily work schedules. In Part Three, the authors take time to look closely at past and present experiences with other people that have exerted important formative influences, seeking and finding relevance to their development as language educators and to ways in which they construct their missions as professionals. The authors also suggest some of the ways that teaching and learning form an inseparable dynamic in the lives of practicing teachers, thus overturning the myth of teacher as knower and transmitter of knowledge. They eschew a quest for certainty in favor of the quest itself (witness Vivian Paley, still pondering questions about good and evil in life, as she listens intently to her kindergarten students' fairy tales). Teachers who see themselves as seekers, learners, and explorers, as people with multiple roles in an unavoidably political environment (Smoke, this volume) are bound to discover things about themselves and their students that otherwise would go unnoticed.

Vivian Paley explains how she uses regular journal writing, recording daily events from her kindergarten classes, as a way to understand how children construct notions about friendship and family, good and evil, and justice and injustice. Through her observations of young children and her journal writing, she expands her own understanding of these major life questions. Trudy Smoke seeks to discover how she and her students can "break the silence" for themselves in a complex teaching environment, where systemic factors increasingly undermine their efforts. She merges her personal background with four anecdotes from her teaching of adult ESL students in New York City, using each one to introduce a new role that she has had to learn to assume. This situation causes her to examine closely the conflicts that arise in her definition of herself as a language educator in a politically and economically divisive environment. In her essay, Jill Bell becomes a language learner herself as a way to take on the perspective of the second-language learners she works with. In the process of finding herself at odds with her Chinese tutor and combating a sense of personal failure as a language learner, she eventually arrives at a new understanding of teaching and learning. Part of her discovery involves her coming to recognize that she had constructed a variety of different stories that helped her make sense of each stage of her learning experience, and her acceptance of these stories as a necessary part of her learning experience. Tom Scovel finds a lesson from teachers and students around him in his early experiences attempting to learn French in the context of a required undergraduate college class. With wit and humor, he recalls that the repeated failures he endured, compared to the successes of those around him, posed a challenging intellectual question for him about the mysteries of foreign language acquisition. His desire to answer this question led him to his career as a second-language educator, and to a stance of intellectual empathy with his own students.

Talking to Myself in a Daily Journal: Reflections of a Kindergarten Teacher

Vivian Gussin Paley

An ordinary conversation is about to take place in the kindergarten. But the tangled web of information passing between Amy, Jamal, Amber, and Jordan would quickly fade were I not in the habit of taping their commentary and continuing the dialogue as I enter it into my daily journal.

Amy: I dreamed about that giant that tried to eat Jack.

Jamal: Guess what? I had a dream too. I was thinking these shoes was dirty but when I took them home they was brand new and clean.

Amy: Because it wasn't really a dream?

Jamal: No, it was. My dad'll laugh when I tell him. I was scared he'd whup me. In my dream.

Amy: Is he a giant? Only giants eat children.

Amber: He said "whup," not "eat."

Amy: Oh, that's good. What's whup?

Amber: You know, whup. It means like a hard slap. Whup.

Amy: Anyway, the giant's wife is nice.

Jamal: Sure. If one person is bad the other has to be nice.

Amber: Right. You can't have both bad. The giant has to marry an ordinary woman.

Jordan: Hey, there could be a good giant. Like in the "Land of Dreams."

Jamal: Oh, thanks. You just reminded me of how I remembered my dream. From talking about that giant.

115

In my journal, I add: The children and I have similar anxiety dreams. Who or what is the giant in my dreams? To nourish this ongoing documentary, I have put away the scorecards and relearned what I once, as a child, could do quite well: make sense of the classroom by watching the children and listening to what they say. We are not, any of us, to be found in sets of tasks or lists of attributes; we cannot be defined or classified. We can be known only in the singular unfolding of our unique stories within the context of everyday events.

My belief that we and the children are part of a larger story-in-progress about the miracle of human differences has opened my mind to the need to consider lines of inquiry that go beyond labels and categories. We may allow science to intimidate us, but we will push stories to the furthest edge of recognizable reality and not worry over unexpected outcomes.

Story listeners and storytellers like suspense. The not knowing about characters makes them more interesting. In a good story, we watch for the unanticipated turn in the plot and we presuppose that we are not seeing the entire picture. The good storyteller dismantles conventional responses and makes us eager to know what happens next. We are disappointed if it turns out to be the same old story. We want sharp differences to appear on every page.

This is what I want from my classroom. It has become, for me, a developing narrative that offers the same intense preoccupation with tiny details found in a good novel, but without the manipulated certainties of fiction. Yet, how do we lay hands on all this storytelling?

I have been rereading Jane Austen lately and she may, it seems to me, help us find our way. These country gentry families of hers, in their carefully constructed societies, pull me into their lives when my own seems too fragmented. Austen knew so well how to fit the pieces together; the reader need not wait long to see the effect of one event or behavior on all the others.

Our classrooms, alas, cannot be described so neatly. They are not carefully constructed societies. They are cultures in the making, we and the children inventing new rules for ourselves every day. We never discover how all the pieces fit or what every behavior means, and the stories we tell of classroom life must, of necessity, end in question marks and untied threads.

Still, although Austen knew the directions all paths would take, her characters do not. They are in the position we find ourselves, where every new event seems to come as a surprise. How these Austen characters attempt to uncover their truths and harmonies gives us much to think about as we go about our special task of discovering individual motivation and societal forces in the classroom.

For one thing, they write letters. Most folks in an Austen novel write letters nearly every day to help them explain what happened the previous day and to anticipate the events of the next. In fact, those who don't write or who write poor letters are often seen as lacking in character. People were known as much by their letters as by their conversation at tea. Friends might correspond several times a day.

Such was the case in Austen's real life as well. She and her sisters, nieces, cousins, and friends transmitted their expectations and disappointments to one another by daily post. Many were not school-educated women—their brothers were privileged to attend school, not they—but they became articulate language users as they carried on extended conversations during afternoon tea and long country walks, as they read novels aloud after dinner and conscientiously recorded their thoughts in letters and diaries.

What would they make of our on-hold, call-waiting phone conversations and our disengaged commentary as we collect messages about more phone calls? What might we be like if suddenly we were transported into a world of uninterrupted dialogue and leisurely contemplation?

In those days, the manner in which one expressed oneself was important. Quite ordinary people scheduled letter and diary writing alongside piano and singing practice. The writing table was a laboratory where the minutiae and mores of life and society were dissected after reviewing them at tea. Each day brought new reflections and fresh misgivings on which to expand and rhapsodize.

A single comment by a visitor could provoke a flurry of written interpretations, each telling a tale of pride and prejudice, sense and sensibility, of good and evil seen through the prism of fantasy and expectation.

As I look back over my daily journal, I realize that these are the same issues that concern Joseph and Alex, two 5-year-olds in my class, although they have not yet learned to write. But they do dictate stories every day that have the sound of morality tales, and the continuity of their written communication grows rapidly throughout the year. They are, in a sense, writing letters to each other, offering ideas to ponder by way of roles to play, while I attempt to read between their lines and fill journals with my own brand of storytelling. It is less spontaneous but, for me, equally useful in figuring out the human dimensions of the classroom.

Joseph dictates, "Once there was a man who lived in a little wooden house. And he loved to go out and play in the grass. And one day he saw a wolf who is Alex and the wolf growled at him. And he shot the wolf and ate him. The end."

When we act out Joseph's story, Alex agrees, hesitantly, to be the wolf. Why does his friend want to devour him? The next day Alex responds with a different scenario. He has learned something about the power of the pen: "Once upon a time a hunter came. And then he saw a wolf. I'm the wolf and Joseph is the hunter. He tried to shoot the wolf but I'm too big and strong and fierce. So the wolf ate the man for dinner. Happily ever after."

These two friends, continually testing power and position in play and conversation, have found the literary means to explore and express life's more puzzling aspects. I record their stories and their talk because I too have found a literary process by which to follow relationships and realities in a classroom. I am as concerned and curious about good and bad as the children are; I want to know how these perceptions affect learning and teaching.

"On guard!" says Alex, pointing a small paper sword at Joseph.

"You don't even know what on guard means," Joseph replies.

"I do."

"What does it mean?"

"I'm not telling you. I'm just saying it."

"See? You don't know what it means. I *do* know what it means."

"Then why do you want me to tell you?"

"I want to know if you know what it means."

"I do know but I'm not telling you because I'm too busy doing my story."

And he begins: "Once there was some pirates and one was good and one was bad but sometimes both of them was good and . . ."

He halts in mid-sentence. "Teacher, you know what, teacher? Sometimes me and Joseph are like enemies."

"You mean sometimes you really feel angry at each other?"

"I don't know." He pauses to examine his sword, then resumes the interrupted story, "And the good pirate said to the bad pirate, 'Are you bad or good? If you're good you can have the gold and the eye patch.' "

Alex stays seated, cutting black paper shapes and waiting for one that resembles an eye patch. Suddenly he asks, recalling a story he had told earlier, after the birth of a baby sister: "Remember that other day I told about a hunter? And the mother that was a wife?"

"The baby with a gun?" I reply.

"Did you like that story?" he asks gravely.

"Very much. The baby becomes a hunter. I do remember."

Later, I write in my journal: Why does Alex recall this strange plot he imagined the day after his baby sister was born? Why does he think of it right now as he tells the pirate story? Joseph's friendship must give Alex some of the same feelings of vulnerability as did the arrival of a new sibling. I know these feelings well. They occur whenever I try to describe puzzling events in my classroom to my colleagues.

Alex and Joseph search for symbols that may, for the moment, help them deal with the good and the bad, help them explain and control the daily gains and losses. And I, through the use of their imagery, am enabled to find some of the words I need to account for the unexpected in this school culture we share.

I have lived in classrooms most of my life, yet I am often as surprised as the children by the events around us. But the more I listen to and record the children's fantasies and explanations, the easier it becomes to bring out my own. And if I do not begin with "Once upon a time" or "Let's pretend" as often as they do, there is nonetheless some semblance of a plot within which to imagine meaning and motive.

Clara's sadness is one such plot. She is too sad to play, she tells us, but cannot remember why she is so sad.

"Clara is too sad to play," I say to the children at snack, turning on my tape recorder. "If we tell her what makes us sad maybe she'll think of what is making her sad."

"When my mom leaves I'm sad," Nell says. "Because I want her to stay." We know this is so; nearly all of Nell's stories end with, "And the mom didn't go to work and stayed home all day to play with the little girl."

"I'm sad if someone pushes me," Carl tells us.

Joseph remembers that dead people make him sad. "Certain dead people?" I ask.

"Everybody that's dead."

"Me too," Alex echoes. "Everyone dead makes me sad."

The next day, Joseph is thrown off a bull in a rodeo and dies. "This is the first time you have yourself die in a story, Joseph," I comment.

"Let me be the one who dies," Alex pleads.

"No, me. It's my story."

"This is interesting, boys. You said yesterday that it makes you sad to think about dead people. But you both want to die in the rodeo."

"In real life dead," Joseph explains.

"I know, but maybe when you tell stories about being dead you don't feel so sad about real life dead. Because the stories are pretend."

"Pretend real," Nell corrects me. "But I don't put anyone dead in my stories only people that come alive quickly."

I could not follow this hilly landscape without securing it to a written road map. Clara's sadness bids us to recall our own, which in turn leads to thoughts of death and resurrection, and these ideas will crisscross many others before they appear on the pages of my journal. It is there I will try to single out the separate themes.

Everything becomes part of the classroom story: Jamal's dream and Amber's knowledge of *whup* and Alex's baby sister and Clara's sadness, as well as the need for good giants and heroic deaths. As a storyteller, I will avoid labels and theories that offer answers before the questions have been imagined.

There is enough good copy to fill any number of journals. It is useful to discuss such matters with colleagues, especially those who work in the same classroom, but talk is not enough. Only as we write down our thoughts and observations may we question and argue with ourselves about the things we do and say. Note: Question and argue with ourselves.

If I were principal of your school or mine, this is what I would announce next September: "Hear ye, hear ye! There will be no faculty meetings this year. And no committees or in-service programs. I am calling a halt to official groupthink for a whole year."

Those who had not already dozed off would clap and cheer, until they heard the rest of my message. "Using the time thus made free, you are to keep a daily journal or write letters to a close friend. You are to write about the things that you do not understand, that didn't work, and try to imagine why. It is only with yourself or perhaps with a good friend that you can learn to be completely honest. Once you begin to bring out the first errors and misjudgments the dam will burst with revelations. One idea will flow into another, reaching deeper into that reservoir of impressions, anxieties, and fragile connections we all keep bottled up beneath the surface."

"But," you will argue, "this can happen when I talk."

"Seldom. You are interrupted and distracted before you can carry any thought very far. Furthermore, when you become too self-revealing or too critical of accepted notions and practices—even of our own—your audience is likely to turn away."

"Wait, not so fast," you urge. "I need my colleagues, their ideas and support."

"True. But you also need to know your own ideas more intimately; you need to know what makes you different from your colleagues. You have your own inner support of memories, feelings, and instincts. Through these you will find your own questions and follow through in your own ways. It is quite euphoric, really, to see yourself revealed on paper."

Your principal and mine will probably not agree to such a plan. The fact is, however, once we stop playing out our feelings and ideas, as the children do, writing—personal, private writing—becomes the tool with which we can best tap the vital store of earlier learnings and instincts that enable us to make real connections in the classroom and in our outside lives as well.

Those signs we see on trucks and taxis, *How am I doing?* can be answered by ourselves alone as we listen, watch, and then record the events of the day, those that make sense and those that don't.

We can write about the problem of the moment or the problems of a lifetime. What do we think, what do the children think, and what do we think about what they think? Never will we fully discover the essential issues for each child or for ourselves, but what we do, as we write, is continually demonstrate the process of searching for solutions as we ask ourselves the questions no one else will ask, including questions about our own classroom experiences.

Jamal dictates a sad story. "Once there was a school with one mean kid. He was accidentally mean but they thought he was really mean. So he went to a different place where people think he is nice."

I write: Is this because I was impatient when he kept interrupting *The Carrot Seed*? Why didn't I ask him to explain why he wouldn't let the characters say their parts? Make sure you discuss this *tomorrow!*

VGP: Jamal, I've been thinking about *The Carrot Seed*. Remember when you wanted the family to say "It *will* come up" instead of "It won't come up" as it is in the book?

Jamal: They was being mean to him on purpose.

Jordan: They just wanted to make him feel bad. They knowed it would come up.

VGP: Why would the mother and father keep saying the seed wouldn't come up if they thought it would?

Amy: Maybe they liked the other brother better. That could really happen, you know.

VGP: I'm sorry I didn't ask for your opinion, Jamal. I was in too much of a hurry to act out the story.

Jamal: It's okay, 'cause we had to go to gym, remember?

This process of examining complaints and imagining solutions gives a great surge of power and communal purpose to us all. And much to write about. There is always a new scenario out there if we care enough to find it. We try in the classroom; we try in our journal; and the next day, we test our reality alongside the children's.

They are our colleagues in this endeavor. They are the ones who will first show us what makes them different and how they connect to everyone else. They will demonstrate the way they think as they continue to develop new roles and rationales. Our own thinking and studying takes place as we observe ourselves and the children moving in and out of untenable positions. This will form the bulk of our daily writing.

One of the things I have learned from my daily writing is that, to me and to the children, the most interesting aspects of the classroom are the vastly different ways people find to behave, even ways that are sometimes disruptive or confusing. These were the most compelling events in society for Jane Austen as well.

How do we begin to write about the classroom? The empty journal page glares accusingly, but we do not feel a bit as if we are Jane Austen or even her sister Cassandra who wrote such sensitive letters.

When I was new at this, I needed safe, planned structures. Those formal discussions that are part of most school days provided me with a relatively controlled arena for practicing the art of classroom reportage. Such discourse is easily accessible, easy to tape, easy to transcribe, and often can be recalled without a tape recorder if not too much time elapses.

The best discussions I've recorded, then and now, often focus on fairy tales. They are treasure chests for open-ended inquiries into the collective imaginations of children and teachers. Indeed, I continually must reassess my position even as I attempt to uncover the children's.

VGP: How would a bad giant find a nice wife? Amy said the wife was nice and Jamal and Amber said she *had* to be nice.

Amy: That giant used to be nice but something made him mad. I don't know what.

Amber: I'm pretty sure he was born bad. Maybe because he was too tall.

Peter: Also he was too hungry. So he gobbled up even people.

Amy: But the mother wouldn't let him. The wife is a mother.

Jamal: When she's there he has to act good.

Jordan: Not a bad giant's mother can't. He's already too bad.

Amy: Don't forget, there still has to be someone nice. Then he re-members that he used to be nice.

VGP: Jordan, can a really bad giant become nice again?

Jordan: Only if he tries very very hard. Then he could.

In my journal, I take the matter further: The children discuss these moral issues, good and bad, fair and unfair, more than we do. It is often easier to be open and honest about my doubts and denials, and errors in judgment, with the children in my class than with other teachers. And easier still to examine these feelings in my daily journal.

The road to discovery lies waiting to be mapped out in each day's journal pages, pieces of a continuing mystery story about individuals and groups who are learning to live together in a school society that seems very different from a sensible home and family only when we arbitrarily make it that way.

Every encounter is full of questions; there is much that exists beneath the surface. Even Jane Austen—who, by the way, apparently wrote her novels at a living room table surrounded by a lively family—even Austen knew there were few answers, only temporary solutions to puzzling behaviors and events. If this were not so, how would there always be material for a new journal page, a new letter, and, in her case, another novel?

There are few novelists among us, and only a small number will have their works published in any form. But we all have the desire to learn more about ourselves and the children who call us Teacher. My way has been to resurrect the daily journal to help me study the most complex society ever assembled in a single place: the school classroom.

Breaking the Silence

Trudy Smoke

Hunter College, City University of New York

People in my family tell me that I learned to read at an amazingly early age. Some say that I started at around the age of 2. My guess is that I had a good memory and memorized the books my mother read to me when I was an infant during her pregnancy with my sister. My mother had toxemia and severe anemia, was weak, and spent a lot of her time sitting and reading. She read everything aloud to me—novels, newspapers, books on the Civil War and slavery, articles on politics and cooking. She also read the traditional children's stories to me, some of them so many times that I began to know the words. I liked to hold the books, look at the symbols on the page, and tell the stories to myself.

I often think that this was what attracted me to teaching writing and literature. The power of writing connected me with my mother and provided the excitement of other voices, other stories. It introduced me to the world beyond my suburban home.

My parents even met through writing. During World War II, my father ran away from his Massachusetts home to join the Navy. When he became lonely, he put his name on a list of military personnel who wanted pen pals. My mother had just lost the love of her life, her high school boyfriend. He had joined the Army and, on leave, met a girl in a bar and married her. Soon after getting this news, my mother sold the wedding gown she had bought for their upcoming marriage, bleached her black hair blonde, and became a volunteer at a New York City USO. She decided to write to the young Massachusetts sailor whose name was on the pen pal list. Eventually, they fell in love through their letters. Although English was not his first language, he prided himself in his knowledge of the language and in his ability to write convincing prose. Two people who had never met were able to overcome huge differences of background and place through writing. Their story was a living example of how writing could be used as a tool to bridge cultural, experiential, and life differences.

They were married before the war ended and quickly had three children. But my parents were independent spirits and they fought and disagreed about many things. She was a Democrat, a liberal thinker, and a political activist who fought to make politicians support personal rights and freedoms. She taught us that individuals have the responsibility to vote, to protest, and to take action for the public good. His was more a private notion of public good. He was somewhat conservative and thought that individuals had an obligation to work hard and take care of their own families, and that social workers like himself needed to be there to help them get back on track, but not fulfill their personal responsibilities.

They argued often and fiercely about how, why, and what should be done to make the world better and make their own children more successful, but even more viciously about painful issues like jealousy, love, and trust.

I was a sensitive child who tried to keep the peace at home. When my efforts to intervene failed, which was often, I felt inarticulate, powerless, and helpless. My only comfort would be to take refuge sitting under the dining table hidden beneath the tablecloth. There I would read and write stories and pretend away the noise and confusion that surrounded me.

One of the ways my parents coped with their problems was to move often. Perhaps because my mother had been jilted, she felt insecure in her relationship with my father. She worried about his friendships with other women and felt trapped by her own responsibilities. Too introspective to spend so much time alone with such small children, she dwelled on her own difficulties and could not overcome them. The only way out of this predicament for her was to continually change her surroundings. We moved from house to house throughout Long Island; I went to more than 20 schools before high school. Although the language in each remained the same, I felt like an outsider in every new location and school system. Maybe this is why I can so easily identify with my students.

Throughout these frequent upheavals, I felt I had only one constant in my life, and that was school itself. The classrooms were similar and the teachers, as I remember them, were uniformly warm, caring, and female. I found it easier to learn the rules of school than to learn the rules at home. In school, all I had to do was be attentive, prepare for tests, and cooperate with my teachers. For this little bit of effort, I got dazzling smiles, pats on the head, gold stars, and straight As. It was a good bargain to my way of thinking. So good, in fact, that I never left school and despite growing up, marriage, divorce, remarriage, loss of both parents, and several apartments and houses of my own, the only constant in my life is still school. I feel comfortable as soon as I step into those chalk-dusted rooms with the big boards on the walls and the familiar arrangement of desks and chairs.

A few months ago, I met with a PhD student who, as part of her research, had observed my ESL writing classroom for a semester. Reading through what she had written, I became disturbed when I read her description of my class as *safe* and *secure*. I wanted her to see the ways in which I challenged my students, forced them to think, encouraged them to find their own abilities, not a teacher who simply made them feel safe in the unsafe new world of college.

Writing this essay has gotten me to reflect on how being a language educator has affected my perceptions of myself and my classroom and this, in turn, has led me to a deeper understanding of my motivations and my abilities as a teacher.

This student's insight was correct: I create a classroom in which students can feel some of the security and safety that I got from school, safety that emboldens students to risk making mistakes, taking controversial positions, and exploring difficult concepts. The need to provide this for others may have been one of the reasons I decided to become a language teacher. Being a language educator has provided me with a place of refuge and a road to personal empowerment. It has helped me gain my own voice, gain confidence, and develop a sense of identity so that I could connect to others and help them feel the sense of safety I try to develop. In this safe world, I have seen students' lives transformed by their exposure to literacy, new ideas, and the power of knowledge.

FINDING A VOICE

Jean Bernard was an 18-year-old student born in Haiti who graduated from a New York City high school and was placed in the upper level of our three levels of ESL writing. At first, Jean seemed sullen and silent. He wore a baseball hat and a team jacket. He sat bent over his desk, fiddling with his pen, and rarely looking up. He did not seem engaged or interested. Jean made it clear that he preferred science and math classes and did not enjoy reading and writing, especially writing because he had nothing to say.

Early in the semester, I had given the class information about a writing contest sponsored by a publishing company that offered cash awards and publication in a textbook. The theme of the essay was to be about how a student had overcome difficult odds. I was stunned when Jean shyly submitted his first draft of an essay for this contest. He was the only student in the class who had drafted an essay for the contest.

Jean's essay was very personal and described the serious adversities, political and economic, his family had faced in Haiti, and the extreme poverty and hardships they encountered in New York City. Among other things, he wrote about not having enough to eat at home and stuffing his pockets with any food he could lay his hands on to bring home to his hungry little sister.

There was a fierce energy in Jean's desire to perfect his essay. He wrote draft after draft and met with me repeatedly in my office. We talked about the content of the essay, and I got to know him and to realize the obstacles he had faced in graduating from high school and beginning college. I also saw his determination to change his life and I identified with it, and with the power he was starting to feel from gaining a voice. Finally, Jean was ready to enter the essay in the contest. A local ESL organization also sponsored a writing contest and Jean entered the essay in that contest as well.

Jean won both contests. He was awarded third prize of $150 in the first contest and won $50 in the second contest. It is customary for the award recipient of the ESL organization to read his essay at the opening session of the group's annual conference. Because of the personal nature of the essay, I suggested that Jean simply say a few words and distribute the essay to the group. When he insisted on reading the essay, I was concerned. I wanted him to be celebrated for his work, but I was worried about the pressure of speaking before a group. He insisted, however, and as the day of the conference neared, I became more anxious. Writing and speaking require different skills and in addition to his shyness, Jean had never spoken before a group nor used a microphone.

More than 200 people filled the auditorium on the day of the conference. When Jean began to speak, I could see that he was nervous. His head bent, his voice soft, Jean mumbled into the microphone, and rarely looked up to make eye contact. Reaching the part of his essay describing his family's poverty and near starvation in New York City, Jean suddenly began to sob and shake. When it became clear that he could not continue, I joined him at the microphone and completed the reading. I empathized with Jean: I, too, have problems speaking publicly and could not even attempt to talk about such personal issues in a public setting. I also blamed myself for not preventing him from exposing himself, yet later audience members congratulated Jean, telling him that his writing had great resonance for them.

In fact, although difficult for both of us, this episode seemed to encourage Jean's expression through his writing. Soon after the conference, Jean asked me to give him feedback on a 20-page love story he was writing. He subsequently became involved in the college Haitian student organization and began to develop a more visible presence and to become more politically active on campus. The experience of writing and publicly presenting may have given him feelings of confidence and power despite the discomfort we both felt.

BECOMING EMPOWERED

Julia Enrique was born in Colombia 26 years ago. She married, had a child, and remained at home with her family. She never had a job outside the home, nor did she have any higher education until she entered my class. On the first day in my writing class, students introduced themselves and told a little about their background. Julia, a petite, delicate-looking young woman with long dark curly hair, said to the group, "I'm not sure I belong in this class. I learned English by myself. I am here because I really want to learn, but I do not know as much as everyone else. I don't know the grammar. I am not a very good writer, really I am not."

Immediately presenting her weaknesses was a strategy with which I could identify from my own early college experiences. Letting people know one's vulnerabilities can be a method of preventing attack. When I entered college, I was also easily silenced and felt that I did not belong. My family did not support my going to college and I was so worried about reinforcing their view that I would fail that I avoided situations where I would have to talk and possibly expose my weaknesses.

As I got to know Julia better, I found even more areas with which I could identify. She had recently separated from an abusive husband. I had had a difficult first marriage and painful divorce. Julia was also doing what my mother had wanted to do; she was going to school and finding an identity outside of marriage. In class, Julia wrote about her family. She articulated the silences I had learned to hide, writing about the difficulties her parents had experienced. Writing stories about her family and her past and sharing them with her peers enabled her to gain her voice and to persevere despite tremendous personal problems. Her stories and life also gave me courage and strength.

Returning to school after a 2-day absence, Julia pulled back her scarf and showed me her bruised neck. Her husband had returned. She was desperate to protect herself and her daughter. Julia seemed so alone; she had few friends and no family in the United States, yet she did not want to return to her country, a place where she said women had few opportunities.

As her situation worsened and her finances dwindled, New York City financial assistance provided barely enough money for food, but not enough for the rent. On the Wednesday before Thanksgiving, Julia sat in my office, sobbing. She was about to be evicted from her apartment and did not know where to go. Afraid of moving to a battered woman's shelter, Julia was distraught. I gave Julia my home telephone number and contacted some of the emergency services in the college. She came back with a check for part of the money but needed an additional $200 to pay her rent and get through the weekend. My own mother had died just months before and looking at Julia, I thought of my mother and her unwillingness to abandon her family responsibilities to fulfill herself. I gave Julia the money. This is something I had never done before in almost 20 years of teaching. I had lent students money for subway tokens and occasionally even bought a hungry student some lunch, but I had never given any student more than $2. Here I was, writing a huge check and believing that I would never see the money again, but I felt I had to do it.

Julia made it through the crisis. Soon after, she got a part-time job making cheesecake while also working as a night shift waitress for a Spanish restaurant in her neighborhood. She was often tired and her eyes were shadowed with dark circles, but she kept working and paid her rent and other expenses. She also gave me back my $200.

The difficulties she was having affected her attendance and her classwork, but she ended up passing all her courses that semester. She found a roommate and started paying her bills. She gained academic confidence and also gained confidence in her ability to take care of herself and her daughter. Her identity as an independent woman had emerged through facing this crisis. I felt that I, too, had gained from knowing Julia and working with her.

DEALING WITH ANGER

Anya Abramova was a 56-year-old former physician from Moscow. She was a sturdy-looking woman, used to taking care of others and taking charge of situations. Anya lived in the Brighton Beach section of Brooklyn, a section sometimes called Little Odessa because of the large number of Russian immigrants living there and the many stores and restaurants in which Russian is spoken and Russian goods and food are sold. There, Anya could speak Russian and use familiar coping strategies. In the college, she faced other, more difficult challenges.

When I met Anya, she had already taken the first two levels of ESL writing classes twice before passing them. She was angry that she was being forced to take another ESL class, even if it was an upper-level one. She was angry at me and at the system that she thought I represented. She attended my writing class, often whispering to the other students in the class in Russian, and arriving at my door, papers in hand, before and after class, refusing to leave even though other students also needed my attention. It is easier to deal with a student for whom you can feel sympathy than one for whom you feel anger and resentment. I had learned to sit under the dining room table to avoid the confrontations and the anger that surrounded me. I continued to have trouble expressing that anger myself. Anya was a catalyst for me to deal with this rough and difficult emotion.

She was also older than I and she felt that she was more of an authority than I should have been. After all, Anya was a medical doctor who was used to dealing with life and death issues. How could English and one English teacher become such an obstacle in her life? She wrote angry essays about the disappointments she felt in the United States—with the social systems that did not provide enough, the overcrowded and small but costly apartments, the miserable health care, and the unsafe, dirty streets and subways she had to travel each day. Other students in the class argued with her and encouraged her to take a less critical stance, but Anya persisted. She reminded me of the negative sides of my mother—demanding, angry, wanting me to take actions that I preferred to avoid. Like my mother, she also made me feel that I was failing her, and I did not know what to do. I felt the need to hold onto some authority, but Anya was pushing me to the limit.

Then she failed the final in the writing class. After getting this news, Anya was waiting at my office when I returned from 4 hours of hearing appeals brought by teachers who wanted their students' essays reread and reassessed. As soon as Anya saw me, she angrily told me that someone had changed her test so that she would not pass. She informed me that someone was persecuting people from her country. I told her that her final was not passing and that I did not believe anyone had changed it. Hearing this, Anya became so enraged that she began shouting at me. She clenched her hand into a fist, and raised her arm as if to hit me. I told her to put her hand down and backed toward the wall. A neighboring professor hearing the noise, called security, and Anya was escorted out of the building.

I understood Anya's frustration as a mature professional failing at simple courses. I easily imagined what I would feel if at her age, I were forced to leave my country, begin a new life, and also have to learn a new language with little or no financial support. I have studied other languages and have had difficulties and embarrassments with them. I remember almost bursting into tears when a French teacher spoke to me rapidly in French, expecting an immediate answer as my brain tried in vain to translate and prepare an acceptable response. Yet as wrenching as the decision was for me to make, I could not in good conscience pass her. Mature enough to accept that she could not manipulate the situation to her advantage, Anya ultimately retook the writing course the next semester and passed it.

Adult students, like Anya, leaving behind lives and careers in their own countries, suffer serious disjunctures. Many of them take their anger at the system out on individuals even to the point of lying, begging, or threatening. It is difficult, as a professional, to tell these students that they have not passed, even when it might mean their being dismissed from college, but it is part of the responsibility of teaching. Making and acting on hard decisions, while painful and troubling, is also part of the process of becoming a fully realized individual.

GAINING INDEPENDENCE

Not all dilemmas are imposed by such dire situations. Yim Lee was a 21-year-old student who had graduated from high school in Korea and served in the Army there. Although he was accepted into college in the competitive Korean university system, Yim decided to come to the United States to study because he wanted to become a sound engineer and there were no programs in his country. He also wanted to be on his own, away from the constraints of his family life. In my intermediate level of ESL writing, Yim was one of three foreign students in a class of 23. His situation and problems were somewhat different from the other immigrant ESL students. He set himself apart from them by making it clear that as a foreign student, he paid more tuition than they did. He seemed to think that because he paid twice as much, he should get twice the attention.

Yim wanted to be hip and accepted as a part of the New York dance-club scene. In describing a place that had made a vivid impression on them, most students wrote about their home cities, but Yim wrote about a Korean dance club in New York where he worked as a disc jockey 5 nights a week. He wrote about mixing music, meeting women, and staying up until 3:00 each morning. He loved to talk about fashion and would compliment me when he thought my clothes were stylish. He used current American slang in his conversations and writing. He made it clear that he had more money than the other students, who were often living hand to mouth.

Despite his interest in being cool, he seemed unaware of many of the social conventions and rules of college behavior. He smoked in the smoke-free hallway, wore audio earphones in class, and lounged in his seat, stretching his long legs so they almost tripped unwary students. He called out and interrupted the class to ask decontextualized grammar questions, "Tell me when you use *in which*. Don't give me examples, I want all the rules. What is the passive form of the future perfect? Why do people say *on the corner* and *at the corner*? Which is better and why?"

After a while, students became impatient with him and let him know that he was disrupting the class. He would smile and apologize.

In a paper about education systems in different parts of the world, Yim wrote that in Korea, teachers function in the parental role when children are separated from their parents. I realized then that he wanted me to direct his behavior, to be the mother he had left behind in Seoul, the parent-teacher he had grown to expect from his experiences in his home country. This attitude revealed the contradiction in Yim's behavior. On the one hand, he behaved like a rebellious teenager wanting to appear hip and independent, but on the other hand, he expected his teachers to be parental and demanding. These are contradictions of growing up, and I felt that behind Yim's bravado was a lonely young man who knew few English-speaking adults in New York City.

He told the class about eating alone in New York restaurants and the vain efforts he would make to meet people in the restaurant. When students showed an interest in his job, he graciously volunteered to bring in music tapes and to tell everyone about how he set up his night's music.

Yim passed the writing class but had to leave Hunter to attend a nearby technical school where the sound engineering courses he needed were available. As is true for many foreign students, living away from his family forced Yim to deal with adult issues for the first time. I do not have children and a part of me responded to his need for me to play a maternal role, yet overall I felt that it was time for Yim to begin to be an adult. Because of my childhood experiences, I could also identify with Yim, the child, who wanted to rely on his teacher to fulfill all the missing parts in his life, yet I knew from my own experience that one needs to find one's own identity and that the support that a language class can provide is the ideal environment for this transition.

REFLECTIONS

Like the four ESL students that I have written about and others I teach, I, too, have experienced in my own life feelings of being inarticulate, disempowered, silenced, and insecure. As a language educator, I help students who are often inarticulate in English—immigrants or newcomers in a strange new world—find their voices, gain confidence, and shape their identities, yet I am often at a loss for words and inhibited and restrained in articulating what I really mean to say. Recently, I was at a college-wide meeting discussing the possibility of decreasing the numbers of courses offered to our ESL students. I found myself sitting there, frustrated and angry at the attitudes I was hearing from my colleagues throughout the college. Suddenly my voice emerged, shaky at first. Ultimately, I was able to speak out with force and certainty in defense of the students. Later, I found out that what I said influenced the final decision to maintain our courses.

At the same time as I am writing this essay and dealing with my own issues, the New York state public college system is facing drastic cuts in budgets, programs, and faculty. How long the students I have described remain in college will, to some extent, be determined not by their desires, abilities, or determination, but instead by the whims of politicians who want to be re-elected or who want to restructure the public sphere of American life. These severe cuts not only threaten the colleges as a whole but they also threaten me. I have spent my academic career trying to help students escape from painful life circumstances with which I can often identify. I have tried to help them experience school as a place of safety, constancy, a place to find a strong voice, connect with others, gain skills, confidence, and a sense of identity. These budget cuts make me feel angry and upset for the students, but also for me. School, the one safe and constant factor in my life, doesn't feel safe anymore.

The continued fulfillment of needs that being a language educator fills in my life feels threatened. Providing a sense of professional identity and connection, of building feelings of confidence and power as with Jean, helping overcome feelings of failure and weakness, enabling me to make social connections as with Julia, of dealing with embarrassment, anger, and frustration as with Anya, and allowing me to be a friend, giver, a mother-caretaker to my students as with Yim are all threatened. All of these roles stir up tensions about the balance between my personal needs and my role as a professional educator. The crisis in public higher education causes anger at the vagaries and injustices of the system, a feeling not unlike the one expressed by Anya. This brings me back to my mother's belief that each of us has an obligation to right the wrongs done by our political leaders, and these political issues have become part of recent classroom lessons. When students come into class with their replies to their letters to various state and federal officials protesting the budget cutbacks, I think of my mother and the connection between her commitment to political action and the power that writing played in her and in my life.

It has been hard for me to write this essay. I am not used to writing about myself, nor am I used to revealing my personal limitations. To some degree, I hide behind my role as a language educator and in writing this essay I am exposing myself. Recognizing the interrelationships of my professional life and my personal needs has made me realize the reciprocal nature of teaching for me. Helping students to find their voices also enabled me to find mine.

Shifting Frames, Shifting Stories

Jill Sinclair Bell
York University, Ontario

As a child, I remember vividly my excitement as I began the study of Latin. I was 11 years old, just beginning an all-girls high school, and Latin symbolized all the new and exciting subjects that only the big girls got the chance to learn. By the end of that first year, when it became clear that school Latin involved a considerable amount of rote memorization of long vocabulary lists and complicated declensions, my enthusiasm began to wane a little. In the second year, an inexperienced teacher struggled without success to hold our interest and we girls soon agreed Latin was unutterably boring. Boring or not, however, we had to continue, since University entrance was contingent on a pass in the national Latin examination following the fifth year of study. Getting this Latin pass became the nightmare of my schooldays. The examinations were offered twice yearly, and twice yearly I failed dismally (setting up an all-time school record in the process). I no longer found Latin boring; I actively hated it. Finally, on my seventh try, following extra classes and private tutors, I managed to scrape up the absolute bare minimum to allow University entrance. Now, many years later, I take some pride in my Latin knowledge and find to my surprise that I make use of it quite often in a variety of contexts. The wheel has come full circle.

I was reminded of these shifting attitudes toward language learning when I embarked on another learning experience more recently. I had been working in the field of ESL literacy for a number of years by this point and had become interested in the question of the role played by first-language literacy in the acquisition of literacy in a second language, particularly when the

133

two languages used different writing systems. When, in my late 30s, I decided to go back to school and get my PhD, this was an obvious area of research. I began work with two Afghan refugees who were attempting literacy in English. Although I did gain some interesting insights from this work, I eventually became frustrated by the process of trying to get inside somebody else's head via an interpreter. Consequently, I decided to become my own guinea pig and attempt to develop a second literacy myself. I wanted to learn a language that had as little in common with English as possible. Consequently, I narrowed my choices to nonalphabetic systems, eventually settling on Chinese.

I looked for a tutor who had learned Chinese through traditional methods and who would teach me accordingly. I was delighted when a mutual friend introduced me to Cindy Lam, who seemed the ideal person. Cindy had grown up in Hong Kong and had all her early schooling there. She had come to Canada as an adolescent and completed high school, university, and a teacher education program in her adopted country, so she was both bilingual and bicultural. She also had considerable experience teaching English language literacy to Chinese learners in bilingual classes, and was intrigued, as I was, by the idea of examining the literacy acquisition process.

Our first meeting was an informal lunch at which we explored the possibility of working together. We discussed the merits of the various dialects of Chinese and decided that she should teach me Cantonese, the dialect in which she herself had first become literate. We agreed that in addition to Cindy's literacy tutorials, I would also take university classes in spoken Cantonese, which would allow me to build up a vocabulary as rapidly as possible. Cindy was at pains to point out that she had no prior experience in teaching Chinese literacy: She wanted me to be aware that she would not consider herself to be an expert. In some ways, I welcomed this lack of prior experience, as I did not want the experience to be neatly packaged for Western learners. I wanted to share something akin to the experience learners from other cultures have when they find themselves, in a North American classroom, being taught by North American methods, which may or may not match their expectations of what education should be. If anything, I was concerned that Cindy's considerable experience with ESL literacy would make her so conscious of Western methodology that she would shape the Chinese literacy lessons into unduly familiar patterns.

I was very soon to receive my first hint that this fear was groundless. Our conversation moved onto the logistics of the study and the amount of time we would spend on it.

"How much of your time will be spent on the research side of things and how much on the actual learning of Chinese? Will you have time to do work on your own?" she asked me.

I explained that in addition to her tutorials, I would be attending an oral Cantonese course at the university and that I would be committed to a considerable amount of work transcribing the tapes of both the oral and the literacy classes, so the demands of the research side would take up a fair proportion of the time.

"But I will have time for assignments," I added, "so if you would set me some work each time we meet, I'll certainly do it. I should have about an hour a day for home-study, I think. Plus of course, I spend 2 hours a day commuting on the subway, so I thought I could use that time to work on the characters."

"What!" Cindy looked astonished. "You can't—you can't do characters on the subway!"

I was baffled. I had had many ESL students who would carry a set of index cards around with them to study on buses and trains at odd moments. I had thought this would be an excellent way of learning characters. I didn't expect to be able to produce good writing under those conditions, but I could surely learn the order of strokes, and the basic pattern of the characters. I suppose my face showed my bafflement, because Cindy began to laugh. "Oh, I'm sorry," she said, "but you just can't learn characters like that. It's a matter of balance. You can't write characters in those conditions."

"Well, yes, I know, it's kind of bumpy, but just to learn the shapes?"

"No, I don't mean that kind of balance. You have to have balance inside to be able to learn them. You'll never learn them properly if you don't have the proper conditions."

I didn't understand what Cindy meant at that time, and I was not sufficiently convinced to let go of the idea that I could use subway time to learn to recognize the characters even if I could not produce them. I was surprised, too, not merely by the content of what Cindy said, but by the immediate and decided way in which she said it, which contrasted sharply with the flexible open-minded tone she had taken in discussing English-language literacy. My surprise must have been evident because suddenly it seemed as if Canadian Cindy resurfaced as she distanced herself from the pronouncement.

"Maybe things have changed now," she said. "For all I know, children in China sit in front of the TV set to do their homework, these days. But when we were children, homework had to be done at a clean desk in peace and quiet so you could concentrate—our parents thought that was very important and the teachers insisted on it. Even in a very poor house, the parents will make sure there is a good quiet table for the children to study on. I really don't think you can write good characters without those conditions—otherwise there won't be any balance."

I really didn't understand at the time what Cindy meant by balance, but I probably nodded sagely and the conversation moved on. We made arrangements to begin the tutoring the following week and I looked forward to our classes with excitement and some trepidation. There were some slightly baffling experiences in this first class. Cindy began by asking me what I would like to learn. Like many learners, I really hadn't considered this issue in advance but had trusted to my teacher to make those decisions. Put on the spot, however, I suggested that I might begin by learning characters that I could encounter in meaningful contexts—characters found on restaurant menus or street and market signs. Somehow, though, it seemed that this response wasn't the right one, and Cindy said that she didn't think we could begin in that way. Next she asked if I would like to learn my name in Chinese, but again we didn't seem to interpret this question in quite the same manner. I thought I would be learning a phonetic version of my name, such as I might put on a business card, but it appeared that the only characters with a sound close to Jill Bell meant something like *idiot*. Cindy rejected this variation, and suggested different meaningfully appropriate characters, none of which sounded to me anything like my name. Eventually, we abandoned the search, and instead focused on learning the characters for the numbers 1, 2, 3, and 4.

In our approach to these first characters, we followed a pattern that was to become routine in the months to come. First, Cindy would demonstrate the character, then she would discuss its meaning, and then provide the new sound. After this, I would write the character a number of times under her supervision with particular attention being paid to stroke order. The characters for 1, 2, and 3 are very simple in Chinese, being basically a matter of one, two, and three horizontal strokes respectively. The number 4 is a little more complicated but still one of the simplest characters. I saw the task of learning these characters as a very simple one, and began to practice enthusiastically under Cindy's supervision. On this first day, I wrote perhaps 20 repetitions of each character and was assigned to do more practice for homework on special paper designed for children that was divided into 1-inch squares. Cindy provided enough for at least 100 repetitions of each character. As it seemed to me that I had already learned these characters in class, I didn't quite understand the purpose of this homework. I began to wonder whether I really was doing the strokes correctly. Perhaps the real test was to line up the characters in each square so they made perfect vertical columns down the page? Or perhaps I should try and capture that slight thickening on the end of the stroke? With each column of characters, I tried some different variant, turning the horizontal into a curve or a slight diagonal, making my lines thicker or thinner.

At our next meeting I showed Cindy my homework, fairly proud of my industry, and described the various ways I had tried to perfect the form. She nodded, commented that the variations in her demonstration characters were really not significant and reassured me that all I needed was some more practice. Things continued along this course for some weeks. Each week I was introduced to three or four new characters, I would write them under Cindy's supervision, and she would assign more repetitions for homework. Her most common feedback was that I needed more practice, but sometimes she would say that I had lost my concentration and that the characters lacked balance.

Over this period, I moved from elation to despair. After about 2 months of study, colleagues began asking whether I could read Chinese newspapers yet, and I became increasingly uncomfortable about confessing that I could barely find a character I recognized, much less read an article. I began counting up the total of characters learned to date—something like 25 to 30—and predicting my likely total count after a year if this glacial pace continued. My progress seemed so slow and I couldn't understand why things couldn't move more rapidly. I fell back on patterns of learning that had proved successful for me in the past, searching for rules that I could apply, and trying hard to link my new learning to existing pieces of knowledge. I began to plague Cindy for more specific feedback so that I could understand what I was doing wrong and correct my mistakes. Was the problem that I was making this stroke too long? Would it be better if I made stroke number two intersect stroke number one precisely at the midpoint rather than slightly above as in the example? To these and similar queries, Cindy would calmly respond that the difference was not significant and I should concentrate and practice some more. I began to feel the pressure of failure.

Failing in an academic endeavor was not something I had anticipated, and as it turned out, I was not well prepared to cope with the accompanying feelings. As I struggled to make sense of this relatively new experience, I cast around for a story that would explain my poor performance. I knew I had a fairly good brain, so this task should not have been beyond me. Unlike those early days of Latin failure, I also knew I was working very hard, so I could not dismiss my poor results as simply the effect of lack of interest. Bruner and Weisser (1990) have pointed out that we have a limited number of stories available to us that we can use to make sense of events. The stories available to me did not include random failure at an academic task at which I had made a concerted effort.

Consequently, I unconsciously began to construct the only other story that seemed to fit the case; that is, a story of poor teaching. I began to cast Cindy, if not exactly as the villain of the piece, then certainly as my opponent. Now, when I was questioned about my progress, I began telling the tale as one where my teacher would not allow me to proceed any more rapidly. Despite my commitment and my obvious control of the material covered thus far, I was being held back by my tutor. I began to question her commitment to our project and to feel irritated by her ambiguous feedback.

What did she mean when she said I had lost my concentration? What was this balance that my characters lacked? How could she tell me I was doing good work when I was still struggling with oversized, childish, squared paper that prevented me from using my adult fine motor skills? If I had had to write the definitive story of my relationship with my teacher at this point, I would have been very negative indeed.

As I have described, from our very first meeting, Cindy had stressed the need for two things if I wanted to succeed at literacy. The first was total concentration and the second was suitable working conditions. I believed I had given the task total concentration. Often, I did think-aloud-protocols as I attempted literacy tasks, so I had records of my tight focus on the production of the characters. The ideal conditions under which Cindy urged me to work were rather more of a challenge to create, however. As a doctoral student, I had access to only a tiny crowded office. At home, I had a husband and three children to distract me. Often, I ended up doing my character practice sitting with the family in the living room, balancing my binder on my knee while the television chattered in the background. Not surprisingly, Cindy's comment on work done in such conditions was invariably, "You lost your concentration."

I'm not entirely clear in retrospect what made me change the way I went about learning Chinese literacy. A number of breakthroughs that came around this time helped me realize that, in part, I was beginning with the wrong base story. Instead of struggling to find a story to account for my lousy progress as a language learner, I needed to question whether in fact my progress even qualified for that description. Maybe the fault lay with my story of what acceptable progress was. A couple of events around this time suggested that perhaps I was making more progress than I gave myself credit for—or was even capable of recognizing.

One such awakening came when I was sitting in a Chinese restaurant, looking at the artist's signature block on a painting, and trying to see whether I could make out any familiar characters. At first sight, none of them were recognizable but, while waiting for the waiter, I amused myself by tracing out the strokes of each part of the signature. Suddenly I realized that one corner of the block contained a pattern of lines that was, in fact, a stylized version of a character I did know. The curves and slopes of the character had been straightened and extended to fill a perfect square but, once I recognized it, the pattern of the character was unmistakable. It was a break-through that helped me understand the importance of the square. Characters don't come in various silhouettes like alphabetic letters where some are tall and thin and some are round and wide. Every character is essentially a square, but somehow I had never understood this. The squared paper that Cindy had me practice on finally made sense.

Around this time I learned, too, that when different characters are linked within a single square, their meaning is different from that when they occupy two squares. Cindy had previously taught me the character for woman, *néui*. In this lesson, working on the large 1-inch squares that I disliked so much, she began by teaching me *jí*, a child. Then she demonstrated that when the two characters for *néui* and *jí* were written together in a single square, they formed the character *hóu*, meaning good. This was my first complex character, and it helped me realize that the base characters I was learning were, in fact, the building blocks for a whole range of other characters.

Perhaps the biggest milestone, however, came out of a practice session where for once I had followed Cindy's advice and provided myself with a clean, clear desk in a good, quiet room. I set the tape recorder on for a think-aloud, but as the tape shows, I drift into silence after a few minutes. When I took that particular set of characters in to Cindy, she was very pleased, commenting on my progress and the sense of balance my work had displayed. At first I felt like a fraud because it didn't seem as if I had concentrated that day, not by my understanding of what concentration was, at any rate. Could we possibly mean something different by the word?

Gradually I began to realize that my assumption that I was making poor progress was unfounded. Cindy was actually quite pleased with my progress and I was indeed learning far more than I gave myself credit for. I had let myself get trapped in the assumption that learnings could be written down, counted, and tallied up. I struggled to discover the systematicity that I was sure underlay all that Cindy was teaching me. I wanted to build up my knowledge piece by piece, linking each new item onto previous knowledge. In an early journal, I describe the learning process using the metaphor of building a web across a lake with bits of knowledge linking to other known items to provide paths across the surface. I comment on how bits of knowledge that do not link to other known materials are like islands that sink back under the surface.

As I began to relax into the study, I became aware that my previous analytic approaches to learning were of relatively little use to me in the task of learning Chinese characters. There was no value in pressing Cindy for a set of rules about the relative length of strokes in a character or the phonetic breakdown of sounds in a word because she had not learned the language in this way. It was necessary for me to approach this task more holistically—to expose myself to the language and to be patient and wait for it to become clear. Gradually, a new metaphor began to show up in my journals—one of a photograph in developing fluid where the hazy overall outline gradually and imperceptibly takes shape and comes into focus. As I began to understand a new way of learning, I began to relax more with the literacy study and to work more comfortably in the ways that Cindy had prescribed for me.

As I took some of the pressure of constant analysis off myself, I felt a growing level of comfort. I found it increasingly easy to reach a state that seemed to satisfy Cindy as concentration, but that seemed almost trance-like

W "active"
E "passive"

to me. I was reminded of the experience I have when I sketch, where as I settle into the drawing, I go into some other part of my brain that doesn't fit well with language. It felt good to realize that I had powers and skills I had not recognized before. I began to feel confidence that this was a good way to learn and a way that I could benefit from using these strategies in other learning arenas.

As I talked to Cindy about this way of learning, much of what she had said to me earlier took on a different meaning. She had told me about the way in which she was educated, "You are supposed to watch and to listen and to practice—and that's in the teachings!" Whereas this had always seemed a passive mode of education, now it began to seem more like the door to enlightenment. I recognized that in nonacademic endeavors, I did learn in holistic ways. I come to know the faces of new colleagues by a process of general exposure and increasing familiarity, not by taking out a ruler and measuring the relative length of their nose and their eyebrows. I pick up melodies by a subconscious process based on repeated exposure, not by studying the score. Why then had I always assumed that literacy was best approached as a series of small, analytic steps? Most likely because a Western education had systematically trained this holistic way of learning out of me. I resented that loss. In my new enlightened state, I began to understand what Cindy meant by balance and concentration and discipline, and I worked hard to incorporate these insights into other areas of my life. I was intensely grateful for this eye-opening experience and felt almost a sense of moral superiority over colleagues still struggling within their limited Western ways of thinking. If I had written the definitive story of my relationship with my teacher at this point, I would probably have written something close to a canonization.

This phase passed too, of course. As we continued our literacy study, other aspects of my personality began to resurface and to have an impact on the experience. I was still impatient for measurable progress and after this phase of blinding breakthroughs, returning to the steady grind of slow character acquisition seemed somewhat flat. Six months after the start of the study, I was still basically practicing individual characters, perhaps copying a phrase of three or four characters, but not generating sentences or, indeed, any meaningful text. In my oral classes, I was developing a fair amount of communicative competence so that I might be asked to do a 3- or 4-minute speech in class describing my weekend activities. I wanted to use my new-found skills to communicate in writing, too, and decided to force progress by beginning a Chinese journal. It seemed to me that I could practice my characters just as well when using them to communicate as I could when writing them in rows. Inevitably, of course, the desire to communicate made me want to use words that I did not know the character for. Sometimes I would know the oral version. Other times, the translation would be completely unknown to me, so I would search the dictionary—a surprisingly difficult task that often had me identifying the wrong character. As a result, I would produce sentences that strung together familiar characters with the occasional phonetically rendered Cantonese word and the odd character deduced from the tiny stylized print of the dictionary from which it was virtually impossible to copy correctly. Grammatically, I am sure that most of these sentences were unacceptable. Nonetheless, I felt this ability to communicate my thoughts to Cindy through the medium of Chinese was quite a breakthrough, and I expected Cindy to welcome my industry and this evidence of commitment and hard work. I remained steadfast in this pattern of working right through to our very last class together.

In retrospect, I should not have been surprised by my tutor's somewhat tempered enthusiasm. She had told me repeatedly that form and content shaped each other. In my efforts to express meaning, I was letting both calligraphic form and syntactic form suffer. It was too late to go back and attend to form after the content was decided. As Cindy pointed out to me, "Sometimes we have to concentrate on more than one thing at a time." By writing improper forms, I was impeding my ability to develop balance and harmony in my text.

I never did resolve this issue to my own satisfaction. I was delighted with the new ways of learning that the experience of studying Chinese literacy helped me discover. I was equally delighted with the skills and abilities I found in myself that had been suppressed for many years. But I could not relinquish the idea that there is a place for analysis and for trial and error in a learning experience. I wanted to play an active role in my learning and to push myself beyond the boundaries of my current experience. Many of these Western patterns of learning seemed to get in the way of learning Chinese. Others, of course, fitted in so easily to support the learning that I was not even conscious of making use of them. Gradually, I came to a slightly more realistic assessment of the learning experience and of the parts that both Cindy and I played in it. So if I were to write the definitive account of my relationship with my teacher now, what would I say? Any comment would be shaped by the fact that Cindy has become a very good friend who will be as amused by my description of her as a guru as by my early attempts to cast her as a villain.

More interesting than arriving at a definitive account, I find, is the question of why, when I tried to describe the experience of learning Chinese literacy, I storied it in such different ways. My first and last tutorial sessions in Chinese were in some ways arbitrary points in the tale of my Chinese learning. My experiences prior to beginning Chinese study obviously affected the way in which the experience took shape. And my understanding of Chinese was not frozen at the point of the last lesson. Some of the knowledge faded, whereas I did not recognize other insights until months later. However, I chose to tell this story as having been framed by my first and last lesson. Consequently, the versions of the story that I spun were affected by their temporal relation to that span of time.

David Carr's (1986) terms, *retention, intention,* and *protention* helped me understand why this story should be seen and told differently at different times. Carr used these terms in relation to the immediate present, but I found them more helpful to me when applied to a longer time period. When I began the study, I had a story of literacy drawn from my experiences as a learner and teacher of ESL literacy. I had a story of myself as a learner that incorporated expectations of how one learned successfully. Although the experiences from which I had developed these stories had taken place over many years, my new exposure to literacy learning brought these stories to mind. They formed the retention, or the held-in-mind past, against which the current moment was understood. The immediately anticipated future, the protention, was inevitably shaped by this retention. We can only predict based on our stories of what is possible. As I came to understand literacy in new ways, the retention changed, and with it, the understanding of the current moment and the possibilities for the future.

When I was both telling this story and still trying to live it, I saw events and interactions differently from the way I would see them once the study was over. Thus, stories I told in the first 3 or 4 months were not merely a history of the past, but narratives that looked toward the future. I believe that we do not merely story our pasts, but that we live stories and shape our futures according to the stories we tell. At the beginning of the study, I saw the impending experience in terms of a source for a dissertation and I was concerned with data collection schemes and logistics. Events that seemed to diverge from the patterns agreed on in the dissertation proposal threatened the future I was trying to write for myself. My stories varied between those that were designed to reassure myself (and perhaps my committee) that a good dissertation could come from this inquiry, and those (usually more secret) that explored the possibilities of total failure. As I became more involved in the study, this *telos* became less in doubt and the language learning began to become an intention in itself. Once again, the future was uncertain; my apparently minimal progress in literacy was seriously threatening when I had no way of knowing whether I would ever fulfill my preconceived notions of success as a literacy learner. My relationship with my tutor was also developing during this period, shifting from a tenuous link that needed protective storying to a stronger relationship that could survive a more honest and critical exploration.

In telling stories about my Chinese study, I wanted to shape the future to include my achieving sufficient proficiency in Chinese literacy to be able to write a dissertation on the process. I wanted that future to include the stabilizing of the relationship with Cindy so that she would continue to be interested in the project. These shaping intentions (MacIntyre, 1981) affected both the way I saw the experience and the way I chose to write about it.

When I look at the same interactions and events from a different temporal vantage point, I see different patterns in the same raw experience. By the end of the study, I had achieved a proficiency in literacy that satisfied my need for success as a learner. I had come to recognize that the kind of data I was gathering would have been adequate for my dissertation purposes even if I had never been able to reach my preconceived literacy goals. I had developed a good friendship with Cindy, and we had laughed together over my fears of her lack of interest, and my attempts to story her as an opponent. It is no longer threatening to describe these problems because their power to shape my future has gone. Thus, the shift in the protention changes both the intention and the retention. In hindsight, I am able to see these concerns about progress and relationship as incidents within larger stories that have successful endings. They become the conflicts without which there can be no resolution to the story.

ACKNOWLEDGMENT

Portions of this chapter are included in *Literacy, Culture, and Identity* by J. S. Bell. Copyright 1997 by Peter Lang Publishing. Reprinted with permission.

REFERENCES

Bruner, J., & Weisser, S. (1990). The invention of self: Autobiography and its forms. In D. Olson & N. Torrance (Eds.), *Literacy and orality* (pp. 129–148). Cambridge, UK: Cambridge University Press.

Carr, D. (1986). *Time, narrative and history.* Bloomington: Indiana University Press.

MacIntyre, A. (1981). *After virtue: A study in moral theology.* Notre Dame, IN: University of Notre Dame Press.

Strength From Weakness, Insight From Failure

Thomas Scovel
San Francisco State University

I subscribe to the individual weakness theory of choosing a career. If you need evidence, look around you. How many attorneys do you know succeed in mediating conflicts within their own homes? How many physicians with whom you are acquainted are known for being good patients when they themselves are ill? And take barbers as another example—they, or at least the male members, all have much too much or much too little hair for someone serving in such a hair-razing profession. And we all know the stories about pastors who preach so effectively against sin from the pulpit— most probably because they have experienced it so intimately in the bedroom of one of their parishioners. But who among us language teachers needs to look at others? All we have to do to find corroborating evidence for this hypothesis is to scrutinize ourselves. Take me for an example.

I grew up in Asia and sailed to the United States on my own for the first time when I was sent off to a small Christian college in Ohio. (A college for small Christians, we students used to jest; later, we grew to appreciate the profundity of the remark.) To admit that I never excelled academically is about as insightful as observing that snakes make poor tennis players. But much of my problem, as we teachers are so prone to observe, was due to motivation. Be that as it may, I was able to stagger through several courses, including classes in science, with some modicum of success and, if not success, with some degree of lack of failure. But language classes were an anathema, and they did much to bleed my already anemic grade point average (GPA). This struck me and my college friends as somewhat odd, given the fact that I had some reputation as a wit with words. On the occasion of our college's centennial anniversary, for example, the student body was polled for a centenary slogan, and mine won a certain degree of acclamation from my fellow students, although, as you might surmise, it was not chosen to celebrate the century of achievement. "Wooster College," I had submitted, "One hundred years, unmarred by progress!"

All of this leads to the embarrassing matter of my grades in foreign language classes. If ever there was documentation for the individual weakness theory of career choices, no more significant evidence exists than my marks in French. Odd, but really not so strange, that someone who was such a failure in language learning at the university would eventually seek linguistics and second-language acquisition as his professional vocation.

In those days, all students were required to pass 2 years of a foreign language in college, and unable to choose easy languages like Chinese or Thai (those alternatives were thankfully available much later on in graduate school), I had the traditional troika of European languages to select from. German was clearly not an alternative. Any language so popular with all the premed students was surely not a sagacious selection for me. Spanish, on the other hand, was seen as the easiest of the three, but I was equally suspicious of a language that was purportedly a breeze. Any language that was so easy to embrace initially must have harbored some convoluted syntax later on down the line. So, true to my Asian heritage, I chose the middle way and went with French. During my freshman year, I eased through the two semesters of the foreign language requirement with Bs and then Cs, but as a sophomore, I met the nemesis of my college career, a veritable leech on my GPA—French 104. Beside it, Principles of Sociology (C) and Comparative Anatomy (D) paled in comparison; only Bacteriology (F), which I took much later in my final year, could compare in the amount of academic anguish inflicted. In fact, to be honest, Bacteriology not only killed my desire to be a biologist, it came close to eliminating me completely. There was that careless moment one afternoon in the lab when I was transferring Salmonella from a test tube to Petri dish cultures, when I absentmindedly sucked on the end of the glass rod I was using for this procedure. The look of surprised horror that transfigured my biology instructor at that moment was the first intimation I had that all was not well, physically or academically. But forgive the digression. Bad as it may have been, French was never life-threatening!

Because the Liberal Arts diploma that I eventually would extricate from the college's stringent Office of Academic Records required that all students had to pass 2 years of a foreign language, I took French 104 again my junior year, after failing it the first time around. My hopes were a bit higher. Blessed with the acumen an upper division student gleans from the campus grapevine, I knew I was repeating French with a much easier teacher—a fresh, young woman, a distinct contrast to the *eminence gris* who had tried to parade me through grammar-translation. She promoted audio-lingualism, and I sensed hope in the headsets and the wizardry of the language lab. I also already knew about the subjunctive and the passé simple, so I would not be ambushed by these deviant tense forms the second time around. Alas, she, the lab, and audio-lingualism failed to keep me from failing, and I entered my first final year desperate for a disparate way to learn French—to pass French.

Fortune smiled like the Mona Lisa. The Foreign Languages Department had just received some films and materials for a new method of teaching, and students in 104 would be given a chance to learn the language via the exciting promise of the audiovisual approach. I was the first to enroll. We went to France via film. I could practically smell the café au lait and croissants at the Parisian sidewalk cafe projected on the screen in our stuffy classroom. Perhaps it was the lack of actual gustatory input, but all the audioism and visualism of this new-fangled method did not nudge me upwards even one rung on the academic alphabet, and I failed for the third time. A new school record, I was told by the Office of Academic Records. "Three years of French, unmarred by progress," my buddies who were graduating reminded me.

Misfortunately, my overall grades were by now so poor, I had to remain for a 5th year of college, and I could relish the luxury that few foreign language students ever enjoy; I could take my final French course for a fourth time with yet another method and teacher. I'm not sure if it was Mlle. Ihrig's formal but empathetic demeanor, or the informed eclecticism of her method, or my status of quiet desperation as a repeating senior whose professional future pivoted around the choice of the fourth rather than the sixth letter of the alphabet next to my name in January when the semester concluded, but the little Christmas party she put on for our class bore positive portent. We sang French carols, and we were each given a piece of holiday *gateau.* Following French custom, one of the pieces contained a small porcelain figure of the baby Jesus as a prize for some lucky reveler. Much to my astonishment, but not, in my retrospective appreciation, to the surprise of Mlle. Ihrig, in the middle of our communal munching, I bit into something hard and inedible. A few weeks later, for my fourth time around in 2nd-year French during my 5th year of college, I received another Christmas gift from my teacher—a glorious C–. To this day, when Advent rolls around each December, the words of a few of those melodic French carols ring in my memory, and somewhere among my cluster of knickknacks from yesteryear, I still possess a tiny porcelain figure—a neonatal symbol of my rebirth as a student of language.

Except for its status as family lore, an anecdote that my children remind me of on occasions when I wax too pompous about the import of scholastic achievement, this unhappy encounter with college French has not played a conscious part of my personal or professional life. Indeed, this is the first time I have shared this story publicly, and because it remains to this day at the margins of my memory, I am still a bit uncertain of its exact relevance to my profession as a language educator. And yet at this moment in my life, like so many personal narratives, this encounter with French appears to be almost a morality play about my career as a linguist and a language teacher.

It is now already patently evident why I espouse the personal weakness theory. After my experiences with French 104, law, medicine, the barber shop, or the pulpit were all inconceivable as career alternatives. I was destined, even at the very first go-around with grammar-translation, to study the process of second-language acquisition. If I couldn't learn French and pass it after one, two, or even three attempts, why was it that so many of my college chums could? Granted, most of them were brighter and better motivated than I, but, to be candid, not all. More vexing still was a question that has continued to haunt me and that encapsulates so much of contemporary second-language acquisition research—why did I have so much trouble when an entire nation of 56 million not only learns this *lingua Franca*, they speak it far better than all five of my American teachers combined? And all of these native speakers have effected this remarkable achievement without the help of grammars, language labs, cinemas, and the Office of Academic Records! Somehow, this academic experience with a foreign language at the university while I was still a young man acted as the catalyst for the early linguistic reagents of my childhood—my exposure to bilingualism and multi-lingualism as I grew up in China, and later when I was a teenager in northern India. Like the heat of a Bunsen burner, the three Fs in college French fused all of my previous linguistic experiences together. This episode leads inexorably to the central concern of the profession I chose (or did it, in fact, choose me?). How can people learn languages more successfully, and why do some learn languages better than others?

Even after 35 years in the business of trying to find answers, these questions continue to intrigue me—all this despite the fact that I have not only learned a lot about language learning, but subsequent to my struggles with French, I have also acquired a couple of foreign languages with a modicum of success and, somewhat surprisingly, a maximum of pleasure. The first question has been studied more intensively and more satisfactorily than the second, and at the very least, we can eliminate some of the answers that were thought to be correct so long ago, when I was still in college. For those of us in the academy, who have spent many years in formal study and many more researching second-language acquisition, it is clear that there is no single method or even group of methods that can ensure success. Contrast this professional conclusion with the lavish claims by language-learning businesses advertised in our media. We are assured of native fluency in Spanish, Japanese, and yes, even French, if we simply purchase their audio tapes and listen to them at our leisure for a few weeks. One very clear lesson from my encounters of the third (and fourth kind) with French was that the method did not seem to matter.

Most language specialists agree that nowadays, we are in a post-methodological era. A generation ago, textbooks, journals, and conventions devoted a great deal of space to methods, but there is now little enthusiasm for prepackaged methods. They have been replaced instead by an interest in underlying principles. So my struggles with French were not due to the wrong method, but to the lack of a number of necessary principles or conditions for successful language acquisition. How could I help myself then if I knew what I know now?

Certainly a key ingredient missing was what Brown (1994) called intrinsic motivation. The fuel that feebly fed me through four encounters with French 104 came from outer forces, not inner resources. It was the extrinsic influence of the Office of Academic Records at our college that goaded me to and through my foreign language classes, not any personal interest within. Later, when my wife and I moved to Thailand, even though there were few extrinsic forces that motivated us to become Thai-tongued, we were captivated by the culture and the people we encountered, and propelled by our intrinsic interest in the language of that new land (and, for me, in almost every word articulated by our stunningly attractive language teacher), we acquired Thai quickly, successfully, and with no small amount of pleasure.

Another principle that was absent in my attempts to become a Francophone was attention to language-learning strategies. This now, of course, is a popular concern among many language teachers and is consciously incorporated into many materials and curricula. Not being a talented language learner myself, I brought very few strategies to my French classes, and I don't recall ever being introduced to any techniques in my French classes to help me remember what I had been taught. Because of this, I resorted to repetition and learned, as psychologists discovered decades ago, that practice doesn't make perfect; it only makes permanent. To split an infinitive to hit the point: I didn't learn French; I learned how to not learn French.

I am not interested in creating a tedious and tendentious litany of excuses why I failed French, especially because intrinsic motivation alone could have effected a scholastic and linguistic miracle, but let me cite one more change in perspective that has transpired in foreign language circles since my college days. In retrospect, it was clear that also absent from any of my coursework was a concerted interest in communicative competence. In essence, whatever the method employed, each of my French courses centered on the linguistic structure of French (grammatical competence, in modern-day parlance). Rarely did I learn anything about how French speakers recognized texts or genres (discourse competence), or decided when to say what to whom (sociolinguistic competence), or how to interrupt someone when they didn't understand their interlocutor (strategic competence). In a superficial way, the math might not add up. After all, if I learned poorly focusing on only one kind, grammatical competence, why would my performance improve if my task were made three times more difficult by the addition of three more types of competence? But this kind of simplistic reasoning ignores the true import of communicatively competent language instruction. Without the other competencies present in the curriculum, grammatical structure was my only window to the acquisition of French. If the other ones had been available, I would have had three different and potentially more motivating opportunities open to me.

So with the gift of retrospective reflection, augmented by the training and experience of the profession, I can begin to explain my poignant experiences as a linguistic failure in college. Second-language acquisition research has helped me to understand how people can learn languages more successfully. But what about that second query: Why do some people learn languages better than others? Holding constant all of the principles that language educators deem necessary, if not sufficient, as conditions for successful second-language acquisition, individual variability in language learning seems to depend entirely on early nurturing and on talent. At our current stage of research, we have only faint hints about the effects of the former, and at present, we can only speculate about the existence of the latter. At best, we can measure and describe individual differences among language learners, but we cannot explain them. My collegiate experience clearly demonstrates that in terms of natural talent, I was and still am an unexceptional language learner. Nevertheless, my subsequent experiences with languages, especially with Thai, suggest that even without much help from nature, nurture—manifested by principled learning and teaching—can accomplish a great deal. This is certainly good news for those of us who have chosen language teaching as our profession. And finally, impoverished though I was by my unfortunate encounters with French, most fortunately, I have been enriched by other language-learning experiences and by my profession.

It is only now, several decades later, when I reflect back on the crucible of those French classes, that I can see my strength as a language teacher was forged from the very weakness that beset me as a language student. Today, so many happy years later, part of the joy I derive as a language educator stems from the fact that my teaching allows me continuous opportunities to learn. It also permits my students to be my mentors. In their faces and voices, I see and hear, and remember and learn. I know I am better for it. God willing, so are they.

REFERENCE

Brown, H. D. (1994). *Teaching by principles.* Englewood Cliffs, NJ: Prentice-Hall.

Explorations for Part Three: Lessons From Teachings and Learnings

1. Vivian Paley observes her classes closely, using audiotaping and journal writing to reconstruct dialogue, events, and contexts as a way to find out how students make sense of their world and how they construct their ethical systems. What is it that Paley seems to be learning about her own life and value systems by close observation of her students? Have you had any similar experiences?

2. Paley claims that, "We are not, any of us, to be found in sets of tasks or lists of attributes; we cannot be defined or classified. We can be known only in the singular unfolding of our unique stories within the context of everyday events." This view goes against much of the traditional work in social sciences, which seeks to categorize, essentialize, and abstract. Do you perceive this as a dilemma or a dichotomy (real or false) in your field? What is your view on where we are "to be found"? How does your view affect how you relate to your students and to the academic work that you are doing?

3. Paley notes that children discuss moral issues easily, then asks, "Why are teachers so ambivalent about taking moral positions?" How do you respond to Paley's question?

4. In her essay, Trudy Smoke discusses the multiple and conflicting roles that she takes on as a female teacher of very diverse, adult, ESL populations. Stemming from her childhood role as an intermediary during family conflicts, her primary goal has been to help herself and her students "break the silence" in a writing classroom that is democratic, multicultural, and activist. Yet she

notes that recently her work as a teacher is expanding in response to her students' different needs and expectations, a burden that has taken on new dimensions since the move to downsize public education. Do you believe that teachers in her situation are professionally or ethically obligated to take on these expanding roles? Why or why not?

5. Review Smoke's descriptions of each interaction that she had with her students. How would you have handled each of these cases? What kinds of circumstances in your own teaching would motivate you to get involved in your students' lives, and what lessons do you feel can be learned from this involvement?

6. Jill Bell reminds us in her essay how important it is for teachers to put themselves in the shoes of learners, as a kind of professional renewal, throughout their careers. Have you had any experiences like this in your own career? What is the value of empathy in language learning and teaching, and what are some of the ways that you believe you can achieve this in your own teaching-learning setting?

7. In the various stories that Bell tells about her learning experience, a strong connection emerges between a language-learning experience and one's perceptions of self, and between the experience and perceptions of a teacher and the culture he or she represents. In light of these many connections, the stories we frame to interpret our successes and failures (and those of our students) shift. What teaching-learning experiences in your own life can you identify that you reinterpreted one or more times as you reframed your understanding of that experience over time?

8. Tom Scovel describes an early learning experience that turned out to be pivotal in directing him toward his present career. What similar experiences of early adversity leading to opportunity do you recall in the path to your own career? What was there about Scovel's (and your own) responses to adversity that helped shape the outcome of the dilemma?

9. Both Scovel and Bell struggled with language-learning experiences that made them feel like unsuccessful learners, although unlike Bell, Scovel was placed involuntarily in a situation where he risked failing. Nonetheless, the experiences of both educators helped them develop an empathy for language learners and teachers that they might not have developed in the absence of these experiences of near-failure. To what extent do you believe that such experiences are necessary in order for language educators to develop depth of understanding for the people they work with?

FURTHER EXPLORATIONS

1. In what ways does writing of various kinds work to help you gain insights about teaching and learning?

2. In your own teaching and learning setting, what expectations and behaviors do you find associated with women teachers? In what ways do you find that these expectations and behaviors change when budget cuts exact especially devastating impacts on students who are poor, minority, and non-English-speaking?

3. With colleagues, exchange specific stories of different roles you have played with different students. To what extent do you control the roles you play? Feel coerced by "the system"? Feel pressure from your own ethical beliefs? Feel pushed to become politically active to help instigate change? How do you define your preferred role as a language educator?

4. Experiment with a variety of metaphors that you could use to explain the ways you frame some of your own stories of teaching and learning (see Bell's metaphors of building a web across a lake and observing images emerge in a developing photograph). What metaphors do your colleagues use to help them frame their stories?

5. In your own language learning and teaching experiences, how have you reacted to what you experienced or interpreted as failure? To what extent have your responses to what you perceive as difficulty or weakness in your own life evolved into areas that you have explored in further study as a way to know yourself better?

6. In what ways does your understanding of failure affect your interpretations of your students' performance?

PART FOUR

Introduction:
Reflections on the Profession

Issues in language-teacher education generally concern matters at the level of individual professional development. We wish to know, for example, how teachers develop identity and expertise, how effective learning and teaching is promoted by contextual factors (cognitive, social, ideological), and what the role of everyday experience is in teacher development.

Some of the after-hours story-telling of language educators, however, also concerns broader aspects of the profession itself. Teachers comment on the status of their departments relative to others, sometimes finding evidence in their anecdotes of patterned discrimination. They notice how the language used by members of professional groups tends to include some people and exclude others, creating what seems like a barrier between those who preach and those who practice. They lament the systemic and structural impediments that prevent them from carrying out their jobs in ways that satisfy them. Many of these stories are told by educators who feel discouraged in the face of struggle. But within the struggle, we also hear stories of courage and creativity as educators reflect on why they remain committed to a particular language education field despite impediments, and how they cope with systemic, structural, and discoursal infelicities of the professions they chose.

The authors in Part Four tell some of these stories. As you read, you will notice not only how intimately the authors' professional identities are linked to personal factors that are brought out in other sections of this book. You will also notice how closely their identities develop in conjunction with ongoing interactions with their professions, and how twists and turns within the career of a language educator are often prompted by issues that reach beyond the local classroom experience while still influencing this experience profoundly.

John Fanselow uses anecdotes from his days as a novice teacher in the Peace Corps and the poetry of Walt Whitman to reflect on the paradox of the teacher-as-authority-figure wishing to liberate students from the dependence that this very image of the teacher generates. In a profession structured into teachers and learners rather than as learners in the role of teachers and learners in the roles of students, he continues to seek ways to reconceptualize his work and his mission. Alan Strand speaks from the perspective of a sabbatical leave from his work as a secondary school language arts (and economics) teacher. By removing himself totally—physically, intellectually, emotionally—from a burdensome work environment, he finds himself looking back exhausted over a quarter-century career. He agonizes over the last decade of systemic and structural obstacles in the language arts field that have led to his sense of defeat as a language-arts teacher. Denise Murray is a second-language educator, a long-time reformer and legislator for change in what she describes as the marginalized profession of English as a second language. Only recently did she recognize that her relationship to the profession was obscuring a conflict between her reformer self (the one dedicated to imposing laws and legislating change) and her image of herself as classroom teacher and colleague (nurturer, facilitator for self-discovery). How to continue her mission of raising standards in the field of ESL without foregoing her classroom self-image constitutes her current dilemma. Christine Casanave searches her personal history of difficulty connecting with academic discourse, including her unsettling encounter with the sometimes inaccessible and exclusionary academic discourse of graduate school, as a way to understand her growing sense of disconnection from her profession. She seems motivated initially only by the conviction that a stronger personal voice and more carefully crafted writing in the texts she reads and writes would help her to form the connections she seeks. However, her dilemma about whether to stay in the field still unresolved, she begins to recognize that her discomfort may stem as much from political disaffection as from her lack of connection with some of the discourse itself.

Postcard Realities

John F. Fanselow
Teachers College, Columbia University

After I fly from one time zone to another one 13 hours ahead, or behind, I invariably wake up at 3:00 a.m. so alert and energetic that I feel much more like playing volleyball than sleeping. This feeling occurs in spite of the fact that I have not played volleyball for 40 years and then did so only under duress, as part of a required gym course. Even if I did regularly play, though, no partners are available at the hour of my jet lag resurrection and there is no place to play, at any rate. Surrounded by silent, dark apartments, I try to focus my energy on attempts to fall asleep. But inevitably, rather than fall asleep, I tumble backward in time and experience all sorts of episodes from the past. I remember the dreamlike episodes more than non-jet-lag-induced dreams perhaps because I'm only half sleeping, or perhaps only 10% sleeping, if that is possible.

Maybe because the reason for changing time zones is almost always to work with practicing teachers in a different location from my regular base in New York, many of the dreamlike/unlike episodes contain incidents from my own first experiences as a trainee/neophyte teacher. One incident I constantly re-experience occurred 35 years ago when I was taking courses at University College Ibadan, Nigeria, as part of a Peace Corps training experience. I, along with around 30 other volunteers, had been living in university dormitories along with Nigerian students, practice-teaching in secondary schools near the university, and attending classes on Nigerian education, history, and teaching methods. All of a sudden, the Nigerian students, who had moments before been symbols of gregariousness, openness and

157

friendliness, stopped talking to us, and, in fact, were demanding that the Nigerian Government expel us all from the country!

We quickly discovered that the instantaneous reversal in attitude was caused in large part by the duplication of a few lines one of our group had written on a postcard. Our fellow volunteer had inadvertently dropped the postcard on the ground in front of a postbox rather than in the slot in the postbox. A passing student picked up the postcard and read the message, rather than posting the card. He shared the postcard with a few other students. And, before the day was out, had typed on a stencil all of the lines from the postcard, along with a demand that the Nigerian government expel insensitive foreigners from the country. (Stencils are waxed sheets used in mimeograph machines—the way we used to make copies before Xeroxing.) In a matter of minutes, hundreds of copies had not only been mimeographed but distributed to students all over the campus.

On seeing her previously thought private message to her boyfriend on a leaflet now not only being read, but being blown about the campus as well, the author of the postcard, together with all of the group, suddenly realized two things. First, her boyfriend wouldn't get the postcard she had sent. Second, there was a distinct possibility that none of us would be in Nigeria long enough to send anyone any more postcards.

Because *Time* magazine and many other international publications soon re-duplicated the lines, the author's fear that the message would not reach the addressee was ill-founded. But the personal nature of the communication was, of course, lost forever.

The message on the postcard, which given even the distance of 30 minutes, much less 35 years, seems particularly innocuous to me and extremely provocative to many, went something like this:

> The people cook in the streets.
> The people eat in the streets.
> The people do everything in the streets.
> They even go to the bathroom in the streets.
> Nothing in training could have prepared us for this!

The part of the incident that has had the most powerful impact on me was not the boycott, nor the lesson that one should make sure to keep one's eyes on the item to be posted as it goes in the slot in the postbox, nor the fact that we should be sensitive to differences when we are guests or visitors—even when we are neither, as far as that goes. No, we had been told over and over that we should be careful about how we acted and what we said. The central focus of the stateside training before we began the in-country component of our training was the need to be aware of differences and accept them. So, if anything, attempts to prepare us were particularly intense. (We had also been told in training that there were some who probably wanted to try to sabotage the Peace Corps programs in some countries—we were in the first group that went to Nigeria and one of the first dozen or so anyplace in the world. But even this additional warning was limited in impact on what we said.)

Rather, the lesson that keeps coming back to me during my jet lag resurrections is the last line in the message: "Nothing in training could have prepared us for this!" We had all written descriptions almost identical to the ones on the dropped postcard, either on postcards that reached the postbox, or in letters. We commented on the phenomenon mentioned in the public postcard constantly in our daily conversations. Yet, during training, we had been told over and over not to make the types of comments that, in fact, we all made. I hasten to add that words similar to ones on the postcard were also used constantly by our Nigerian hosts and colleagues. The Nigerian press published much less-flattering comments than those on our postcards and in our letters. But, of course, citizens have privileges/rights that noncitizens do not have.[1] (Another lesson, taken up next, is how what to one is innocuous can to another be incendiary.)

The postcard incident has become significant to me for other reasons as well. Bateson's reminder of Korzybski's (1941) dictum that "the map is not the territory" could be paraphrased "the picture postcard is an idealized image of the territory" (Bateson, 1972, p. 183). I've never seen a fly or a mosquito in a scene on any picture postcard. Yet when I've visited the scenes depicted on many postcards, my first experiences, as yours, have involved mosquitoes, flies, and garbage.

The pictorial message of Nigeria on the postcard my fellow volunteer dropped represented one view of reality; the volunteer's written message represented another view. The pictorial side of the postcard was not duplicated, partly, of course, because mimeograph machines could not make copies of pictures. But even if the incident had happened in more modern times, when color Xerox machines would have been available, I doubt that the picture would have been copied.

When I hear or read professional rhetoric—be sensitive to students, make language meaningful, increase communication—I sometimes consider the clichéd rhetoric as postcard images. But ironically, just as the Nigerian students were more angry with the words on the back of the postcard than with the idealized picture on the front of the postcard, so many of us tend to see the questions about the clichéd rhetoric in our profession as the problem rather than the idealized/unreal rhetoric itself. Thus, when teachers

---

[1]It is perhaps critical to point out that the 1961 postcard incident was the exception rather than the rule; no other incident since has caused a comparable stir in spite of the fact that tens of thousands of Peace Corps volunteers have subsequently been living in scores of countries for 30 years plus.

say their experience contradicts a theory, they sometimes question their experience rather than the theory. When some teachers do not understand a technical term, they see their own misunderstanding or lack of insight as the problem rather than the term and the ability of the person using the term to provide examples that enable others to engage the term.

Why didn't the university students say that the picture on the postcard was farther from reality than the written words? Why did I and fellow volunteers not realize that what we considered innocuous was incendiary and insulting to our hosts? Why are we constantly taken in by what on one level we know does not represent the territory? And on another level trapped by our own view of reality as if our view of reality and reality are identical? But who of us can easily resist the palm trees and glittering skies on picture postcards? And who of us wants to buy postcards with pictures of a beach under swaying palms that also shows flies, mosquitoes, and garbage, with a paper mill close at hand spewing out waste water for good measure?

When we buy picture postcards with one view of reality, we are free to compose our own view of reality in the blank space reserved for messages. But the blank space provides less freedom than we realize. For one thing, the amount of space available is limited. For another, the message is public, even if we manage to get it into the slot in the postbox. Those who collect the mail, sort it, and deliver it all have access to our words. Finally, the place we mail it from often provides a context within which we compose our message. Although I could send a picture postcard of the Manhattan skyline on one side and a message about sheep farming on the other, the words we write are usually related to the place we are in as well as the picture on the postcard.

In the same way, the freedom we have in our professional lives is more constrained than it seems. When I and others write, teach, and present at professional conferences, the representations of reality we share, as well as the way we present our realities, are our choice. But the word *freedom* might be too strong. The usual question after a presentation at a conference is, "How did it go?" with, "Great." being the expected answer. Almost all course evaluations have items on clarity of aims, clarity of expectations, and clarity of the syllabus. My response to "How did it go?" is usually, "I don't know how it went. Ask some who came, or, better, overhear them talking about the session." Participants in my courses or workshops are likely to say things such as, "There is no course outline?" "I enjoyed the guerrilla theater presentation you made." "What was he getting at?" "What does he want us to do?" These comments remind us of constraints we have, and thus make me say that the word *freedom* might be too strong. Why is a presentation that does not start with aims and frameworks guerrilla theater and not just something different, even if the words *guerrilla theater* are meant in a positive way? Why are unclear aims an anomaly, or even considered different, rather than one of many options?

The subtle constraints that surround us in the form of course evaluations, formulaic questions about presentations at conventions, and in expectations of students have a powerful impact on us all. In fact, perhaps the subtle constraints are no less powerful than the more direct set of constraints I was introduced to soon after I arrived at the teacher-training college where I started my professional career.

Picture yourself, or anyone you wish, sitting on a stool around 10-inches in diameter and 24-inches high in the front of a classroom of 40 to 50 first-year pupils in an elementary school—surrounded with picture postcard palm trees, believe it or not! (But with infinitesimal sand flies too small to be seen even if photographed for the picture postcard ferociously biting us.) Sitting next to you is a person who has been supervising teachers for 30 years, on the same size stool and in the same location: in front of the classroom facing 80 to 100 eager/excited/vibrant eyes—none with glasses.

My mentor—he of the 30 years of experience—is wearing knee socks, spotless, perfectly ironed white shorts and a perfectly ironed short-sleeved shirt, wearing a necktie—"tied up," as the practice teachers used to say. I am wearing baggy trousers and a wash-and-wear, button-down blue shirt, ironed, but not perfectly. In common, we are wearing sandals. (Many of the students do not worry about sandals versus shoes as they have flip-flops on, at the most, their own feet in their natural state, at the least.) Heat and humidity, close to the figures we always wished we had earned on any test we took, add atmosphere.

The practice teacher we were observing was less shocked than I at the command shouted by my mentor: "You call yourself a teacher! Sit down and let me show you how to teach!" By less shocked, I mean that the teacher remained standing in a balanced position, not visibly shaken, while I almost fell off my stool. But maybe he remained balanced because it is harder to fall when standing than when sitting on a stool 10-inches in diameter. At any rate, the practice teacher moved to the side—not accepting the proffered space on my mentor's now vacant stool next to me.

The practice teacher and I then watched as he of the perfectly ironed white shorts took over the class. The practice teacher appeared to me to watch without moving one muscle/nerve/hair—as if he was frozen stiff, in spite of the high temperature and humidity. (The only movement was his flowing perspiration.)

After around 10 minutes, what now became our mentor rather than my mentor moved toward his vacant stool and simultaneously shouted this crystal clear admonition: "Now see if you can teach right." He resumed his position on his stool as if he had just gotten up momentarily to express a warm, pleasant greeting to a passing friend. I thought of the students' rage at the lines on the postcard and their benign neglect of the lies/distortions/exaggerations in the pictorial representation. I seemed to be the only shocked person in the room, however. Neither the practice teacher nor the students, nor perhaps not surprisingly our mentor acted as if anything untoward or unusual had happened. My view of reality seemed to be the only one affected. The lenses that I had worn until this time were shattered. Partly as a result, I have since that time tried to develop multiple lenses, the more the better, so I've got a lot of spares even if a few are shattered at the same time, which is not that uncommon! To accept and believe the first interpretation that comes to my mind, to assume we know rather than to accept the ambiguity of life as well as the need to realize that not knowing can lead to genuine questioning and the potential of seeing something we did not see before have become central to me.

No subtle constraints of a course evaluation form our mentor. No subtle implication that a presentation should go well. No. Instead, we had direct constraints from our mentor. Our mentor knew what was right: his reality. Had our mentor trained me and fellow volunteers, would we have mentioned what we observed in our letters and postcards? Or would we have kept our reality to ourselves?

At the end of practice teaching—around 3 weeks after my initiation into what might be called intense direct method—I received another lesson in direct constraints. The profound lesson in direct constraints and stifling of dissent from he of the "sit down; I'll show you how to teach" school was shortly followed by a similar lesson showing me again why we all have a tendency to go along and accept, at least outwardly, or why constraints constrain us. An inspector from another area of the country was scheduled to evaluate all the practice teachers from our teacher-training college. Official title: External Inspector.

A few days before the External Inspector's visit, as soon as the practice teachers found out the name of our External Inspector, the practice teachers asked me to reserve the school vehicle for the day of the inspection. It seemed that our External Inspector was into the use of pictures and objects. So, on the morning of the inspection, one hour before our usual meeting time, when we ordinarily met to walk to the primary school we used for practice teaching, less than 2 miles distant, I parked the school vehicle near the houses/dorms where the teachers lived. Three trips to and from the school were needed as the teachers had assembled what amounted to three vehicle loads of objects and pictures. (No teachers could fit in the vehicle; their materials alone made up the loads.)

For 3 weeks of practice teaching, they had used nothing more than graphic and striking chalkboard sketches and objects they had picked up around the grounds of the primary school or had asked the pupils to bring to class. But for the External Inspector, three vehicle loads of objects and pictures were needed. A new reality was taking over. New lenses were going to observe us or project another reality on us.

My mentor (who was really our mentor, as all the practice teachers also experienced his reality) and the External Inspector would probably not have accepted the claim in the last line of the postcard: "Nothing in training could have prepared us for this!" They would have probably argued that had the training been prescriptive enough, it would have been effective. Their beliefs, reflected in their behaviors, also seem to contradict Whitman's oft-quoted line: "You must travel it (the road to learning and experience) for yourself" (Whitman, 1950, p. 46).

But there is more to the story of our mentor and the External Inspector. When our mentor was not observing teachers he had set models for, these teachers were not following his models. And recall that the three loads of visuals were only necessary on one day: the day of the inspection. Remember, before the day of the inspection, no visuals were used other than sketches and objects gathered around the school compound. The behaviors of the teachers raise profound questions about the power of prescriptions and lend power to the claim that "Nothing in training could have prepared us for this," short of experiencing a wide range of possibilities.

Between demos—demonstrations, not demolitions, or maybe a bit of both—my job was to make suggestions to the practice teachers. All the practice teachers had at least 2 years of experience more than I had—a prerequisite for entry into the teacher-training college where I had been assigned, but not a prerequisite for teaching there. Many had as many as 20 years of experience. Partly as a result, I was not immediately ready to assume our mentor's model. I had a very unclear picture of the reality around me—looking at first with my lenses as a major in English and Spanish literature, with a bit of Peace Corps training, and subsequently with even these lenses shattered—and, as a result, could not impose my reality on anyone else.

Additionally, the teaching material was all news to me. In history class, Lord Lugard was as unknown to me as the elementary-school students the practice teachers were instructing. *Poles, rods,* and *perches* as units of measurement were as foreign to me as *pounds, shillings,* and *pence.* I joined the children in grappling with the conversion of pence and shillings into pounds during math lessons. Remember that in 1961, the monetary system in countries such as Nigeria and Kenya, which used money based on the British monetary system, had not yet been decimalized.

Add to the totally new information, the extensive experience of the teachers under my charge and the need to deal with 40 kids in each class sitting three or four to a bench designed for two, books often shared by groups, and there was no question about my showing the teachers how to teach: imposing my reality! Even if I had not been inclined toward believing in traveling a road on my own to learn, there was really no option. Both the teachers and I had to travel many roads for ourselves.

Fortunately for me, partly as a result of the fact that there were two streams of each class—two first grades (two standard ones to be precise), two second grades, and so forth—we did not have to travel the roads by ourselves alone. We were able to travel many as genuine partners. The teachers and I agreed that I would spend half of each period observing one of the two practice teachers in each grade. I took copious notes of each part of the lesson, during times when I was not struggling with the conversion of shillings to pounds or the distinction between the exploits of Lord Lugard and Mungo Park.

During planning and critiquing time, I would use my notes to describe to both teachers of each grade what the other teacher had done. Each practice that one teacher used that the other did not became an alternative practice for the other to try. I did not hide the fact that the suggestions for alternatives were not mine. Nor did I hide the fact that I did not know the material being taught. In fact, not knowing the material enabled me to ask genuine questions of the teachers, which in many cases enabled them to demonstrate or illustrate the meaning in ways that they could not have done had I already known and understood the material they were teaching. I also could ask questions about teaching practices that I did not have the answers to, as I had never before been in Nigerian primary schools. We were able to jointly build a reality or two and exchange a range of lenses in a genuine way.

Over time, I began to notice some practices that had consequences that the teachers liked, and, because I was observing, I could sometimes point out something about their practices that they had not noticed. It is almost always easier to see how another does something than to see how one does something oneself. A golf coach can point out moves to a golfer who would fall over if he or she tried to observe a movement as the movement was in process. Because I was genuinely ignorant, and thanks to the fact that the External Inspector determined their future, I was able to play a role that I prefer to play but which over time has been more and more difficult: a joint traveler. Not a fellow traveler.[2]

Immediately after I completed teaching in Nigeria, I became a trainer of other Peace Corps volunteers. From the role of ignorant observer, traveling various roads with teachers more experienced than me, I was placed in the role of experienced guide and mentor, with a bit of External Inspector thrown in, as my opinions were asked for during the process of selecting and weeding out volunteers.

As I took more courses and had more training experience, the asking of genuine questions became more and more difficult, due in large part to the role I was in. No matter how much I said that I really did not have an

---

[2]During the McCarthy Congressional hearings in the 1950s, some individuals, although themselves not members of the Communist Party in the United States, were accused of associating with known members. Such individuals were often called "fellow travelers."

answer in my mind to questions I posed, those in my workshops and classes assumed that I was asking questions to lead them to a particular place. The expert mantle encapsulated me all too quickly. The trap of expert status on those of us in supposed expert positions is set both by the constraints of expectations of what a course should be, together with how one should make a presentation at a professional meeting. The function rooms at hotels and convention centers hosting conventions contain a podium, with a microphone and pitcher of water and a drinking glass in the front of rows of chairs facing the podium. In a subway car, unless there is an accident and a doctor is requested, roles are less differentiated. All are fellow passengers—joint travelers.

I sometimes wonder whether conferring so-called expert status is a way for those who do the conferring to absolve themselves from some responsibility. If I make the dentist responsible for my teeth, and at the same time fail to follow the dentist's suggestions to floss and brush my teeth, I can still blame the dentist for my cavities. As long as I am considered an expert, those I'm working with also have a reason to depend on me rather than on themselves. Even if my intention in modeling a practice is to illustrate possibilities—to free others—rather than to prescribe a practice, the potential exists that stultification will result, rather than freedom, as the meanings of intentions are jointly determined.

We might also confer expert status because of our lack of trust in ourselves. Let's say I brush and floss my teeth with so much vigor that my gums bleed excessively. When I continue in spite of the pain and blood, I might be valuing the words of advice of an expert above the reality I am experiencing. "As a result of vigorous brushing and flossing, my gums are killing me, but the dentist said brush and floss. And the dentist knows and I don't."

Having been reminded of what we do not know on many tests and in many classroom encounters and exchanges, it is easy to see how self-doubt might occur. After all, we are much more likely to have been asked to underline the words we do not know as we read rather than to cross them out and underline the words we do know. The possible reasons we confer expert status, like the reasons we resist learning, and like most explanations, are multiple.

Each time I do a workshop, make a presentation at a professional conference, teach a class of teachers in a graduate program, discuss a lesson I have observed with the teacher of the class and other observers, write an article or book about teaching practices or other ways to observe, the line "Nothing in training could have prepared us for this!" comes to my mind. Although I had read Whitman's "Song of Myself" in *Leaves of Grass* in college, I have reread the following closing lines a number of times since the postcard incident, finding that they continue to express a central dilemma of my entire professional and personal life.

I tramp a perpetual journey, (come listen all!). . .
I lead no man to a dinner-table, library, exchange,
But each man and each woman of you I lead upon a knoll,
My left hand hooking you round the waist,
My right hand pointing to landscapes of continents and
   The public road.
Not I, not any one else can travel that road for you.
[In spite of a thorough Peace Corps training program at
Harvard University and University College Ibadan.]
You must travel it for yourself.
[Nothing in training could have prepared us for this!]
                                                        (Whitman, 1950, 46)

Whitman's claim is, of course, paraphrased by me and countless other teachers on a regular basis in questions such as, "What can I do to free rather than constrain those I teach? And in the process, can I or anyone else make a real difference? Or, would those we think we free have been able to free themselves without us? What difference, if any, does any of my teaching make? To what degree can I get another person to don my lenses to see a slice of reality I consider critical? To what degree can my experiences prevent others from falling the ways I have fallen or enable others to ascend in ways I have ascended?"

Again, Whitman (1950) said what I and those I work with must do: "You are also asking me questions and I hear you./I answer that I cannot answer, you must find out for yourself" (46).

While during normal waking hours, I am sometimes slowed down by these questions; while experiencing jet lag at 3:00 a.m., the skepticism of these questions has excited me. At 3:00 a.m., I can entertain the assumption that whatever I do is potentially a total waste of time. Accepting this assumption means that any insight I or a person I am working with gains provides evidence to negate the assumption! The questions thus lead me on to continue to play with what I do as I seek to find out for myself.

However, seeking to find out for myself by myself, alone, is like trying to use a pair of scissors with only one blade. Simultaneously asking what difference my work with teachers makes in my own teaching and beliefs about teaching and the way I live provides the other blade of a pair of scissors for me. Scissors, to cut, like the tango, require two: a pair of blades. Without others, neither I nor anyone can find out much, as learning must be giving up as well as gaining.

The need I have for others to enable me to travel roads on my own at first seems to be paradoxical, if not contradictory. But I feel I need others to have experiences with so I can make choices. The insights, knowledge, and advice of others provides me with choices as well as stimulation. With choices, I can compare. Information and insights from others can also serve as benchmarks to see to what degree the changes I perceive I am making in words I am, in fact, making in actions as well. Finally, I can make discoveries others might have already made my own.

When one of my daughters was around 3, she suddenly put her hand in her pocket and shouted "Pocket!" She had used her pockets for a long time; we had used the word *pocket* as in "the candy is in your pocket; I have the key in my pocket; empty your pockets." Yet for some reason, all of a sudden, she was able to discover on her own the connection between the phenomenon and the word that those she had been around had already made (Bronowski, 1956). "You must travel the road for yourself" would be Whitman's explanation, with the implicit reminder that there are almost always others on the road to observe and get information from.

Why do people act lines in plays over and over? There are excellent films of the best actors and actresses acting the lines. Does not each want to reinvent the lines just as my daughter reinvented *pocket*? Each of us yearns to create and recreate for ourselves what has already been created by others for themselves. Yet, the frequent remark: There is no point in reinventing the wheel. In fact, each of us has to reinvent the wheel even as we see others using wheels! Why do we even consider preventing people from reinventing wheels? Think of the excitement those who first discovered wheels must have experienced!

Of course, models and prescriptions and advice and information are needed for each of us to experience and recreate our own ways of teaching. But models must be presented and seen as samples of possibilities or prods to question what we do. If they are given as samples of what is true and right, they are more likely to be stultifying rather than liberating. Guidelines from professional organizations, degree requirements, and experiences required for teaching licenses try to ensure quality. But they also limit freedom and stifle change. The lenses from these sources are ground in exceedingly similar ways and the tints vary less than is needed for encouraging freedom.

To help others to see models as samples of possibilities in a teacher education setting rather than as samples of what is right and acceptable, I require constant flip-flops of models rather than mastery of the models. After I see a show-and-tell lesson, I ask that the teacher reteach the same lesson as a problem-solving lesson. But when I see another teacher provide a problem-solving lesson, I ask that this teacher reteach the same lesson as a show-and-tell lesson. Require? No matter how much pressure I might bring to bear, in the final analysis, although I can require anything, I cannot guarantee compliance. Resistance is part of learning and teaching. Allowing others to travel their own road can lead to as much resentment as trying to have others conform to a set of steps to follow. But I prescribe flip-flops of various teaching practices—urging us all to try the opposite—as firmly as our mentor and the External Inspector had urged adherence to their realities.

The matching and rematching of labels such as *show and tell* with practices is my way of trying to enable myself and others to experience traveling the road by ourselves through joint exploration. It represents my attempt to illustrate the negotiation required by Bakhtin's (1981) assertion that "the word in language is half someone else's . . . it is populated—overpopulated—with the intentions of others" (p. 292).

The matching and rematching of labels requires constant shifting of the lenses we have, the trying on of new ones, and the shattering of some, as well. The matching also forces us to look beyond talk to action. As Portia reminded us at Shylock's trial: "If to do good were as easy as to say what were good to do, chapels would be churches and poor men's cottages, rich men's palaces" (Shakespeare, *The Merchant of Venice*, Act I, Scene ii, lines 13–15). Talk unrelated to actions becomes empty rhetoric, bromides and clichés, eye patches that obscure reality rather than lenses to refocus and multiply our views of reality.

I am afraid that my attempts to explore along with those I work with is my own illusion. Can a person seen at conferences for 25 years be viewed by those new to the field as a fellow explorer? Can teachers at workshops see a person who is affiliated with an old/large/expensive graduate school as a fellow explorer? Can a person whose name appears in a bibliography now and then and has had some journal articles reprinted in anthologies and had books advertised in catalogs be seen as a fellow explorer by those who attend workshops I am invited to give? Thinning and graying hair alone contribute to expert status, even without these other badges of rank and power and authority.

Can I as a professor enable others with less official status in the club called schooling to jointly create? Can I and those I work with construct meaning together and discover together rather than try to please each other, even when courses are pass/fail and the pass is written on the grade sheet well before the course is over? Can I really try new lenses at the same time that I am engaging those I work with in activities similar to ones I had provided in a previous term? Can I discard, or even hold in abeyance, perceptions I have developed through years of observing and analyzing lessons so that those I am working with can discover the perceptions on their own?

My students pay more for each class session than for a box at the opera or a couple dozen seats at a movie theater or sporting event. With such an investment for each session, how do they feel when I share self-discoveries with them and point out how their comments and questions taught me? "Hey, you're the one who is being paid to teach us!" is an unspoken thought of at least some students. Why do I not supplement travels and explorations with some slide shows? Provide more of what many seem to want?

I push others to try alternatives. How can I not try alternatives? I keep asking myself whether I am resisting change as much as those in classes and workshops, and in the same ways. Except I have less pressure on me to decrease my resistance. Concerns, such as getting positive letters of recommendation, provide impetus to some to stop resisting, or at least to pretend to cooperate. But I have no pressure to stop resisting. I am tenured. I have enough requests for consulting to keep me busy. I have enough opportunities to get what I write published. I have been president of TESOL, as well as of one of its largest affiliates.

But to resist simply because one is in a secure position makes no real sense. Do I avoid lecturing and reading papers because I am unable to? Or because I see these modes of delivery as symbols of the expert telling the nonexpert what is known? I have enjoyed many lectures and papers others have given. I have been stimulated by them. And if I really wanted chapels to be churches, why do I not expand my repertoire and supplement my guerrilla theater/travel routine with lectures in class and the reading of papers at conferences?

I lecture little because of the difficulty of transferring what I know. Some might be impressed by my telling what I know. And I might instill the hope in some that when they get to my state, they might know as much as I do—hopefully more. No, I don't mind telling an apartment guest that the round key is for the front door and the square one for the back door of the apartment. I overlook the fact that trying both would only take a second and that my guest might get the right key in the right door by chance. I feel a bit bad if my guest forgets my instruction, uses the round key for the back door, and then curses himself for being stupid as I told him which key was which. But I can do the usual now and then, for small things. A bit of direct information can decrease tensions and make guests feel that they are not going to be visiting in the apartment of a madman. I even give short lectures now and then in spite of my reflections on why I consider them a very minor part of my practices.

On the other hand, why must we assume both in our professional and personal encounters that the other person does not know what we know or cannot do what we can do? Does not my experience and reading have the potential for limiting my vision as well as expanding it? Too many lenses can slow down our take on a situation, make it more complex than it needs to be for the conversations we are having at the time.

"I don't have any previous experience in the field"—not meaning the place to frolic or play ball—is a frequent plea or admission or statement from some MA candidates in my classes at the beginning of each term. Some seem to be asking for a reading list, others for a few office hours so I can share my great knowledge/experience with them and bring them up to snuff. My comment, "Lovely, you will be able to provide a perspective I might not have" is variously reacted to. Some no doubt consider requesting a tuition refund, others think I am simply trying to reassure them. The fact that I am genuinely delighted with the possibility of a potentially fresh perspective seems not to be accepted. The idea that I, a professor, can be ignorant, and thus learn requires a change in expectations for some (Ranciere, 1991).

But in the end, I return to Whitman.

> YOU must travel it for yourself.
> You MUST travel it for yourself.
> You must TRAVEL it for yourself.
> You must travel IT for yourself.
> You must travel it FOR yourself.
> You must travel it for YOURSELF.
> YOU MUST TRAVEL IT FOR YOURSELF.
> You must travel it for yourself. (46)

And these variously stressed renditions are only a few of the possibilities. Tone of voice, pitch, speed, emotional overtone, accompanying gestures, body movements, and breath stops provide a wider range of possibilities.

I recently had my first class meeting of the semester in a park, with a group of largely inexperienced teachers. I was bringing up the end of the lines of students so they all had sat down and arranged themselves before I arrived. You guessed it. They formed a large half circle with a large space in the middle so that I could sit in front of them all and expound. Few of them had previous experience in the field. But when allowed to sit in any formation in what was a new field, literally, for none of the students had previously visited the park where we were sitting, they assumed the canonical positions with teacher/expert in front. No directions were given, and none seemed to be needed! The podium, microphone, pitcher of water facing rows of chairs model at professional conferences was recreated in the park.

Some anthropologists urge that when we look at reality, we need to try to discard our previous perceptions of reality. We need to both don new lenses and shatter our present ones. But as 35-year-old postcard messages and recent seating arrangements in the park for a first class remind me, the discarding of previous perceptions of reality—the shattering of old lenses or the donning of new lenses—is not easy. "We don't have conversations; conversations have us" is a claim that has been intriguing me recently more than almost any other. The variation, "We don't acquire language; language acquires us" is equally intriguing (Gadamer, 1975, p. 62; Heidegger, 1962, p. 252 and 262, quoted in Arcario, 1994).

When I speak to my children and suddenly realize that I sound like my father, when I pucker my lips and make faces at babies and realize that I am acting like my father, and when my comments to a relative at a funeral sound like comments others have made to me, I begin to wonder again about the degree to which we can move beyond the boundaries that encompass us, to not only try new lenses, but to have them genuinely affect our realities. While we might have to travel the road by ourselves, the road has boundaries and directions and other travelers that might restrict us more than we perceive.

Montessori (1967) told the story of a nanny in the park who told the child she was caring for that it was time to leave. The child was in the midst of filling a small bucket with stones as the announcement was made. As the nanny wanted to arrive with her charge at the appointed time, she started to put some stones in the child's bucket. The child started crying as soon as the nanny started to help her. The lesson from the encounter to Montessori was, "Let them fill their own buckets." Ironically, for some, by the time graduate school comes around and professional preparation begins, help in filling buckets is still sought and expected.

My original professional goal in life—after discarding early ideas of being a chef or a dentist—was to be a kindergarten teacher. Working with kids seemed very, very appealing. Observing some using their noses to taste food by inhaling it, observing others making mud pies and realizing that dirt and puddles are things to be relished rather than avoided, wondering about outbursts of anger and crying spells, being amazed that running noses seem not to interfere with anything, and seeing the exhilaration of kids zooming down slides and not caring whether those who come to play have degrees or experiences but hoping that anyone around can join in jumping rope or lying on the grass to be amazed and mystified by the insects crawling around, as well as the grass itself.

Whitman tried to remind us of the mystery of grass in *Leaves of Grass*.

A child said *What is grass?* fetching it to me with full hands,
How could I answer the child? I do not know what it is any more than he.
I guess it must be the flag of my disposition, out of hopeful green stuff woven.
Or I guess it is the handkerchief of the Lord,
A scented gift and remembrancer designedly dropt,
Bearing the owner's name some way in the corners, that we may see and
    remark, and say *Whose?*
Or I guess the grass is itself a child, the produced babe of the vegetation.
Or I guess it is a uniform hieroglyphic,. . .
And now it seems to me the beautiful uncut hair of graves.
Tenderly will I use you curling grass. . .
I believe a leaf of grass is no less than the journey-work of the stars.

(6, 31)

Whitman somehow retained and symbolized the exuberance, freshness, curiosity, and ability to keep wondering about the multiple meanings of experience, the exhilaration that genuine questioning of convention and accepted perceptions can bring. No pat answers or picture postcard realities for him. And, I hope, no pat answers or postcard realities in my work as a teacher/learner, either. What would kindergartners have drawn or written on a postcard from Nigeria? Would some have drawn flies on the beach or market scenes? Would they have drawn messages unrelated to the pictures? Had I taken them to the park for their first class, would they have sat in a half circle, expecting me to sit in the middle to teach them?

A lot of buckets filled by others to arrange for getting emptied and filled in different ways. A lot of different postcard realities to try to see with new lenses and to write about. A lot more different time zones to induce more dreamlike episodes to help free me from the restraints and doubts of day-to-day postcard realities in the same time zone.

REFERENCES

Arcario, P. (1994). *Post-observation conferences in TESOL teacher education programs.* Unpublished doctoral dissertation, Teachers College, Columbia University.

Bakhtin, M. M. (1981). *The dialogic imagination* (C. Emerson, & M. Holquist, Trans.). Austin: University of Texas Press.

Bateson, G. (1972). *Steps to an ecology of mind.* New York: Ballantine.

Bronowski, J. (1956). *Science and human values.* New York: Ballantine.

Gadamer, H. (1975). *Truth and method* (2nd ed.). New York: Seabury Press.

Heidegger, M. (1962). *Being and time* (J. Macquarrie, & E. Robinon, Trans.). New York: Harper & Row. (Original work published 1927)

Korzybski, A. (1941). *Science and sanity* (2nd ed.). Lancaster, PA: International non-Aristolean Library Publishing Company.

Montessori, M. (1967). *The discovery of the child.* New York: Ballantine.

Ranciere, J. (1991). *The ignorant schoolmaster.* Stanford, CA: Stanford University Press.

Whitman, W. (1950). *Leaves of grass and selected prose.* New York: Modern Library. (Original work published 1855)

Sabbatical Blues

Alan Strand

Howard S. Billings High School, Châteauguay, Québec
Châteauguay Valley Teachers' Association

I am writing this from the point of view of a year's sabbatical with no strings attached. I have intentionally chosen to plan nothing and perhaps do nothing this year. I certainly have no intention of doing anything that reminds me of teaching if I can possibly avoid it. I am not taking courses; I am not doing research; I refuse even to cross the bridge that separates me from my school beyond the St. Lawrence River's broad (perhaps, in the context, not broad enough) expanse. After 23 years teaching whatever to whomever, I am, as we say in Québec, royally *tanné*.

I am not sure to what this unhappy pass in my career is attributable. It may be that teaching is not something mortals were intended to do for more than 20 years. Certainly, as I grow older, I have increasingly less patience with adolescent caprice. I prefer my situations somewhat slower and more predictable than are commonly encountered in a high-school classroom. I am more inclined, however, to believe that my battle fatigue is attributable to the sense of failure that I feel in doing my job—a failure that seems intrinsic to the task as it has been defined by society and educational administrators.

It was not always thus. I became an English teacher for a number of reasons. I am verbal. I love language. I respect words and use them carefully, with love and, often, to good effect. I toyed with the thought of working in theater, but the insecurity of that career does not appeal to me. Fresh from McGill University with a B.A. in English and philosophy, I and two friends applied for positions teaching English at a small rural school (under

500 students K–11) in New Richmond on Québec's Gaspé peninsula. Despite the anxiety that afflicts all new teachers, I loved teaching. In those days of Québec's emergence from the dark days of conservatism, clericalism, and social repression, teaching was a great experiment—not in any scientific sense, for there was not the rigor of controls nor the necessity to produce findings that could be validated. It was maybe a bit of a free-for-all. Roethke and rock were both worthy of serious consideration; a conference I attended in the Spring of 1970 in Toronto was formally adjourned so that we could demonstrate in front of the American consulate against the invasion of Cambodia. For all that, I had some sense that I knew what I was doing, despite my lack of formal training.

In 1971, I returned to McGill to obtain the teaching certificate without which I could not obtain permanent accreditation. The 1-year post-graduate program touched rarely on the real experience of being in a classroom with adolescents. My two methods courses, in English and drama, dealt superficially with a few techniques and strategies. A psychology course was an insubstantial salad of Skinner and Piaget. A philosophy of education course focused on anarchy and, appropriately, ceased to exist as a formal entity.

I emerged from this experience with no clearer sense of what I was doing than I had had when I entered. Still, I wasn't bothered immeasurably by that confusion. Times were good in Québec, my working conditions and salary continued to improve, and I was usually pleased with classes and found the experience of being a teacher intellectually stimulating. Those were the early 1970s, when the economy appeared stalwart and there were still plenty of jobs.

Things started falling apart in the early 1980s. For one thing, the world changed. The recession of 1982 threw the schools into turmoil. Society blamed the schools for unemployment and expected them to do something about it. Teaching and testing to objectives were the instrument the Ministry of Education was to use to scrutinize the process. At that time, tens of thousands of green-covered documents describing the new provincial curricula deluged staff rooms. Innumerable meetings and workshops were convened to explain them.

In the case of the language arts, which were still my principal assignment, the objectives, while more or less clear, were no less general and self-evident that they had been in the faculty of education: We were to inculcate the skills of reading, writing, reasoning, and effective communication (both oral and written), a sensitivity to language, and an understanding of literature, including its forms, its history, and its practitioners. Detailed descriptions of these objectives, as well as suggestions for their attainment, are contained in dozens of volumes detailing content and objectives for language arts and literature for all secondary levels as well as recommendations for a more specialized study of such fields as drama, the electronic media, journalism, and public speaking. This *pot-au-feu* has even been seasoned in some cases with such topics as *personal and social development* and *career choice education.*

Unfortunately, torpor and lack of time have not permitted me to assimilate all of this. In fact, I find it so overwhelming as to constitute a hindrance. The objectives remain so general as to be useless, and the responsibility continues to redound to me to decide when—or even whether—I should be teaching the appropriate use of semicolons. Given the social, cultural, and intellectual diversity of the school population, the fashion for whole language in elementary schools has produced students of divergent skills with equally different needs, and I am instructed that the appropriate response to this is grouping for cooperative learning. At the same time, economic crisis across Canada, but especially in Québec, has produced classes that grow consistently larger from one year to the next as well as fewer and fewer support services. In that context, I am generally dissatisfied with the way that group work functions—at least as I have been able to implement it.

As a consequence, I find myself confronted with the conflict of a society that is imposing an increasingly more conservative vision on schools, and a curriculum and methodology that continue to recall the liberalism of 25 years ago.

Fortunately, though, it has been possible to ignore many of the edicts that constitute make-work for the thousands of bureaucrats in the Ministry of Education. No one is inspecting my classes with any regularity, and evaluation continues to be based on writing samples which, if they are not marked by me, are marked, more or less subjectively, by my colleagues. Consequently, nobody has been nipping at my heels with accusations of incompetence or insubordination. Nonetheless, I feel a profound dissatisfaction in my job, which makes me understand why people want to get out of the classroom.

To put it simply, too much is expected of teachers of language arts. I could not do, even under ideal circumstances, everything described in the aforementioned curriculum guides. I cannot teach sensitivity to tone or point of view to students who have not mastered elementary reading skills. In truth, as a high-school teacher, I was never taught how to teach reading. Nor am I particularly interested in teaching reading. But I will teach reading if it is clearly understood that that is my task and if I am given the resources to do it. All I ask is that my responsibilities be reasonable, attainable, and clearly defined. Is this too much?

One of the corollaries of our declining enrollments combined with the job security provisions in our contract (negotiated in better times), is that specialization is extinct. The trade-off for having a job is becoming an *uomo universale.* Four years ago, I persuaded the school board to finance a degree in French. The consequence of this Faustian pact was that I was expected to teach in our French immersion sector once I became qualified. Since the election in 1976 of a separatist government and, subsequently, two referenda on independence (defeated), Anglophones have become nervous about their future in Québec. French immersion courses seemed essential if their children were to remain within driving distance after graduation. Many of reproductive age have fled to Toronto, resulting in the depopulation of our institutions. These various historical circumstances combined to create of me a teacher of various subjects in French. After a false start in moral and religious instruction, or rather *éducation morale et religieuse* (a subject to which I am in no way temperamentally suited), I became, first, a teacher of *géographie* and, more recently, of *éducation économique*. It should be noted that I have no background in either of those disciplines, apart from a casual acquaintance with the business section of the newspaper and a less-than-successful foray into the fools' paradise of the stock market. Furthermore, while I now have a second degree in French, it must be understood that it is a second language learned as an adult, and thus a language in which I will never be as comfortable as in my mother tongue.

Despite that, and much to my surprise, I have enjoyed my immersion classes far more than my English language classes. First, while streaming has become decidedly unfashionable, there is a de facto streaming in that unmotivated students do not customarily elect immersion courses, nor are they encouraged to. More important, however, to me is the fact that the economics curriculum provides clear compulsory objectives that are sufficiently specific so that I can be certain whether or not I have achieved them. In fact, they are such that objective, summative testing can measure my success. I am finally relieved of the burden of subjective and norm-referenced evaluation. I can compare my results with those of my colleagues. Even when those comparisons are not favorable, I have some sense of how I'm doing. I rarely have that in teaching language arts.

The expectations of the economics program are reasonable. Although it is a comprehensive course covering everything from personal chequing accounts to the international money market, it is possible to cover the entire program in the time allocated. Circumstances even permit some enrichment and exploratory activities.

Finally, the course is accompanied by a good textbook that provides structure and content for me as well as my students. For the first time in my teaching career, I was not responsible for the creation of a curriculum, the selection of texts, the preparation of materials, and the formulation of criteria for evaluation. I was able to concentrate on presentation and evaluation that, given our workload, I find sufficient. And, despite the structure, I feel freedom to perform, to provoke, to play.

I came to realize that teaching language arts is unlike teaching the vast majority of subjects that are taught in schools, and that the demands made on language-arts teachers are far more onerous than those on other teachers. The freedom that I once valued became, with changes in the institution, the clientele, the working conditions, and, perhaps, my own personality (I am now incontrovertibly middle-aged), an increasingly insupportable burden.

I want to say to society that I can't do everything that is expected of me. I have reached a point where I want somebody else to at least participate in the inevitable choices. If you don't tell me to teach grammar, don't blame me when my students don't know what a participle is. If you don't tell me to teach Romantic Poetry, don't blame me when they have never heard of Byron. If you don't tell me to teach public speaking, don't blame me when your children aren't cynosures at a public meeting. I am tired of being the fall guy for the failure of our language arts programs' success in being all things to all people.

The fact is that when a child doesn't learn to solve quadratic equations, the school hears nothing about it. But if he leaves a note to his mother full of errors in grammar, punctuation, and spelling, there is hell to pay. That visibility, which derives from the importance society imposes on effective communication, places on teachers of language arts a responsibility, an accountability that is becoming increasingly more unreasonable, especially given the expansion of the language teacher's task, which now includes various aspects of socialization, reasoning skills, and media literacy, as well as all those skills more traditionally associated with the teaching of language arts.

The enormity of that task has taken its toll on most of us. I find myself spiritually and intellectually drained much of the time. I feel the failure of not being able to attain objectives. I feel confusion about what those objectives are. I feel the frustration of working under conditions that make my task virtually impossible. And I feel resentment that I take much of the blame for a situation that I did not create.

I am enjoying this year off. I do not spend my evenings worrying about what I did not get done today and what I won't be able to do tomorrow. I have time to read books, write letters, and cook—even to indulge these catharctic reflections on my professional tragedy. I am frankly not looking forward to going back. And, unless something changes to make teaching English easier and more joyful, I think I would prefer to teach economics.

Changing the Margins:
Dilemmas of a Reformer in the Field

Denise E. Murray
San José State University

I have always been a rebel with a reformist zeal. Over my lifetime, this zeal has lead me to activism in many arenas—from politics to the environment. The field of ESOL has provided me with many opportunities to help bring about changes vital to the field because ESOL[1] is a marginalized field, one in which both teachers and learners receive little recognition either by the populace in general or within the broader field of education. Ironically, however, in this struggle for change, I have uncovered a dilemma I face almost daily: As a reformer on the political level, the victories are deductive, top-down solutions, but this contradicts my own inductive, nurturing philosophy of management and teaching. How can I continue to be a rebel with a reformist zeal? To do so, to continue to work to demarginalize the field of ESOL means imposing my values on other people. Let me explain by beginning with a personal story, one that made me focus my reformist zeal on issues of professionalism and qualifications of teachers, in particular. While this is my own story, my conversations with other ESOL educators throughout the world convince me it is not an isolated case.

When I arrived in California in 1980, having married a North American, I had already been teaching ESOL at both the adult level and in college

---

[1]ESOL refers to English for speakers of other languages. I prefer this term to others because it acknowledges that the learner already has at least one other language. However, in the text I also use ESL (English as a second language) where it refers to a particular program that uses that term.

intensive programs for over 7 years in Australia and Thailand; I had also taught university courses in ESOL methodology and language acquisition. I had a master's degree in linguistics, specializing in TESOL[2] and had been a frequent presenter at conferences and workshops. My job search in California, however, did not lead to a full-time job, nor to a position in an intensive program, which was my major area of expertise. But I did get a part-time position in our local adult-education program, teaching every morning, 5 days a week. This work was both fun and rewarding, despite the large rotating enrollments of 40 students in my class. During my time in this adult program, I was asked to give demonstration lessons and help develop curricula. The functional/notional approach was just appearing in textbooks in the United States, and I had helped develop such curricula in Australia. I worked with some wonderful colleagues, who helped ease my transition into life in the United States.

Our adult program was organized through a consortium of several K–12 school districts. One district decided to withdraw from the consortium and rehire many of the teachers, but without offering tenure and at lower pay rates. Two of the adult teachers in that school district had earned tenure with the consortium and clearly did not want to be rehired with no tenure and lower pay. They could only be accommodated into the now-reduced joint program if some of the more recently hired teachers were fired. The school district for whom I was working was asked to take one of the consortium-tenured teachers. Given the district's policy of last hired, first fired plus my ESOL qualifications and experience, I thought my own job was secure. The most recent hire was a guitar teacher. However, several weeks before the reorganization, the district for which I was working hired the guitar teacher to teach one of our ESL classes. She had no ESL experience, but a life general secondary high school or adult credential, which licensed her to teach any subject in high school or adult education. In addition, she was tenured to the adult program as a guitar teacher and thus could not be let go. So, I was bumped. This eye-opening experience started me down the twisting path to where I am today. I vowed that this would never happen again. I decided to go back to school and get a PhD, and, probably even more important, I decided to become actively (politically) involved in debate over professional standards for teacher certification through CATESOL, the professional organization for ESOL educators in California.

My story illustrates how our profession and the people in it are marginalized. But, let me sketch some other scenarios to demonstrate the breadth and depth of this marginalization. Although the characters in these scenarios are composites of people I have known personally, they represent many

---

[2]TESOL refers to teaching English to speakers of other languages. Also sometimes referred to as TESL.

types of educators in the field. Their experience may strike a familiar and uncomfortable chord with many second-language educators.

My friend Lesley is a freeway flier who cobbles together a living by teaching ESL in several different locations. (I use a female name deliberately because our profession is dominated by White women.) Lesley teaches three classes of freshman composition in my department at San José State University. She works Monday, Wednesday, and Friday, teaching 3 hours and holding office hours 1 hour each day. From San José State, she drives to a community college 15 miles away, where she teaches two listening classes that meet each day in the late afternoon, early evening. On Saturdays, she teaches composition at another community college, with 35 students in the class. Although she is married with two children, she rarely sees them because most of her spare time is spent grading the endless composition papers. But she considers herself lucky because San José State University gives her full medical and dental benefits, unlike the other colleges.

Fran is an elementary school district ESL specialist. Many years ago, she decided she wanted to make ESL her specialization. She went back to school, took a TESOL certificate, and then passed the Language Development Specialist Examination, which authorized her to teach ESL in California. She attends conferences and workshops, constantly keeping herself up to date on innovative methodologies and research on language acquisition. Although her district has several bilingual Spanish classes, the district also has numbers of Punjabi, Laotian, Hmong, and Portuguese students. In spite of the large numbers of students in the latter groups, they are insufficient at any one grade level to form a class, nor are there sufficient bilingual Laotian, Hmong, or Punjabi teachers.

So, Fran travels from school to school in her district, teaching Limited English Proficient (LEP) students. Her students are from different language groups and grade levels, have different educational backgrounds from their home countries, and come from a wide range of socioeconomic backgrounds. The single commonality that identifies them as a group is that they are not yet proficient in English. All that Fran has in common with them is English. In one school, she holds class in the library, where she and her students must keep quiet so as not to disturb classes using the library facilities. In another, her classroom consists of an anteroom through which other students stream as they go to their lockers. Fran's car houses the proverbial traveling ESL resource center. With no place to call her own and with visits to different schools each day, she must carry with her all the materials she knows are essential to the language development of her students—the realia and manipulatives needed to help beginning learners acquire concepts in a new language. And, of course, these materials are her own, bought out of her own salary. Her requests to the school district to provide her with such materials fall on deaf ears—after all, her students are unobtrusive, the superintendent argues—they cause no trouble. The district needs to spend any spare money on truancy and discipline problems.

Several years ago, my own campus created a brand new Department of Linguistics and Language Development, born out of a decade's struggle for the right of language-minority students (who comprise more than 40% of our campus population) to become part of the university's mainstream. We refused to settle for second-class status. Many people on campus argued for an academic skills program, a separate unit that would report directly to the Academic Vice President; that is, a program that would not be part of the regular academic structure. We argued, and won, an academic department that would be the equal of any other department on campus. The department was formed—with three degree programs and the responsibility for the academic reading and writing of language minority students—ESL and second dialect speakers. We felt we had finally won a major battle.

Perhaps. But let me conclude this series of scenarios with one of a different sort—one that shows how pervasive the attitude is that language minority students do not belong in a real university department. Not long into our first semester as a department, I was talking with colleagues in Special Education, defining our mission and discussing ways we could cooperate. In all seriousness, a colleague who defines our mission solely as ESL welcomed me and the department as the new kids on the block. "I am especially pleased there is a department of ESL," he told me, "because now there is someone lower on the pecking order than special education." This is a colleague who visits schools, sees the need for ESL and bilingual instruction, and really cares about the education of children! Imagine what colleagues in other departments think about the new kids on the block. They not only resent the formation of a new department in economic hard times; they especially resent the formation of a department designed to educate students who they think do not belong in a university at all. From their perspective, if students' English is not at university level, they should not be in a university, even if they are successful in their field of study, often making GPAs of 3 or higher.

It is situations like this that spur the reformist in me to fight this continuing marginalization of the field. I have been actively involved, especially in California, to ensure that what has happened to me will not happen to others. Through the professional organization CATESOL, I have lobbied state bodies that control education to develop professional standards of qualifications for ESOL teachers at all levels—K–12, adult, and post-secondary. We have been successful in getting new legislation and regulations to ensure that ESOL teachers are appropriately and adequately educated. However, just as my conversation with my colleague in Special Education helped me realize the fight is not over even when you think it is, recently several groups in California have worked to weaken these standards. The teachers' union, in the name of preserving jobs, has successfully lobbied to have current teachers undertake minimal preparation (45 hours of in-service) to become ESOL teachers. Would anyone take such a suggestion seriously if the subject matter were math or science?

Although the legislation and regulations that I have worked on have been developed with broad consultation from educators, this legislative solution essentially represents a top-down approach. By reforming the field, by working to demarginalize the field, I have helped legislate external standards for professional teacher preparation. Yet, as much as I have struggled to achieve standards, standards and a top-down approach contradict my own teaching and management philosophy, which is essentially inductive, bridging, nurturing, and encouraging of self-realization. I believe that education is not a process of telling others what to do, but of dialogue and shared discovery; yet, at the same time, I clearly have my own agenda and views, which, of course, I hope that my students and colleagues will share. This dilemma plays out in my classroom on a daily basis.

One semester, for the first time, I taught a graduate class in cross-cultural literacy, one of the primary areas of my own scholarship. I was very excited to be teaching a class in which I could use some of my own research and writings. I had become interested in literacy by accident. As a graduate student, with some reluctance, I took a class on literacy with Shirley Brice Heath. I was reluctant because I had always taught ESL writing at advanced levels and had no interest in people who were pre-literate. This course, however, made me reevaluate my own notions of literacy. I began to understand that literacy is socially constructed, that is, as involving (socio)culture-specific ways of taking meaning from texts and using texts to create meanings. Over the years, as I continued to do research and read, my ideas of what literate behavior means have changed. I came to think of it in terms of literate behaviors and practices rather than of the technological skills of reading and writing. So, when teaching this class, I wanted to help my students to discover, as I had, their own definitions for literacy through reading and research.

In the first class meeting, I asked my students to do a freewrite on what they thought it means to be literate, telling them we would come back to those freewrites at the end of the semester when they could evaluate how their concept of literacy had changed. I then asked them to keep a journal of their literacy activities over the next week, to be shared in class the following week. When the class next met, small groups shared their journals, developing categories of literacy events that they then shared with the rest of the class. In one group, two students discovered that they were both servers in restaurants, and talked about reading the customer. A heated discussion broke out about whether this could legitimately be called literacy. I deliberately avoided giving any indication of what I thought. Over the course of the semester, the class proceeded in this way, through research, readings, and discussions. At the end of the semester, we all shared our new definitions of literacy and I explained my own, giving them a paper I'd written on the issue.

When I read through students' evaluations of the class, I found that some were thrilled to have had the opportunity to find their own meanings; others were frustrated that I had not given the class enough direction by telling them what they were to discover. One student said I let students discuss their own opinions too much; another said I was a strong personality and this prevented students from expressing their own opinions. Of course, instructors often get mixed evaluations. But, for me, this exemplified the dilemma I have. How can I help students discover the meanings I have discovered and thus share the excitement of the discovery? Or, how can I help them make discoveries that may be different from mine? Also, is it more manipulative to lead students inductively to a point of knowledge than to tell them up-front where I think they should go? Would such an approach allow for more open discovery? Am I, in fact, really committed to inductive learning and self-discovery if I want students to find what I have, but just in a more indirect way? Am I then still a reformer in the classroom, trying to impose my own standards and world view? But just using a different approach?

I experience a similar dilemma in much of my professional life—in com-mittee and organization work. Recently I asked a couple of colleagues work-ing with me on a state-wide committee to write a letter of support for my promotion. I was delighted when they stated that I was valued for having clear and theoretically supported opinions, for expressing them forcefully, but for not imposing my ideas on others. This sounds like a contradiction— and it is. In meetings, I find myself pulled between the need to get the task done and the need to nurture other people's ideas; between the need to have a product and the need for process. It is very easy to merely respond, "yes, but . . ." The reformer in me examines an issue, sees a solution, and wants to apply it. The nurturer in me wants to help others find solutions. While I wrote the first drafts of this chapter, I was on sabbatical in Australia, thousands of miles away from my home university. An interim chair was filling in for me during my absence. I was sorely tempted to keep an eye on the department, even from such a distance. Yet it was more important for me to let the department operate without me. Now, as I'm writing final drafts, I am deciding about whether to run as chair for another 4-year term. The reformer in me wants to run because there are still many things to accomplish. The nurturer in me wants to stand aside and let someone else accomplish and find resolutions. Interestingly, my greatest fear is that another chair might not be as collaborative and inductive and might impose her/his view on the department.

For me, the dilemma in my career has been the conflict between this caring, nurturing aspect of the profession and a sense of the importance of professional standards. On the one hand, I am attracted to the field and many of my colleagues because they value self-actualization, wanting to help students realize their full potential. On the other hand, I am angered by the lack of professionalism we display—as if caring were enough. Caring is a two-edged sword. Because I am caring, I don't want to criticize my colleague who does not have the appropriate credentials or who does not return student papers on time or behaves in other unprofessional ways. I hope she will value herself as a professional and act accordingly. But what if she doesn't? For me, this is the essential contradiction in the field and my professional life as an ESL educator: I work on one level to develop standards of professionalism so that others will not lose their jobs to unqualified teachers, and to change the marginal status of our nonnative English-speaking students and their teachers; but, in my own classrooms, I want students to take control as adults capable of determining their own lives. How can I change the world without imposing my values on other people to the end of producing clones? How can I value individualism and honor self-actualization and yet work for standards of professionalism that imply conformity? It is that unresolved contradiction that now characterizes my professional life.

I realized when I lost my adult education ESL job that the decision was not personal, but political. Being, by nature, a rebel with a reformist zeal and determined not to be cowed by the system, I threw myself into reforming the field—working to demarginalize the discipline, ESL students, and the professional status of ESL educators. In the process of engaging in this battle, I recognized the personal dilemma described in this essay that characterizes my professional life: Political reform creates top-down, deductive solutions, but I advocate nurturing and inductive management and teaching. Writing this essay has sharpened this awareness (see "On Getting There From Here," this volume). As a result, the question of how to help change the world without imposing my values on other people is now central to the way I see myself as a rebel with a reformist zeal within a profession that continues to be marginalized. There is a great deal of work left to be done.

Body-Mergings: Searching for Connections With Academic Discourse

Christine Pearson Casanave
Keio University, Fujisawa, Japan

As a child, though I did well in school, I was not an avid reader or writer. Although I was competent in both and always loved language (especially language-based humor and foreign languages), I recall few school reading and writing activities that interested me. It is curious, therefore, that I was drawn to a career in a school setting in which reading and writing lie at the heart of the profession. Having made the commitment since completing a graduate degree to continue working in the world of second-language education at the university level, I have, in recent years, been faced with the dilemma of how to survive comfortably in a field where people read and write for a living, yet where I don't connect with much of the academic discourse I encounter.

It is a push–pull, love–hate relationship, in that I have been drawn in compelling ways via academic discourse to fascinating issues in the broad field of language education, and equally often bored, angered, and thus distanced by discourse that seems inaccessible and irrelevant. Part of my survival involves understanding the complex relationship that I have forged over the years between my own personality and habits—some of which are not well-suited to a life in academia—the demands (or my perceived expectations) of my field, and the specific positive and negative reactions I have to varieties of academic discourse when I read and write. This relationship is inextricably intertwined with my view of myself as a language educator, and given the ongoingness of the ups and downs, I am no longer sure how to position myself within my profession. It does not help that for

187

6 years I have lived as a geographical outsider, in Japan, where I am foreign and illiterate, far from easy access to the inviting worlds of American university libraries. So even though I am usually perceieved as an insider by my Western colleagues, I feel a growing sense of distance from any of the niches within the second-language field, niches that are (like all academic communities) partly defined by the discourse they use. This sense of being an outsider surfaces especially tangibly on those days when I try to read or write, and cannot.

It has been easy in the past to blame myself for finding the reading and writing so difficult at times, and on my low IQ days I wonder if I chose the right field. Yet I am comforted to learn that I reside in familiar territory, if I am to believe the private confessions of many students and colleagues who also find it difficult to forge connections with some of their reading and writing. It has been equally comforting to see my own concerns reflected in a growing body of literature since the mid-1980s (some of it wonderfully accessible, by the way) on the nature of academic and scientific discourse—what it is, how it gets produced and admitted into the field as knowledge, how novice scientists and academicians learn how to "play the game," and how political factors help shape the decisions we make about what to read and write and about what to ask our students to read and write. Other literature by writers about writing has helped me realize that some of the problems I have connecting to written text stem from prose that meets few of the criteria for clarity, simplicity, and grace, considered basic to good writing by these authors (e.g., Becker, 1986; Williams, 1981; Zinsser, 1980).

I have come to understand a little more from these external sources about why I sometimes feel so disconnected from some of the things I read, why I view myself at times as an outsider, playing at the margins of the field; in short, why I and many people, especially those outside the mainstream (e.g., people of color, women) feel excluded from some of the important conversations that take place in academia via the written word. So I am not alone. What I write in this essay, therefore, will probably strike no one as new, and many people will find it familiar. I want to bring this familiar struggle out in the open so that it becomes easier to talk about without characterizing myself as intellectually challenged or academically mislocated. I want to expland my own conceptualization of what the academic discourse game is all about.

DO I WANT TO PLAY THIS GAME?

If I feel misplaced in finding it difficult to connect to some academic discourse, it may be that I am realizing that I don't want to play the mainstream scholar game, where some writers seem to be hiding themselves behind a facade of jargon, statistics, or pseudoscience, performing a politically charged show according to rules they think should not be broken. In research I did in graduate school, I watched some sociology doctoral students learn to emulate the very prose they found inaccessible, and so perpetuate the show. In that same period, as a student member of a faculty hiring committee, and as a novice who was learning to write for publication, I became aware that others, such as gatekeepers in the form of tenure committees, publishers, and journal editors, also perpetuate the show to the extent that they hesitate to risk changing the rules or cannot see beyond established discourse conventions.

Where do I fit in this game? How do I survive in a world where, at times, one of the functions of written discourse seems to be to exclude (often in the name of maintaining standards) those who don't comply with the rules? How can I interweave the personal and political dimensions of my relationship with different kinds of academic discourse in ways that push me to read with less resistance and bolder discrimination, and to write well—flexibly, purposefully, and accessibly? How can I make my home in academia more comfortable; that is, figure out how to position myself in a variety of professional contexts in ways that help me maintain my intellectual self-esteem, despite my lifetime of difficulty becoming absorbed in reading and writing? Should I fight, flee, or play the game?

TROUBLE CONNECTING FROM THE START

I probably have always been restless about reading, in the sense that since childhood, it has been difficult for me to sit quietly and read with concentration. As a youngster, I spent afternoons after school and weekends as a horse, galloping and grazing on neighborhood lawns with one or two other small horses my age. During quiet time alone in my room, early Saturday mornings, my bed was piled high not with books, but with crayons of the most delicious colors and scents, soft pencils, and piles of white paper. In both cases—the running, whinnying, and pretend-riding through weedy backyards and ravine paths, and the tactile and visual experiences with the waxy colors and fragrances of the Crayolas—I felt integrated, powerful, immersed in a world of both mind and body, where I had physical energy and strength, fantasy, focus, and control. I felt connected to a life force even when I was just interacting with marks on paper, as long as I was creating my own images and the stories that went with them. The worlds and creatures that I created merged with my own body during these periods of play and picture-making. I did not know the words *dichotomy* or *fragmentation* until much later, but began experiencing these rifts in school. My body and the words in my school textbooks never really merged in the same way they did during my life as a horse or as a picture-maker, so effortlessly. I know this now because I don't remember my school textbooks, but I recall vividly my imaginary life as a horse and the worlds I created with pencil and crayon.

I think that since childhood, I have sometimes felt pulled apart by dichotomies like these—mind and body, insider and outsider—even though these days we are not supposed to speak of dichotomies. We can speak only of false dichotomies. But this essay is about connecting to, and feeling disconnected from, some of the ways language is used in the academy. In this regard, I find it appropriate to reflect on the concept of dichotomies because, in the academy, I have felt pressured not to employ dichotomous thinking. But in a postmodern world, where nothing is real, or at least not objectively real, where discourse creates and controls worlds for us, then concepts created out of discourse and perceived to have meaning are real for the people who perceive them. Thus, I hesitate to say these dichotomies are nonexistent, or even false, unless I intend to silence my own voice. As conceptual organizers for my everyday thinking, such dichotomies work for me. It is true that I perceive many different contexts in which I am insider or outsider, and thus many kinds of mind–body interweavings. I see and feel the overlaps and the wholeness of experience as well as the ruptures. Dozens of similar dichotomous and tri- or multichotomous conceptualizations help me make sense of a world too complex and chaotic to leave in the hands of postmodernists who have few solutions to their deconstructionist activities. So if I discuss my experiences with some of my school-based reading and writing activities, beginning in childhood, in terms of a disconnection between body and mind, I do so because this is what my discomfort feels like, in a quite tangible sense. I find this imagery real and meaningful, in spite of the fact that I acknowledge wholeness, continua, fuzziness, multiple voices and stances. When I don't connect with written text, my mind feels separate; it constructs little, it does not integrate, blend, mesh, merge its workings with my body. The dichotomy is real in terms of my lived experiences.

STRUGGLING FOR MEANINGFUL MERGINGS IN GRADUATE SCHOOL

Although I happily surrounded myself with books in graduate school (and continue to do so today), I did not feel connected to much of the reading I did there (having books is one thing; reading them all is another). As was the case when I was a youngster, my grades did not reflect how difficult I found it to concentrate on my reading and writing. In graduate school, there were at least two of us in this predicament, and I spent a number of tortured hours with a similarly beleaguered classmate who also had trouble focusing. Occasionally we discussed especially difficult texts together, trying to untangle ideas we thought resided in criminally long sentences full of abstract nouns whose meaning escaped us. I assumed at the time that there was meaning there to be discovered, and suspected that because the discourse was so complex, the ideas necessarily must be too. I naively thought that everyone else but us understood all the readings, and some of the more jargon-laden class lectures as well, and that I could access these ideas if only I tried harder, knew more, were brighter, and so on and so forth.

As a first-year doctoral student, I reached an intolerable level of intellectual discomfort in a qualitative research class in which one of the professors, a well-known White male researcher with a congenial but imposing presence, had repeatedly used the word *hermeneutic* over several class meetings, a word that peppered the readings we had been doing as well. I could not match my dictionary definition with his use of the word or with its use in my readings, so it became clear it was a concept I needed to internalize. I finally flung up my hand, motivated more by frustration than fear, and asked what it meant. I didn't understand his explanation, which of course just added to my frustration and sense of inadequacy. I blamed myself for this inadequacy, feeling ill-prepared and out of place, partly because there were some students in this class who spoke up regularly and confidently, challenging and questioning the teachers, and conversing comfortably in a disciplinary jargon apparently familiar to all of them. It turned out that several other of the quiet people left the class that day with similar feelings of puzzlement and inadequacy, and not just the nonnative English speakers in the class. I wondered why more people had not spoken up to request clarification of key concepts. Were we supposed to know all this stuff already? To already speak this foreign language? Because this man was considered a skilled teacher, it never occurred to me that he might have failed as a teacher to recognize and address our level of knowledge, failed to recognize that terms and concepts new to us had long been breakfast-table conversation to him.

So began my continuing professional curiosity about several things: about what good writing consists of; about disciplinary jargon, who uses it, and why; about the wide variety of writing and speaking styles in the academy, some accessible and some not; about how over time, people whose bodies have merged with specialized language and concepts no longer recognize the extent to which their use of academic language has distanced them from novices, the very people they are supposed to be reaching. I recall the embarrassment I felt during an incident with my advisor, for whom I was writing a paper on reading research, when something she said about my paper implied that I should not cite certain people together. I presumed I had misread and therefore misrepresented some of them, and vowed to be more careful next time. But noting later that several of the names in my reference list never appeared in her own writing, I began to get a sense of the factions and families within areas of inquiry, the different perspectives that people adopted about the same issues, the different language and conceptual frameworks they used to discuss them, and the political implications of citing one group of scholars and not another. This sense of which group(s) she belonged to came naturally to my advisor, as it no doubt did to my qualitative research professor, yet neither recognized the distance that I felt as a novice from feeling connected to any kind of home base in the world of academic discourse.

Then, over the next 4 or 5 years, as I waded through mountains of prose I sometimes found inaccessible, a number of concepts and writing styles that had once been inaccessible did find their way into my body (the only way I can describe it adequately), becoming part of me in ways I could not have imagined in that first year. I was not aware of how or when this happened, but a distance was beginning to form between me and people outside my program. I remember feeling shocked when going home one weekend and chatting with my sister about some of the ideas that were beginning to spark my interest for a dissertation project, only to have her cut me off midsentence with the curt request to speak in real English. The shock was especially profound because I had consciously tried to express myself in ways she would comprehend, and I did not know how to further simplify or rephrase. After this experience, I did not really know how to talk about my graduate work with my family. I apparently, at that point, had one foot in the door and another one out. This experience added to my growing curiosity about how and why connections do or do not happen as people struggle to interact with academic texts, and so helped shape my dissertation project.

In this project, something that one of my informants said to me struck me as a real déjà vu encounter. A young woman of Puerto Rican background in her first year of a doctoral program in sociology told me that she always checked how well she was connecting with her reading and writing by asking herself whether she would be able to explain to her mother what she was doing. By the end of her first semester in a dense and jargon-filled theory course that included 400 pages of readings exclusively by White European and American males (her comment), she claimed she could no longer talk about her work with the people she felt closest to. The new language and concepts, plus the intensity of her immersion experience in this doctoral program, effectively isolated her from those she loved.

I perceived that this young woman, a novice sociologist, was probably misplaced in an elitist institution that did not care about what she could bring to the sociology program. My perception highlighted my awareness of my own marginal but shifting status, and of my continued struggle to connect with my academic reading and writing in ways that were meaningful to my life outside school as well as inside. I was still finding myself feeling disconnected and excluded from some of the texts I was asked to read. I puzzled over jargony and pretentious scholarly articles, filled with lifeless, boring prose where people were replaced by abstract categories and faceless group identities, by symbols and numbers, and where actions happened miraculously, without anyone taking responsibility for them. I wanted to read about real human beings—actors, agents, participants, populations, ethnic and racial groups, young and old, rich and poor, interviewer and interviewed, surveyor and surveyed, observer and observed, humans with histories, intentions, and values. I asked myself then—and continue to ask—the questions that the Puerto Rican woman was asking herself at the end of her sociological theory course: Who are the professors talking to? Who are the authors writing for? Where are the women and the non-Whites, except in the mostly silent audience of people who pay tuition? How am I supposed to connect with some of this dense and lifeless literature? If the literature in sociology (and psychology and linguistics and education . . .) is about people and their behavior and their language, where are the people in some of this academic babble? And then I recalled a paper I wrote for Elliot Eisner.

THE EISNER PAPER

A paper I once wrote for Elliot Eisner in graduate school came closest of anything I've written to letting go of the act—to liberating myself from the real and imagined constraints of so-called academic discourse and thought. We had to write about what the act of teaching involved, and what our notions were of what a "teacher" was. Eisner convinced me that—for this assignment at least—he was a genuinely interested reader, and that there was no penalty for letting our language and thinking soar, which I did with gusto. But he was the only reader. There were no gatekeepers in the form of journal-article reviewers, publishers, or conference program organizers, six of whom heap praise and half dozen of whom condemn. For that paper, there were no mainstream genre conventions to be followed, no bodies of literature to situate myself in (always with difficulty), no procedural trail to cover up my intellectual and compositional meanderings, no models to emulate, none of the struggles with academic writing that are described in the literature that I would later read as part of my dissertation work.

I recall sitting down at the typewriter, a warm cat in my lap and a martini on a soggy coaster, and finding that the ideas were coming faster than my fingers could type. My list of metaphors for "teacher" alone reached a full page. The permission Eisner gave me to liberate my prose style helped liberate my thinking, and I had fun doing it. Once. It was difficult to nurture that sense of liberation outside Eisner's class, where I was, for the most part, immersed in mainstream literature, and where I was learning the rules, implicitly for the most part, for situating myself in that literature.

Not all of this literature left me feeling like a mind without a body. Occasionally I was stunned at the humanity and eloquence of some of the things I read. Could I become a writer whose work was both accessible and accepted? Eisner's own clear and elegant writing, as well of that of many other academic scholars, convinced me that it is possible for people in academia to write well and to connect with readers like me. What is it about their writing that helps it to merge with my body? I can't explain it well, but I feel the presence of life in their discourse. I get a strong sense of who the authors are and why they are writing—an honesty of purpose, perhaps, and a strong commitment to reaching out to readers rather than just to impress a gatekeeper. I wanted to learn to write like that.

WRITING WELL (BUT WHO'S THE AUDIENCE?)

Like many other people who live in academia, I am not used to revealing who I am in print, to making a point by demonstrating it with life-filled language, without teaching it or explicating it to death. I realize that this is a common problem, stemming partly from the fact that many of us simply are not very good writers. In other words, it's not a case of consciously choosing not to fill our prose with life. In my own case, sometimes I just don't know how to write well for a particular purpose, or I am afraid to risk experimenting with unconventional genres even though I know they can be as analytically rigorous as the genres modeled on science, or I do not have the time, energy, or discipline that it takes to polish a piece of writing.

What do I expect from myself, and what message do I wish to pass on to my students about how to write well, and at the same time, how to position themselves, and myself, within a field? I found it interesting that Lillian Bridwell-Bowles (1995) admitted that she can experiment with her own academic discourse, pushing against the narrow conventions, because she has tenure and does not need to play the political games in the academy that she knows her students and less well-established faculty face in making their way through the system. So while she encourages her own students to put more of themselves into the writing they do in her classes, she also sees their dilemma. Outside her own classroom, outside my classroom, my students and I are caught in the larger political web of learning how to write and interpret what we read in ways that fit a variety of strategic (read: political) purposes and that don't rock the boat too much, if we want to find our way into the academic community of our choice. As to where good writing fits into this picture, I didn't get the impression that many of my own professors valued it much, although they recognized and appreciated it when they saw it. In my research on academic writing in a sociology department, I remember asking several professors about the value they placed on helping students learn to write well in a field notorious for its inaccessible writing. It can wait, was the answer. They need to learn the issues first.

I think that people don't talk often about good writing because we all know how much time and effort is required to produce it. When I'm feeling particularly depressed about not being able to write, I sometimes reread Annie Dillard's (1989) wonderful book, *The Writing Life*, about how difficult it is to write well, each time delighting in the craft and polish of every sentence. In this book, Dillard demonstrates and describes by personal example what writing means to her. I see Annie Dillard herself—her humor, her imaginings, her sense world, as well as the agonies she goes through when she writes. I see all the physical and mental tortures she imposes on herself and doggedly endures in order to pull out one reluctant sentence after another, to give readers the impression of a rich, effortless flow of language and thought. All the while she is at the center of her prose, even when she is not talking about herself. I connect with her personally when she portrays herself as a procrastinator, one whose mind wanders away from the task at hand and onto details of life—particularly things in nature—visible from her study window; one who needs to enforce solitude on herself as a kind of self-discipline, to immerse herself in a barren environment, too small and empty to tempt her with distractions outside the whirlings and imaginations of her own mind. She shares with readers like me the meanderings of her mind, the minute details of her environment, the frustration of days and nights in which she cannot write. Her stance is personal, situated, experiential, rather than just conceptual (Connelly & Clandinin, 1985), yet it is just this stance that draws me in and opens me to her messages. With her, I unite mind and body; I share her thoughts, I see myself in her words; and merging with her words, I become her words.

Annie Dillard's writing connects with me partly because it is written in the first person, but more so because it is rigorously crafted, with care for her readers. If every academic writer worked as hard as Dillard does to write well, we would all write less. Not a bad idea. I am sure that I would feel more connected to the professional literature that I read if there were less of it, and if it demonstrated the writers' care for their craft and a sincere interest in their audience.

Audience? I am the audience for the literature in my field, yet often feel that the authors of some of the professional literature I am exposed to, and some of the professors who assign such literature, don't recognize, or accept, the diversity of which I am a part. My awareness of the diverse audience in my field developed first-hand, as I looked around me in several different school settings, a diversity all the more remarkable because these settings on the surface looked very White and middle class. I realized over time that I shared physical and intellectual space with people from ages 22 to 60, with lots of White people to be sure, but Whites of all kinds (no, we are not a homogeneous group), with Asians from many countries, with Hispanics and Middle Easterners, with too few African-Americans. There were privileged elites and working-class people, gays, lesbians, straights, bisexuals; several blind people, hearing impaired, and people in wheelchairs; people with strong disciplinary backgrounds and people new to a field; people with years of working experience and others recently out of an undergraduate program who were just starting out. Lots of women, some married, some single, some in both groups with children. Meek and passive people, angry and abusive people; people who were confused and searching, and people who believed they had found what they were seeking; complacent people, and those who were driven; loners and social butterflies; optimists and depressives. Politically astute people and those whose naiveté got them into trouble; people with a polished act designed to help them fit in and those who preferred to display their resistance publicly. All alive, all inquisitive about issues in language education, all with our own voices, all interacting with texts as we sought ways to fit in, to forge identities, to make connections. And for me, connecting with the literature in a field is connecting to the field. It's just that as someone who reads and writes as part of my normal work activities, I haven't been sure lately how much effort I want to continue making, either to forge connections with existing literature or to help change the literature (happily a job already started by others). What do I expect for and from myself in the second half of my career?

SHIFTING PRIORITIES

As an aging language educator embarking on the second half of my career, I seem to be getting more restless, not less, about spending quiet, focused time reading and writing. I may always have trouble sitting for long periods reading and writing, partly because of this physical restlessness that I've lived with all my life. I am learning to compensate somewhat for this intellectual handicap by acquiring the ability to read and walk at the same time, particularly when I am reading at the early stages of a writing project. This is possible as long as I am traversing a familiar terrain, one that is free of potholes, roots, and ridges, of traffic, auto exhaust, and stop lights. A paved bike path works well. My body settles into a walking rhythm, where sensations move from the ground up through my legs and back, where sunlight warms my face even on a cold day and reaches my brain through my retina, where temperature and breeze create sensations on bare skin and on skin sheltered by textured clothing. My vision drifts from page to path to plants to water to trees to buildings to horizons to clouds to page. My mind focuses on ideas. The experience as a whole reminds me at every step that I am alive. This sense of aliveness, of diffuse focus away from sole concentration on the physical presence of the printed page, seems at times to assist me in my struggle with academic discourse that I find difficult, to assist my thinking when I need to write, to assist in the process of body-merging. The walking is becoming increasingly a regular part of my search for connections, but I'm not sure at all where the path is leading me.

I do know that I am much less patient today with what I read and write than I used to be, and much more aware of how important it is for me to connect both mind and body as I interact with text. I want to experience academic discourse the way I do other bodily experiences over which I have a sense of wholeness, belonging, integration, authority. When I do connect with print, words fill me not with meanings per se, but with sensations. Usually it is with sensations of something alive, often people. I don't mean to say that I expect authors to narrate personal experiences and feelings in everything they write. Even without a first person confessional from them, I believe I can experience an author, and certain histories, intentions, and passions that emanate from them in well-written prose. I can observe myself constructing meaning (or not) with the assistance of an author, provided that I can make the initial connection, the initial merging of a discourse sensation with my body. This goes for my writing as well, where I need to be in touch with my own intentions and passions in order to find my way into the prose. With this hook into the discourse, I feel (on high IQ days) willing to struggle to continue constructing meanings that eventually seep into my system. When these connections happen, I experience interaction with a sentient being (including myself if I am the writer) who wishes to express something, who has a reason for communicating, and who cares if someone listens. I sense life in the discourse.

But because much academic discourse that passes before my eyes, especially in professional journals, does not merge with my body, I am tending to spend less time struggling with it. When my reading and writing activities do not connect with the whole of me that experiences life most fully (with my sense of sight, sound, touch, with my intuition and sensibilities about things human), when what I read remains as marks on a page or screen or as noises from a speaker (much as does a new foreign language), when it does not trigger a process of meaning construction and connection (a process that begins with my eyes and ends not in my head, but in my toes), then I feel myself slipping gradually further away even from the margins, and ponder more and more whether I belong. I am not talking here of problems with academic discourse in areas in which I have no professional expertise or interest. What discourages me, on those days when I am easily discouraged (after a night of poor sleep, after a conference where I've allowed myself to compare myself to others, after critiques of my own writing that focus too much on what's wrong and not enough on what's right), is not being able to connect with so much of the academic discourse that ostensibly deals with language and with people. Discourse from disciplines that educators like me routinely draw on—psychology, sociology, philosophy, anthropology, feminist literature, applied linguistics—in short, discourse about people, their language, their places in the world. Is it partly that, as an educator of the sort that I have become, I am not a true insider in any of the disciplinary groups on which education draws, and feel estranged for not belonging to a more clearly defined discourse community? Or is it that I am a closet feminist, finally coming out and beginning to reject the inevitable political games that scholars play as they vie with each other to achieve insider status within a patriarchal educational system? Maybe this is my new path to walk.

In the second half of my career, if I become a feminist of the sort I would like to become, I will read only those well-written texts that truly excite my interest, even though I will probably miss much of the literature that the field of second-language education presumes I should know. What I do read will merge with my body and help me feel whole. If I choose this path, I will write nonmainstream academic discourse, even though my voice will probably not be heard in conventional circles. What I do write will express who I am in ways that better suit my personality. In a move that I see now has already begun, I will help my students rebel against the narrowly circumscribed discourse conventions of the mainstream second-language education literature, and will help them develop the courage to speak from the heart, yet with analytical and theoretical rigor that all good thinking requires. I will do this even though this approach may not prepare them to compete in the conventional academic discourse game. If I become the sort of feminist that I would like to become, however, I will help them learn how to recognize the game, and play it if they choose to, without compromising their integrity. But I think if I choose to drop out of the academic discourse game altogether, my professional satisfaction and development may suffer. In fact, the love–hate, tug-of-war relationship I have with academic discourse no doubt contributes to my intellectual growth, an insight that has surfaced after 2 years of wrestling with this essay. So if I become the sort of feminist I would like to become, I hope I will be able to make myself step into the fray as often as my hermitish personality permits, and to talk back with the courage that has eluded me for much of my professional life, courage whose absence I have heretofore hidden from the public eye.

REFERENCES

Becker, H. (1986). *Writing for social scientists: How to start and finish your thesis, book, or article.* Chicago: University of Chicago Press.

Bridwell-Bowles, L. (1995). Freedom, form, function: Varieties of academic discourse. *College Composition and Communication, 46,* 46–61.

Connelly, F. M., & Clandinin, D. J. (1985). Personal practical knowledge and the modes of knowing: Relevance for teaching and learning. In E. Eisner (Ed.), *Learning and teaching the ways of knowing* (pp. 174–198). Chicago: National Society for the Study of Education.

Dillard, A. (1989). *The writing life.* New York: Harper Perennial.

Williams, J. (1981). *Style: Ten lessons in clarity and grace.* Glenview, IL: Scott, Foresman.

Zinsser, W. (1980). *On writing well: An informal guide to writing nonfiction.* New York: Harper and Row.

Explorations for Part Four:
Reflections on the Profession

1. John Fanselow is very concerned, or one could argue obsessed with, his responsibility in ensuring that his students develop a spirit of free thinking; yet the many questions that he poses throughout his essay suggest unresolved doubts. What are your responses to his questions? To what extent can those we hope to free reach that state without us? What difference, then, does teaching make?

2. Fanselow uses images of postcards, scissors, and glasses with different lenses to help him express the multiplicity of ways we can construct and interpret reality. How well do these images, and the messages Fanselow associates with them, resonate with you? In a language-teaching profession, do you believe that teachers have a responsibility to help students, as well as themselves, "try on new lenses"? How would this work in your own setting?

3. In both the cases of Fanselow and of Shea (his conflict with Jason, see Part Two), we see evidence of how teachers and students struggle with conflicting expectations in the teaching–learning context. To what degree can teachers get another person, a student or colleague, to see a slice of reality or to share expectations that they consider critical? Compare how Fanselow and Shea deal with this issue, contributing your own views as well.

4. Alan Strand narrates his struggle to fulfill the curriculum objectives in his area of English language education, noting that "society and educational administrators" have defined for him (and for other English teachers) an impossible task. Which aspects of this "impossible task" do you particularly

relate to? If your curriculum is mandated in any way, are you in possession of documents describing the current local, state, or provincial curriculum objectives for your subject area? What critiques would you offer in response to these visions?

5. In his essay, Strand contrasts the existential condition of teaching English language arts subject matter with that of economics. What is your interpretation of where these differences came from? If you have had experiences in two or more very different subject matter areas, how do they compare with Strand's?

6. In the first half of her essay, Denise Murray recreates a number of scenarios that are intended to convey the depth and breadth of the marginalization of her profession. For those of you who are TESL educators, how representative do you find these scenarios? What scenarios come to mind in your own professional experience that depict experiences of marginalization that you might have lived or witnessed?

7. In what ways do you identify or not with Murray's dilemma between upholding professional standards through legislating and encouraging the development of independent ideas on the part of others?

8. Christine Casanave depicts her long struggle to connect with academic discourse. What have been your own experiences with, and responses to, the various discourse styles in the educational literature you read?

9. Casanave finds it difficult to explain why some of her experiences with what she calls "inaccessible" academic discourse have not been satisfactory. What do you believe some of the reasons are that make it difficult for some people to connect to some academic discourse? To what extent do difficulties reside in the language itself, in the way that language is used, or elsewhere? What do you consider the obligations that readers and writers have in forging these connections? Do you believe that there are cultural differences in how people define these obligations, as has been suggested in the literature on contrastive rhetoric?

FURTHER EXPLORATIONS

1. Have you ever experienced teacher burnout? What circumstances contributed to this sense of fatigue or defeat (as Strand described it, the sense of feeling "spiritually and intellectually drained")? How did you come out of the situation? What constructive suggestions can you make as to how burnout might be averted? In your particular setting, would it be useful to compile your suggestions into a document that could be distributed to colleagues at your school?

2. What changes do you feel need to be made in your field of language education? What choices do you believe you have in helping to bring about

change, and at what level(s) does action need to take place? Interview several professional language educators outside your class and include their views in your discussions as well. For those who are interested in taking action, consider collaborating with colleagues to design a small piece of legislation (a petition, a proclamation, a list of objectives, a letter to an administrator, etc.) for a specific purpose in your field that could then be submitted to an appropriate audience.

3. In several of the essays in this section, we encounter issues concerning the badges and behaviors of rank, power, and authority—people who have authority and wield it, people who have it and claim they don't want to wield it, people who don't have it. In your own field, what do these badges look like, how are they created, and who wears them? If possible, identify concrete instances of how men and women in your educational setting use language and behavior to reveal or conceal their badges.

4. Several of the authors in this section express either a deep dissatisfaction or a profound frustration with certain aspects of their field and their work. Do you sense a thread of dissatisfaction running through the professional discussions among practitioners in your field? Interview a number of seasoned professionals with whom you come into contact regularly, query them about this issue, and compare the responses you get with those procured by your colleagues. What commonalities and differences do you find among those you spoke with? If you are a newcomer to your field, what messages can you glean for yourself from these reflections on the profession? What factors seem to be keeping you, and the people with whom you talked, committed to staying in the fray?

PART FIVE

Introduction:
Conversations

When we began requesting essays for this book, we believed that contributors would appreciate (we hoped relish) the opportunity to write a story about themselves, from the heart. Select an issue or dilemma in your professional life, something you feel is important in language education, we stipulated, and let the wheels spin. Set aside the staid and sterile conventions of scholarly discourse. Give us dialogue and drama, colorful analogies and metaphors. Write about yourself in a way that demonstrates how you wrestled with an issue that may be commonplace in our professional lives but that does not get discussed in the literature. Give us the gut-wrenching story that you have told repeatedly over drinks or dinner because it was so consequential in your development. At last, you have the opportunity to be yourself in print.

Little did we surmise how challenging this task would prove for some of us. Some folks bailed out early, stating openly they did not feel comfortable going into print with personal revelations. Others were intrigued by and committed to the task, but faced great difficulty in realizing it. As editors, we found ourselves sending drafts back to authors with advice to become more personally reflective and less teacherly or researchy, with requests to use a story to demonstrate a point to readers rather than to explicate or preach it. We received revisions, parts of which inspired and moved us with their insight and color, and other parts of which distanced us with their objectivist, academic stances and rhetoric. Words sailed over phone lines and airwaves, and where possible, over long lunches, coffee breaks, and happy hours. We all learned things about ourselves—about how we are prone to take refuge in the safety zone that conventional professional discourse allows us to build, and how rarely we emerge from this safety zone to examine in detail our beliefs and behaviors.

But why eavesdrop publicly on some of these conversations that took place as the book evolved? What can they contribute at this point? Why are they important? In the first place, a finished piece of writing, whether it is a traditional scholarly article or a reflective narrative, hides the trail of thinking and composing that the author has traveled. So it should, you may say. It should not be the purpose of published writing to reveal every nook and cranny of the writer's mind, the false starts, clumsy beginnings, the tortured procrastinations, the pondering, doubting, and musing, the critiques from friends, colleagues, and editors that leave us feeling deflated or defensive, as well as determined to go on. We don't disagree. But in this book, intended in part to reveal how and why people become language educators, it makes sense to share a few of the many substantive discussions we have in our profession that ordinarily never end up in print. They reveal the successive peeling back of layers of thought, bringing to the surface what lies beneath. What lies beneath can teach us a great deal about why we chose to become language educators, and how we respond to the daily challenges of our profession. These discussions contribute greatly to who we are, who we are becoming.

Moreover, many pieces of writing never get finished, and may not even really get started, even though much thinking, discussing, and note-making have already transpired. No one would claim that such meanderings are a waste of time. Whether or not they result in a printed piece, they contribute to shaping our professional personae. Often, these meanderings take place not in isolation, but as conversations among colleagues, between author and editor, and among our various selves. They lead to complex interminglings of personal and professional issues that all feed into who we are and what we write. These conversations are an intrinsic part of how people become language educators. They remind us that our knowledge and beliefs—our own and our students'—are jointly constructed in the process of writing and speaking with others.

Finally, the conversations further one of the goals of this book—that of forging connections between readers and writers. We have a sense that readers will find relevant to themselves the issues brought up in the conversations about the search for personal meaning in professional life, the struggle to shape inchoate ideas into language, the importance of friends and colleagues in the isolating profession of teaching. The conversations can thus encourage readers to learn to value the tensions and connections they experience in their own professional lives, to embrace the sometimes painful process of becoming a language educator.

For the record, we did not have lengthy conversations with all of the authors, and with those we did, we have a trail in writing from just a few. The conversations that we include here represent different but equally insightful experiences of three people who did provide written documentation, through retrospection, fax records, and e-mail. Two, Denise Murray and David Shea, completed essays for this book, and their conversations with us document the struggles we all had with this task. The third, Judy Winn-Bell Olsen, eventually chose not to participate in this project in the way we had originally intended. In all three cases, we see a number of common issues.

A fundamental one has to do with decisions the authors made about what to reveal about themselves in print. Self-disclosure, personal storytelling, as it turns out, is not so personal when it is laid out for all to see. When does a self-disclosure become a confession that most appropriately remains private?

Additionally, the conversations reveal that both the authors and editors need to consider carefully what the purpose of such self-disclosure is. The purpose must extend far beyond insider gossip and storytelling for its own sake, to narratives and dialogues that will potentially have some lasting and purposeful impact on readers, something (insight? engagement? connections?) they cannot ordinarily get from the more scholarly literature.

Last, these conversations, which illustrate the interactive nature of the relationship between authors and editors, caused us, as editors, to questions our goals and methods and to reflect on our own willingness to do ourselves what we asked the authors of the essays in this book to do. To what extent do we as editors encourage others to help us peel back the layers of our own professional lives? To what extent have we insisted that authors' stories match what we think they should be saying rather than what authors believe they want to say?

What follows are three conversations that differ greatly in tone and purpose, all of which helped the authors and us as editors reflect on the issues that surfaced as we worked with each other over the several years in which the book evolved.

On Getting There From Here

Denise E. Murray
San José State University

A dominant metaphor in English is "life as a journey." In this "conversation," I want to take you on a journey, a writing process journey that vividly demonstrates the need to bounce ideas off an interested, engaged reader—in this case, Chris Casanave, a co-editor of this volume. I want to take you on the journey that produced the piece that appears elsewhere in the book. In keeping with the book's goal to turn inside out the usual remote, pompous prose of the field, I've turned this experience into a dialogue, reconstructing some of the discussions Chris and I had over nearly 2 years—in person, by letter, and by e-mail and across three countries—the United States, Japan, and Australia. The dialogue is presented in our own voices. Chris's are exactly those she wrote to me by mail or e-mail.

In fall of 1991, Chris invited me to participate in this book project, after a discussion about a plenary address I'd given at CATESOL in San Diego— "Ending Marginalization: An Agenda for Change." Because all of the issues I addressed in this paper are dear to my heart, I thought it could be reworked for the book. Chris agreed. In January 1992, I received the formal letter of invitation. Being pressed for time, I merely mailed off the original plenary paper for feedback. Chris wrote in response:

> ". . . [T]he theme of professionalism is great. The substance of the paper is also right on track, such as your descriptions of how ESL does not enjoy the status of a profession. We're particularly interested in how *you* came to be aware of this as a problem, and how *you* have worked and are continuing to work through it as a driving force in your career as a language educator."

I began to try to revise the paper, but just could not get anywhere with it. I had no sense of audience and certainly no sense of what I wanted to tell them, except the pain I felt because our field was marginalized, and the urge I have always felt to change the world. I sent a new draft to Chris, only slightly different from the original—that is, I made a paper-to-be-read-aloud into a written paper and I shortened it considerably. Chris sent me another letter asking me to change the title ("This should not be a 'We need to . . .' piece, but a personal sojourn"), the tone ("Avoid arguments for and against making ESL a discipline"), and the conclusion.

I was devastated by the letter. She wanted me to take out what I thought was most important to me—how to end marginalization. I was stuck in this theme, unwilling to let it go.

Chris and I had lunch a few months later. We talked and talked. From this conversation came tumbling out feelings and events from my childhood: my anger at a system that had let my father be a temporary employee for the same organization for more than 20 years, to retire without any retirement benefits save the federal government's age pension; of how hard he'd worked and what tremendous responsibilities he'd had—so much so that when he retired, he was awarded a medal from the Queen. I talked about the insecurity of my parents, both of whom had left school at age 12. Of how they were conservative in behavior and dress and voting habits to mask their insecurities, how they had to have control over these parts of their lives because neither had any control over their work lives. I rebelled, determining I would never let any system control my life.

Our conversation helped me see the reformer in me—the person who has always wanted to change the system, right the wrongs—a trait that led to my professional activism in California. But it also touched on the nurturing side of the profession and of myself—I said that I liked the profession because of the caring people in it. Was this then my dilemma—feeling pulled between changing the system, ensuring standards for TESOL educators (an essentially controlling activity) versus my love of the nurturing, caring side of the profession?

I immediately wrote a new draft, somewhat different from my first. But I could still not let go of the "here-is-how-to-end-marginalization" tone, even in the title, which now read "Negotiating Standards of Professionalism: Reform or Self-Actualization?" I had tried to accommodate what Chris and I had discussed, but, at the same time, I still wanted to take control by sneaking in what I wanted to do. Chris responded by pointing out that "for our book, what's important is not 'Why do educators in the field of ESL experience marginalization?' but why you, Denise Murray, have a professional life that is partly characterized by a dilemma." She suggested that I "talk about your urge to solve these problems through legislation—a top-down approach that essentially tells other what do do" and also to include "some scenarios from the other side of your life . . . illustrating your commitment to self-actualization. Then we could SEE the dilemma you face."

Try to give scenarios about self-actualization? What scenarios? I panicked. Did I really have any? Was I merely claiming I believe in self-actualization? I realized that a story I'd told Chris about changing my teaching style was a scenario illustrating this dilemma. I thought of other professional settings and activities in which my desire to control from the top threatened my belief in process and self-discovery. I wrote a very different paper and sent it off.

Finally, in the more relaxed atmosphere of a sabbatical in my home country, I realized I was telling MY story, MY dilemma—not advocating for change. This was in fact an odyssey of conflicting professional values: Was I a nurturer or reformer—or both?

Reflections by Fax and E-mail

Judy Winn-Bell Olsen
City College of San Francisco

April 18, 1993

Dear Christine and Sandra,

. . . It is not yet clear exactly what my contribution to the
book should be, but I've suggested that either of my keynote
speeches, "Focus on the Teacher" and "Focus on the Teacher,
Part 2," be considered. . . .

Chris, for the TESOL panel [based on evolving ideas for the
book] I could elaborate on the "Burnout" stage in a teacher's
development. . . .

I trust you'll let me know in due time if my ideas are hitting
the mark(s) you had in mind.

Best,

Judy

* * *

May 3, 1993

Dear Christine and Sandra,

Thank you for the draft of the proposal.

About the abstract [for the TESOL panel based on the book]:
Looks like you and Sandra plan to be managers more than
sharers of personal experience. Since this idea was yours, why
not your own stories too? . . .

About the book:
Since your fax when you asked "Where are YOU in your stories
of burnout? What happened to you?" etc. I've been struggling
with the writing I said I'd do for you. I think I finally understand the level of personalization that you want, and I'm
not sure I can give it to you very extensively on a topic that
I've already synthesized into publishable prose. I've been able
to articulate my thoughts on the subject of burnout because
I've put it at some distance from me, and after generalizing,
I've lost the personal particulars.

. . .

I've been asking myself what I *can* give you that has the personal immediacy that I think I now understand you're looking
for. I'm working on something now with a working title "On
Teacher-ing and Getting Beyond It (and Figuring Out When To)".
It's a reflection on what kind of learning has been most meaningful for me, what I notice is most meaningful for people in
my inservice workshops, and what my students respond to best.
The "teacher-ing" refers to straightforward didacticism and
overly structured "communicative exercises" which leave no room
for people to express who they are, shape their own learning
to some extent, or be creative on their own terms. This may
come closer to what you want in terms of personal voice, because I'm thinking it all through right now.

Although this letter feels unfinished to me, I'll send it along
now so you can finish your abstract [for TESOL]. I'll keep wrestling with the book topic. This is harder than I'd anticipated.

Best,

Judy

* * *

January 16, 1994

Dear Chris,

Sorry to worry you [about the long silence]. I've been very
busy writing and editing, but not the project I promised you.
That's coming up next.

I hate to respond to queries until I have something new to
show, which is why I've been holding off a reply. But I'd better let you know I'm alive . . . and working lots on various
projects, and very shortly on yours again.

. . .

Best,

Judy

                                *   *   *

Feb. 5, 1994

Hi Chris—

. . . I'm rather relieved to hear that many other people seem
to be having a difficult time of it too. I think it's particularly hard for people who have polished one style and stance
to be "up close and personal"—and still professional—in print.
Trading stories over drinks is one thing—that's backstage kind
of stuff. But anything in print with one's name attached is
definitely front-and-center stage, and it's tricky. Also, I
think some of us said "yes" to this project with something
else in mind, so aligning perceptions has taken a bit of time,
and I gather is still going on with some folks?

Yes, I'll definitely want feedback from you, but not . . .
quite . . . yet.

Judy

                                *   *   *

Feb. 24, 1994

Chris—

Thanks for your fax. I was about to send you one to give you
an update.

About our presentation [at TESOL]: seems to me that what is effective in a written collection is not necessarily "grabbing"
in a presentation. Also, I've been struggling with what else I
want to say that you want to hear.

With that in mind, I just tried out two different versions of
a presentation on the topic to colleagues who were kind enough
to listen and give feedback. . . .

I'm taking their reactions to each version—what they liked,
what they thought didn't work—and am designing one presentation
with the best of both versions. It will be largely extemporane-
ous (I'm lousy at reading papers to an audience!) and supported
with some OHP visuals: some pictoral/symbolic, perhaps a head-
line or two.

The basic thesis is this: As a developing language educator, I
frequently find myself in "overload." Why keep doing so much in
so many areas? (teacher-facilitator/trainer-researcher-partici-
pant). . . .

I have pretty good evidence that with the right delivery, it
will go over well with an audience of teachers and teacher-edu-
cators. Whether it is what you ultimately want in your printed
collection should perhaps be a separate issue to be dealt with
after the presentation.

I hope you will find this satisfactory. It's what I can do
with authenticity—it really does spring from my gut.

. . .

More soon,

Judy

* * *

Nov. 13, 1994

Dear Chris,

. . . Somehow a "personal story" is not so personal when it's
down there in black and white for anyone to read (one can no
longer choose the audience, setting, etc., for disclosure, and
degree of disclosure) and when anyone can do anything with/to
it, you know not what. One loses control of something very central to oneself.

And I think decisions involving real disclosure have more to do
with intuitive/emotional factors in the immediate situation
rather than the intellectual factors involved in planned written discourse. The people who do written self-disclosure best,
I think, are the poets, playwrights, novelists—though they fashion their own veils and drape them just so to reveal just what
they choose to.

But many of the rest of us are at a distinct disadvantage here—
not only are we not used to diving into our own unconscious
murk for pearls, but we may not recognize them when we find
them, and when we do, we're at a loss what to do with them.

I think maybe I've just said something very important someplace
back there, but I'll leave that to you to judge.

Another expansion of above: In a personal story, the choice of
audience can be crucial to the teller's comfort. Witness my continued exchanges with you halfway around the planet, however
slow my responses, and the fact that I have not once initiated
contact with Sandy, who is probably not 30 miles from me. I respect her but I don't know her.

. . .

Anyway, I had a thought for you on "how I got to be this way"
(which strikes me as the deep-structure title or subtitle of
your book) which no doubt will pertain to some folks in your
volume . . . maybe it can contribute to your "final fold-in"
(think cooking here) in your conclusion.

I think part of this ongoing development/struggle (for those of
us who keep doing more beyond the sphere we're expected to
work in, and get known for it) is wanting to be immortal.
Which may be stronger in some of us who are childless, I don't
know.

I think it's immortality in two senses:

First, and I think this is the "best" sense—to develop and
pass on some idea(s), some seed(s) that will grow and enrich
others who come after us. So we (certainly I) have been anxious to share these ideas at conferences like TESOL. And I certainly can't complain that the ideas haven't been well-received.

Second, and I think this is the not-best sense—to have our
name respected and remembered for what we've done.

I think this second not-best thing can go to our heads and ultimately cramp the first, best-sense stuff. It's what makes us
paranoid that other people will rip off our stuff without giving credit (as indeed they do) and makes us bitter about it.
The selfish part begins to fight the procreative part and
strange things happen, internally and externally.

I'll give you a personal example: the dyad maps I developed in
the early 70s and shared at TESOL '75 and after.

I have pretty strong proof that I did them first. And it is
satisfying to see that the formats are being realized in so
many different ways in so many textbooks, teacher books and the
like these days.

But sometimes it gives me a little twinge—sometimes a big one—
to know that I'm never credited with inventing them—they are
just part of the communicative lore. . . . If ego demands lasting name recognition, maybe I'll be happier in the long run putting my creativity into academic projects.

We'll see.

. . .

Best,

Judy

*   *   *

Jan. 16, 1995

Hi Chris,

.   .   .

The reason that I'm dropping everything for the moment to send
this is to share the enclosed with you (which I just ran
across, and if I don't do this right now, I'll lose it).

Enclosure A is part of the conclusion of a discourse analysis
paper that I wrote in a Speech Communications class in 1978.
I'd been trying to apply a Labov and Fanshel model to several
taped interactions between myself and several people in my life.

What my analysis showed me about my own behavior was rather embarrassing to me, but provided a lot to reflect on about myself, human behavior in general, and the whole process and
goals of discourse analysis.

I'm enclosing part of my conclusion to that paper, because I
think it touches on some of the issues that we've been back-and-
forthing about on your project.

.   .   .

Happy New Year,

Judy

• • •

Enclosure: Final Comment on 1978 Paper:

This study has raised a question in my mind as to the place of
self-disclosure in serious scholarship. At what point does serious examination of one's own behavior for academic reasons become an exercise in "True Confessions"?

Until now, most intimate glimpses into human linguistic behavior of an intensely personal nature have been through analysis
of therapeutic discourse—where the patient, viewed as a helpless individual, is exposed to all who would care to see—

through no conscious choice of his or her own. S/he may be
anonymous in the transcript, but there is still a sense in
which s/he is a victim, and the scholar is a voyeur. . . .

We will find, I think, feelings and motives every bit as powerful, hidden and complex in the everyday interactions of people
judged competent and sane. It is, of course, much more painful
to scrutinize our own behavior. Literature, to some extent visual art, and lately film have been the safest ways to express
the truths that we come to realize about ourselves. But what
art has long expressed of our intuitive knowledge, linguistics
and communications studies are now trying to quantify—by looking at the "victims" of our society, seemingly at a "safe" distance. Dare we now take our "truth-finding lenses," formerly
ground, polished and focused on "fictional" personalities, then
on pathological personalities—and turn them on ourselves?

Correspondence With an Editor

David P. Shea
Heisei International University, Saitama, Japan

Sandra R. Schecter
York University, Ontario

June 29, 1994

Dear David,

. . .

Let me first say that I'm responding to the draft received in
the Center office on March 22. If that is not the more recent
of the two drafts you sent, forgive me. That is the one I have
before me. In truth, I did not pay too much attention to which
version I took home with me because my issues with your piece
are not the ones you were responding to in your second draft.
In fact, it kind of irritated me that you were revising to be
more fair to your dissertation advisor, or to consider his perspective additionally. Your concern with your representation of
Jason's perspective came across plenty strong in the original
draft. I even had the impression that this concern ·dominated
your writing process.

Before receiving your piece the running title I had for your
contribution was "Whose Dissertation Is This Anyway?" I'm not
sure if that header was one of Chris' inventions (sounds like
her humor) or yours (it wasn't mine), but I liked it and now I

know why. It places the emphasis where I thought it belonged
(the accent on the right sylla'ble, as we used to say when we
were tots), that is, on your struggle with issues of intellectual property, as opposed to where it rests with your current
title, which is on your advisor's agenda, i.e., gender bias.
Also, throughout the piece you reaffirm the dominance of your
advisor's agenda—from the very first phrase of your Acknowledg-
ment note, to the very last sentence of your story. It is almost as though Jason is looking over your shoulder as you are
writing.

Basically, you can tell one of three stories. You can tell the
story of your longstanding concern with issues of intercultural
communication, your original conception of the scope of that
concern, how as a doctoral student you were asked/told to go
in search of gender bias which did not fit into your notion of
what your thesis was about, how you did this because you felt
you had no choice, and how as a result your concept of the
role of gender difference in discourse developed. Your title
would then be appropriate. With this scenario, we wouldn't need
as much information about Jason as you have provided—the debates around the time of your proposal hearing would suffice;
we would, however, need more text on your original notions of
conversational participation—perhaps some texts or authors that
influenced you and framed your thinking—to situate us squarely
in the subject matter at the start and to set your transformation in relief.

Or, you can tell the story of your struggle over issues of intellectual property and authorial voice in this implicitly coercive situation, how you felt "discouraged and abused by the
usurpation" of your dissertation, how you "resisted at first,"
how eventually you did what you needed to get through, how you
started to identify with Jason's perspective (which made it easier to do what you needed to get through), what reckoning you
have come to about this accommodation strategy and/or how much
of the toxins you feel are still in your blood. In this scenario as well, we won't need as much about Jason after the initial contests of will.

Or you can tell the story of the wisdom of a teacher named Jason, how at first you resisted his ideas—poor ignorant slob
that you were—and how you came, as a sign of maturity (would

you entertain several alternative hypotheses—eventually you learned to love your captor, perhaps you were vampirized?) to see the wisdom of his way. With this scenario, you can write as much as you care to about him.

I don't advise your attempting to tell all three stories in the same piece unless the reader understands that you have done some heavy-duty reflection on the manner by which each has vied for your soul, and the torment this struggle has caused you, a "three faces of David" scenario, as it were. Whatever you decide, get the monkey off your back, David. Tell the story that would emerge under hypnosis, not the one that Jason would most sanction. We'll wait. We've got time.

Sandra

* * *

Date: Monday, December 18, 1995

From: David Shea

Hi Sandra,

. . .

At the moment, I am sorry, but I think there's no way that I can give you the response you requested for the Language Educator book. First, I'm simply swamped with things to do, with school work, family matters, and other pressing professional obligations. Second, (perhaps just as important) I don't feel an authentic response inside. That is, plain and simple, I don't think I have anything to say. It's hard to try to force something out at this point about the struggles with that paper.

I will make a confession, though. When you wrote to me last June offering your response to the first draft of my paper, I had already heard from Chris about the gist of your comments (based on conversations you had in America, I think) prior to actually receiving your letter. As I recall, Chris mentioned something to the effect that you thought I waffled in my argument and had sold out to Jason's authority. The criticism stung. It's hard enough to write anyway, so I simply put your

letter away without opening it and passively sat on my paper
for a couple of months. During the following summer vacation, I
went back to work on the revision and came up with the present
draft, where I make the "waffle" toward Jason even more explicit (because I think the matter of professorial authority is
a dialogic process, not a matter of either student voice or
teacher control). You liked this version better, not because
you "agreed" with my "conclusion" but because it was more coherent. But I think it's significant that I didn't respond to
your comments to produce this positive result. I mean, I did
but I didn't.

I find my reluctance to be criticized particularly interesting.
I didn't open your letter and read your comments until after I
had a final approval from you that the revised version was all
right. Then I read what you said. In a sense, I knew on the basis of your not so positive original response that what I had
written wasn't "right." But in a sense, I didn't need anyone
to tell me what to write (or think) in order to revise successfully. What I had to say was inside and articulating it was a
matter of listening to my own voice, not responding to an outside editor.

Yet as I write this I know that if it weren't for outside readers, both you and Chris as editors, reading and responding to
what I had written, asking questions ("What on earth do you
mean here?"), making comments ("This seems inconsistent!"), and
so on, I would never, ever, not in a million years have written that paper.

The process is entirely social and absolutely personal at the
same time. It makes me think not only of the multivocal character of writing, as a conversation among readers and a writer.
It also makes me think about the pain of writing, about how aw-
fully difficult it is to sit down and articulate ideas so that
they are coherent and persuasive. Maybe it's different for some
people, perhaps for academics who write fluently in pre-pol-
ished prose. But for me, writing is like bleeding on the key-
board, and I rarely go in search of opportunities to bleed on
paper unless I am pushed or forced by external pressure, such
as an impatient editor.

I don't know where this is leading, really. Perhaps it's just
to say that my relationship with you (and Chris) seems to parallel my relationship with Jason, as it seems to parallel my rela-

tionship with my students. Perhaps it's just to complain that
writing is a mysterious blend of fortuitous discovery and frustrated despair.

At any rate, I'm late and must get this off to you now or
never. Have a Happy Holiday Season.

Belatedly,

David

* * *

Dec. 25, 1995

Dear David,

First, I want to thank you for your "non-response" to my letter. I would like to include a substantial portion of it in
the book actually: Your non-response proved more thought-provoking than any response I could have imagined receiving.

I owe you both an apology and a personal debt. The apology is
for the three story lines by which I sought to circumscribe
your options for reflection on and resolution of the Jason dilemma. No scenario, no matter how well formed, is worth abdication of an authentic voice. In any event, I believe that the
path you ultimately chose will be more satisfying for the
reader than any of those I suggested. As you know, I loved
your final draft, and am moved by your power as a writer.

I won't prolong the apology part: I'm not the ingratiating
sort. About the personal debt: It is for the insight that you
provided me into the relation between writing and engagement
with the world outside one's front door. In your non-response
you assert that you find writing painful; however, in illustrating that assertion, the example you use refers to interactions
that you have been drawn into with other people over/as a result of some of the issues raised in your writing, or by the
very act of writing. I'm not so much signalling a contradiction
in your representation as I am coming to terms with a confusion in my own way of thinking about a matter that has assumed
some importance in my life. Like you (and most serious writers

everywhere, the relevant literature reassures us), I have for a long time associated writing with pain. However, curiously, for the past seven months—since I have been on my own research money—I haven't minded writing nearly so much. I dare to say that sometime I find sitting down and composing/revising to be downright enjoyable.

I'm realizing that it wasn't so much the writing that I found difficult, but the engagement with individuals over the writing. Thing is, until recently, the writing has gone hand-in-glove with the other part—writing for bosses, for editors, for professional groups. Now that I have more control over my day-to-day environment—a welcome, albeit too brief, respite from the vicissitudes of the workplace—I find responding to feedback on my writing an altogether non-traumatic experience. Historically, though, my choices over whether and in what manner to engage with critical feedback have been more limited, and I have been unable to associate writing with anything remotely connected to emancipatory experience. Of course, now I will need to consider the hypothesis that it may be relationships—as opposed to writing—that I'm not very good at. I may yet regret that you did not leave me in my state of false consciousness.

You too, Happy Holidays.

Sandra

Explorations for Part Five: Conversations

The conversations in this section depict only some of the editor–author interactions we have had as this book took shape over several years, and suggest a real struggle going on in some cases between authors and editors. How far should the editors of a book go in pushing an author to shape a piece that fits their goals for a book? Likewise, to what extent should editors respond to input from authors on their own (the editors') writing? Whose book is this, in your opinion?

Contributor Biostatements

JILL SINCLAIR BELL

I was born and raised in England. I drifted into teaching ESL by accident, when I was trying to find a way to put myself through graduate school. I soon discovered both that I liked it as a profession, and that it provided great opportunities to travel. The first stop was for a contract in the Bahamas, followed by a few years in Curaçao, then Canada, then Singapore. Along the way I acquired a husband and three children, with whom I now live in Toronto, where I teach at York University. I have a weakness for hands-on research methods, which in recent years has led me into the Chinese study detailed in my essay for this book, and into an intensive course in refrigeration mechanics, where I learned to weld a nifty seam.

CHRISTINE PEARSON CASANAVE

Like many daughters, I never wanted to be like my mother, but here I am describing how in some important ways I am. Self-conscious and solitary as she was, she spent 9 years of her youth as one half of the comedy song-and-dance team The Wallace Sisters in the long-running show *The Drunkard* in Los Angeles. She played music all her life (piano, and then recorder) and performed with local groups once or twice a year until her emphysema got the best of her, but continued, simultaneously, to be solitary and uncomfortable around people. Shortly before my mother died, my sister asked her how she could possibly have performed on stage, given her character.

Her answer was simply, "People clapped." My own youthful forays into public performances (folk singing, parody shows, singing groups), combined with an intense attraction to solitude, suggest some kind of influence from home or genes. When I found myself in front of an ESL class at age 26, and nightly in the quiet of my apartment alone with stacks of papers and books, I realized I had found the perfect combination: a profession that offered me periodic public exposure from which I could periodically escape. I'm still doing that—teaching, writing, presenting, and escaping—usually with a deep sense of satisfaction, even since taking a job at Keio University in Japan and becoming a foreigner, and even though people don't clap very often. However, if there is such a thing as reincarnation, I would like to be reborn as a Pointer Sister.

D. JEAN CLANDININ

I am a university teacher educator with a passionate commitment to coming to understand who I am in the stories that I live and tell with student teachers, university teachers, teachers in schools, and children. I think that paying close attention to my own lived and told stories helps me to understand a great deal about the ways we construct the landscapes on which we live with each other. I have worked at the University of Calgary and at the University of Alberta and have, in both places, tried to experiment with alternative programs in which we learn to teach. I began to work in narrative inquiry with Michael Connelly when we realized that people lived storied lives and told stories of their lives. It was as we worked with others that we realized that we need to pay the closest attention to our own stories and to who we were in others' stories.

JIM CUMMINS

I grew up in Dublin, Ireland, and went to Canada in the early 1970s to pursue graduate studies in Educational Psychology. I hold both Irish and Canadian citizenships and feel a strong identification with both societies. This is more than I can say for my sense of disciplinary belonging. Although my roots are in psychology, the work I do skirts the boundaries of education, psychology, sociology, and linguistics. My focus is very much on applied educational issues and I try to draw on whatever theoretical perspectives are necessary to interpret and act on these issues. I would rank as my number one professional and personal frustration the fact that we see glimpses in virtually every country of how teachers can create contexts of empowerment for both themselves and their students, and yet so very few children around the globe actually experience this form of education on any consistent basis.

CAROLE EDELSKY

I'm standing at the kitchen sink in this photo, either chopping or washing—a fitting place. I get my best ideas with the water running or when talking with others while cooking or eating. I wrote my dissertation in the early 1970s, by hand, at the kitchen table. For the past 20 years as a professor at Arizona State University, my reading and writing (still by hand) has never been far from a food source. I've received more nourishment as a result of my work in language education than I could have imagined possible. My three children have witnessed the feast and each in different ways has also taken on working with language. Right now, I am working with a local group to counter moves to privatize public education. I just mailed the manuscript of the second edition of *With Literacy and Justice for All* to the publisher. Indeed, my cup—but not the sink—runneth over.

JOHN F. FANSELOW

One of the most frequent questions I am asked by colleagues at Columbia University's Teachers College and by almost everyone else I know is "How did you get the way you are?" or a variation, "How is it that you are able to wing it so easily as you teach?" My usual reply is that I have no idea why I am the way I am. In fact, I have never been able to explain why I do what I do, except that doing things differently always has felt natural. For example, when I was finishing elementary school, at about the age of 12, I used to deliver newspapers with a wagon. All the other boys had bicycles. For me, using a wagon was normal; for my peers, it was abnormal. Living in a house was also normal at the time, although most of my friends lived in "six flats"—apartments. I have now lived in apartments longer than I had lived in a house and wonder why I felt sorry for my apartment-dwelling friends. Over and over, I am surprised by what I think is vital at one point and at another point, trivial. One of my favorite cartoons shows a person saying to a waiter: "I want some imported cheese, and be sure it's imported, because I can't tell the difference."

LILY WONG FILLMORE

I am happiest hanging out in schools, observing teachers and children as they work with one another. I have done this formally in connection with my research on second-language learning by children in school, and more informally in visits to classrooms whenever and wherever I happen to be near a school. I consider myself a linguist, children's advocate, and life-long student of culture and communities. My early work in the farm labor camps in California's Santa Clara Valley led to interests in children's second-language learning, educational policies and practices that affect children who speak languages other than the one used in school, and socialization practices by which families impart the language and culture of home and community to their children. These experiences propelled me into university work and into six major research projects on second-language learning and the education of language minority students in California in the last 25 years. I have also examined the conditions leading to the loss of indigenous language by individuals and communities, especially in Alaska and in the Southwest. I am currently director of a Kellogg-funded initiative, which offers Indian leaders from several Pueblos in New Mexico opportunities to work on doctorates at the University of California at Berkeley while they investigate ways to strengthen their communities linguistically, socially, economically, and educationally.

MICHÈLE FOSTER

I grew up in an extended family comprised of my mother and maternal grandparents, in a house built by my great-great-grandfather, Luke Goins, a runaway slave who fled bondage in Harpers Ferry, Virginia, now West Virginia. I am the mother of a recently married 29-year-old son who is the sixth continuous generation to live in the house. My grandmother, who was a showgirl in the Black Broadway musicals of the 1920s, wanted me to pursue a career in show business. So when I was 1, she began giving me dancing lessons and later got me involved in show business—acting in summer stock theater, cutting a record, and performing on the Ted Mack Amateur Hour. I have a lot of interests—racquetball, swimming, cooking, and sewing—which I haven't had time to pursue since getting into academia, most recently at the Claremont Graduate School. However, I recently began studying American Sign Language and taking tap dance lessons.

NORMA GONZÁLEZ

I am a third-generation Tucsonan. This long-term residential history in Tucson, Arizona, deep in the Southwest, has profoundly affected my views on language and language use, since Spanish, in its various forms, has been intertwined with both my personal and professional identities. My own schooling is a hybrid of *barrio* parochial schools and nonminority schools, and my B.A., M.A., and PhD are all from the University of Arizona in my hometown. Because my training is in cultural and linguistic anthropology, language use in the borderlands is an exciting emergent topic for me. In my work as an educational anthropologist, I hope that work that underscores the multiplicities of experience of Mexican-origin students can impact public perceptions of school, school success, and school failure. At the Bureau of Applied Research in Anthropology at the University of Arizona, I have attempted to look at the lived experiences of Mexican-origin households and students, beyond the traditional emphases on surface language features and cultural markers.

DENISE E. MURRAY

Unpacking my career and my accent reveals the many identities I have accumulated along the way from being a high school mathematics and English teacher in rural Australia to a chair of a university department in California. Growing up in a monolingual family and community, I didn't even know that my future field—ESL—existed when I first started teaching at 19. I fell into it when I was asked to tutor some Japanese students at the high school in England where I was teaching mathematics. Eventually, I decided I really needed to get more background knowledge, and so did an M.A. in linguistics—what fun that was! Then I decided I really needed the experience of living and working in a country where English was not the dominant language, which led to a job in Thailand. There I met and married my husband, Bill. I followed him to California and, because I couldn't get a full-time ESL job, went back to school for a PhD. Since childhood when I taught my dolls, I have always loved teaching, language, and different cultures. It still amazes me that I have been able to combine all three into a career at San José State University—that I can actually get paid for doing what I love to do.

JUDY WINN-BELL OLSEN

I live in San Francisco's Sunset District, about a half a block from Golden Gate Park, in a small house with my husband, Roger, two cats, and a roaming rabbit who is slowly demolishing the carpet that I never much liked anyway. I was born in Montana, and spent most of my infancy with my father (Winn, a printer) and mother. My school years were spent in Hawaii with my mother and late stepfather (Bell, a professor), both of whom favored books, education, and creative projects, but not, alas, balanced budgets and tidy households. For many years I have taught in the noncredit (adult education) ESL program of the City College of San Francisco. I've been an active participant in the TESOL organization, and have led seminars and workshops in 10 different countries, and have written and coauthored several books. I credit much of what I have accomplished to the support of Roger, who has been by turns a street artist, small shop owner, comptroller for a leather wholesale company, ESL publisher (The Alemany Press), researcher in needs assessment, and most recently consultant in ESL marketing and teacher training. My current professional goal is to talk less and read, think, and write more. My current personal goal is to decide how to dispose of my recently deceased mother's lifetime collection of artworks, craft projects, clothes, and household effects, the containers of which are blocking access to most of my professional library in the basement.

VIVIAN GUSSIN PALEY

Two decades into my teaching career, I decided I was a schoolteacher who writes books. My search into the social and moral landscape of the classroom began with *White Teacher* in 1979, and continues through my most recent book, the ninth, *The Girl with the Brown Crayon* (1997, Harvard University Press). In all these, it is the children's play and stories, their logic and thinking, that propels me into the next adventure.

PETER V. PAUL

As an individual with a profound bilateral hearing impairment, I have found it difficult in my personal and professional lives to become part of either a hearing world or a deaf world. Although English was my first language, and I later in life was introduced to signed English and American Sign Language, my views on the appropriateness of this approach for children with severe hearing impairment have been challenged, and have subsequently changed (and continue to do so) over the years as a result of my own educational experiences, my teaching, and my research. In the public school system, at the elementary and the high-school levels, I have taught students with severe to profound hearing impairment. At present, I am a professor at The Ohio State University, where my major responsibilities include teacher education for individuals interested in the education of deaf students. My research has involved work on inclusion, vocabulary, literacy, and ASL/English bilingualism, as have my scholarly publications. A new twist to my interest in literacy has surfaced in recent years as I contemplate the issue from the perspective of a parent of a child with Down's syndrome.

SANDRA R. SCHECTER

Soon after completing this essay, I resigned my administrative post at a U.S. university and accepted a faculty position in education at York University in Toronto, Canada. My current work milieu presents a talented, dedicated faculty cohort, and incisive, engaged students at both the pre-service and graduate levels. My professional responsibilities also provide scope for honoring my commitments—as an ethnolinguist, to the study of bilingual/biliterate development in families, communities, and classrooms, and as a teacher, to the preparation of skilled, responsive language educators and an informed general public.

I'm pictured here with my two young sons, Jacob and Zachary. I could explain their presence as representing a convergence, a fusion, of my two equally compelling interests, teaching and research, but that would be stretching things. To be sure, as a parent I perform many instructive functions. However, after I'm done yelling at them for spilling their juice on the rug, neglecting to throw their popsicle wrappers in the trash, and fighting in the car ("He's looking on my side!"), I have little energy or inclination for collecting text samples for the purpose of analyzing emergent literacy behaviors. I have to lie down. Nonetheless, I am happy to avail myself of the opportunity to include my children in a published collection.

THOMAS SCOVEL

I was born and raised in China, and was educated largely by my mother while growing up during World War II. I attended Woodstock High School in the Himalayan foothills after my parents were reassigned to India. Upon graduation, I left my parents and my Asian home of 17 years and sailed halfway around the world to begin college. It was there that I encountered culture shock and French. Happily, I survived French, college, and culture shock and went on to find a wife, a vocation in linguistics, and a career in university teaching. By grace, I still enjoy all three. My professional home is San Francisco State University, where I educate future EFL teachers. My profession also affords me opportunities to return to Asia and to spend time writing. At home, I keep busy and healthy by corresponding with international friends, volunteering at church, and training for triathalons.

DAVID P. SHEA

I live on the margins between two cultures, a long train ride from Tokyo in the rural suburbs of Japan where I teach at Heisei International University, and a longer plane ride from American universities and academic conferences, and a recently purchased house in my home state of Georgia. In the balance, I struggle to be an academic with a conscience, and a good father to my two kids at the same time. It's hard, of course, trying to integrate theory with practice, trying to make a difference in the classroom when most people I run into are talking about tenure and promotion, making me feel like I'm going to miss the boat if I don't. All in all, though, I like the margins, perhaps because they're the natural environment where bilingual diversity and the assimilationist politics of monoculturalism, so prevalent in language education policy, come together in ways that keep me watchful and involved. I also enjoy the fact that living outside the center allows me the chance to take the bicycle to work through the rice and wheat fields.

TRUDY SMOKE

I have been teaching in Hunter College, one of the senior colleges of the City University of New York system, for 20 years. I am a firm supporter of affordable and good public higher education, which I believe has the ability to transform human lives and society as a whole. I am troubled by recent political decisions to cut back on public higher education that have been made at the expense of a generation of young people. At Hunter, I am an associate professor in the English Department, and in addition to teaching a wide variety of courses in writing and literature, I coordinate the Developmental English program. I received a PhD in rhetoric and applied linguistics from New York University, and have since written and presented on a variety of topics relating to ESL and developmental writing. Although I grew up on Long Island, I have had a love affair with New York City since I was a child. I moved to the city when I was just under 20 years old. My husband, Alan Robbins, and I live in a prewar apartment building on the Upper West Side with our golden retriever, Max.

ALAN STRAND

Born, according to my mother, in a rat-infested maternity home in Elizabeth, New Jersey, I would like to suppose my origins were humble. I suspect the conditions were not so Dickensian as my mother pretended. I was raised in the Bronx, in a neighborhood that I probably would not now feel comfortable visiting. Passing through suburbs of New York and Philadelphia, I found myself in 1964, part student, part refugee, at McGill University in Montreal. Teaching found me, and adventure led me to the Gaspé peninsula, a remote (Gaspésians consider the Bronx remote) corner of Québec jutting into the Gulf of Saint Lawrence. At a critical juncture, I defined myself as urban and returned to Montréal, where I have been teaching (with occasional lapses for recovery) since 1973. I have lately found haven in a position with my union that has removed me from the classroom.

Author Index

Subject Index

A

Academic discourse, *see also* Language
  education profession; Research,
  university
  audience for, 194–196
  concept clarification, 190–194, 202
  connection with, 193–194, 196–198
  disconnection with, 187–188, 189–190,
    202
  playing the game, 188–190
African American community, 20–21, 24–26
American Sign Language (ASL), *see* Hearing
  impairment
Authority issues, *see* Sociopolitics; Tutelage

B

Belief systems, *see also* Bilingual education;
  Catholic school education;
  Hearing impairment; Second
  language acquisition;
  Sociopolitics; Whole language
  modification of, 1–2
  study questions, 69–71
Bilingual education, *see also* Bilingualism;
  English as a second language
  (ESL); Second language acquisition
  effectiveness, 36–37
  influence on teaching, 60–61
  Ireland, 57–61
  and nationalism, 57–58, 59
  psychological influences on, 64–66
  religious influences on, 61–64, 70
  sociopolitics, 61–67, 70

Bilingualism, *see also* Bilingual education;
  English as a second language
  (ESL); Second language acquisition
  Cantonese–English, 29–30, 36
  Catholic school, 20–21, 23–24
  code–switching, 77
  French–English, 20–21, 23–24
  Irish–English, 57–61
  Spanish–English, 34–37, 75–76

C

Cantonese, 29–30, 36
Catholicism, 61–64, *see also* Catholic school
  education
Catholic school education
  African American community, 20–21,
    24–26
  bilingualism, 20–21, 23–24
  grammar emphasis, 21, 26
  influences of, 20–27
  instructional methods, 21–23, 25–27, 69
  public performance, 24
Classroom environment, *see also* Teachers as
  learners
  anger issues, 128–129
  empowerment, 127–128
  independence, 130–131
  public speaking, 125–126
  safety/security, 125
  for second language acquisition, 29–37
  teacher experience of, 123–125,
    131–132, 151–152
Code-switching, 77
Critical theory, 52, 53–54
Culture, *see* Bilingual education; Sociopolitics

241